C-104   CAREER EXAMINATION SERIES

This is your
PASSBOOK for...

Building Inspector

Test Preparation Study Guide
Questions & Answers

COPYRIGHT NOTICE

This book is SOLELY intended for, is sold ONLY to, and its use is RESTRICTED to individual, bona fide applicants or candidates who qualify by virtue of having seriously filed applications for appropriate license, certificate, professional and/or promotional advancement, higher school matriculation, scholarship, or other legitimate requirements of education and/or governmental authorities.

This book is NOT intended for use, class instruction, tutoring, training, duplication, copying, reprinting, excerption, or adaptation, etc., by:

1) Other publishers
2) Proprietors and/or Instructors of "Coaching" and/or Preparatory Courses
3) Personnel and/or Training Divisions of commercial, industrial, and governmental organizations
4) Schools, colleges, or universities and/or their departments and staffs, including teachers and other personnel
5) Testing Agencies or Bureaus
6) Study groups which seek by the purchase of a single volume to copy and/or duplicate and/or adapt this material for use by the group as a whole without having purchased individual volumes for each of the members of the group
7) Et al.

Such persons would be in violation of appropriate Federal and State statutes.

PROVISION OF LICENSING AGREEMENTS – Recognized educational, commercial, industrial, and governmental institutions and organizations, and others legitimately engaged in educational pursuits, including training, testing, and measurement activities, may address request for a licensing agreement to the copyright owners, who will determine whether, and under what conditions, including fees and charges, the materials in this book may be used them. In other words, a licensing facility exists for the legitimate use of the material in this book on other than an individual basis. However, it is asseverated and affirmed here that the material in this book CANNOT be used without the receipt of the express permission of such a licensing agreement from the Publishers. Inquiries re licensing should be addressed to the company, attention rights and permissions department.

All rights reserved, including the right of reproduction in whole or in part, in any form or by any means, electronic or mechanical, including photocopying, recording, or by any information storage and retrieval system, without permission in writing from the Publisher.

Copyright © 2024 by
National Learning Corporation

212 Michael Drive, Syosset, NY 11791
(516) 921-8888 • www.passbooks.com
E-mail: info@passbooks.com

PUBLISHED IN THE UNITED STATES OF AMERICA

PASSBOOK® SERIES

THE *PASSBOOK® SERIES* has been created to prepare applicants and candidates for the ultimate academic battlefield – the examination room.

At some time in our lives, each and every one of us may be required to take an examination – for validation, matriculation, admission, qualification, registration, certification, or licensure.

Based on the assumption that every applicant or candidate has met the basic formal educational standards, has taken the required number of courses, and read the necessary texts, the *PASSBOOK® SERIES* furnishes the one special preparation which may assure passing with confidence, instead of failing with insecurity. Examination questions – together with answers – are furnished as the basic vehicle for study so that the mysteries of the examination and its compounding difficulties may be eliminated or diminished by a sure method.

This book is meant to help you pass your examination provided that you qualify and are serious in your objective.

The entire field is reviewed through the huge store of content information which is succinctly presented through a provocative and challenging approach – the question-and-answer method.

A climate of success is established by furnishing the correct answers at the end of each test.

You soon learn to recognize types of questions, forms of questions, and patterns of questioning. You may even begin to anticipate expected outcomes.

You perceive that many questions are repeated or adapted so that you can gain acute insights, which may enable you to score many sure points.

You learn how to confront new questions, or types of questions, and to attack them confidently and work out the correct answers.

You note objectives and emphases, and recognize pitfalls and dangers, so that you may make positive educational adjustments.

Moreover, you are kept fully informed in relation to new concepts, methods, practices, and directions in the field.

You discover that you are actually taking the examination all the time: you are preparing for the examination by "taking" an examination, not by reading extraneous and/or supererogatory textbooks.

In short, this PASSBOOK®, used directedly, should be an important factor in helping you to pass your test.

BUILDING INSPECTOR

DUTIES
Performs technical work in field inspections of building construction, alteration, and repair to enforce adherence to building codes. Performs related work as required.

SUBJECT OF EXAMINATION
The multiple-choice written test will cover knowledge, skills, and/or abilities in such areas as:
1. Inspection procedures;
2. Building construction, including methods, materials, and components;
3. Building, housing, and zoning laws and codes;
4. Interpretation of building plans and requirements;
5. Fire prevention and understanding and interpreting fire codes; and
6. Understanding and interpreting written material.

HOW TO TAKE A TEST

I. YOU MUST PASS AN EXAMINATION

A. WHAT EVERY CANDIDATE SHOULD KNOW

Examination applicants often ask us for help in preparing for the written test. What can I study in advance? What kinds of questions will be asked? How will the test be given? How will the papers be graded?

As an applicant for a civil service examination, you may be wondering about some of these things. Our purpose here is to suggest effective methods of advance study and to describe civil service examinations.

Your chances for success on this examination can be increased if you know how to prepare. Those "pre-examination jitters" can be reduced if you know what to expect. You can even experience an adventure in good citizenship if you know why civil service exams are given.

B. WHY ARE CIVIL SERVICE EXAMINATIONS GIVEN?

Civil service examinations are important to you in two ways. As a citizen, you want public jobs filled by employees who know how to do their work. As a job seeker, you want a fair chance to compete for that job on an equal footing with other candidates. The best-known means of accomplishing this two-fold goal is the competitive examination.

Exams are widely publicized throughout the nation. They may be administered for jobs in federal, state, city, municipal, town or village governments or agencies.

Any citizen may apply, with some limitations, such as the age or residence of applicants. Your experience and education may be reviewed to see whether you meet the requirements for the particular examination. When these requirements exist, they are reasonable and applied consistently to all applicants. Thus, a competitive examination may cause you some uneasiness now, but it is your privilege and safeguard.

C. HOW ARE CIVIL SERVICE EXAMS DEVELOPED?

Examinations are carefully written by trained technicians who are specialists in the field known as "psychological measurement," in consultation with recognized authorities in the field of work that the test will cover. These experts recommend the subject matter areas or skills to be tested; only those knowledges or skills important to your success on the job are included. The most reliable books and source materials available are used as references. Together, the experts and technicians judge the difficulty level of the questions.

Test technicians know how to phrase questions so that the problem is clearly stated. Their ethics do not permit "trick" or "catch" questions. Questions may have been tried out on sample groups, or subjected to statistical analysis, to determine their usefulness.

Written tests are often used in combination with performance tests, ratings of training and experience, and oral interviews. All of these measures combine to form the best-known means of finding the right person for the right job.

II. HOW TO PASS THE WRITTEN TEST

A. NATURE OF THE EXAMINATION

To prepare intelligently for civil service examinations, you should know how they differ from school examinations you have taken. In school you were assigned certain definite pages to read or subjects to cover. The examination questions were quite detailed and usually emphasized memory. Civil service exams, on the other hand, try to discover your present ability to perform the duties of a position, plus your potentiality to learn these duties. In other words, a civil service exam attempts to predict how successful you will be. Questions cover such a broad area that they cannot be as minute and detailed as school exam questions.

In the public service similar kinds of work, or positions, are grouped together in one "class." This process is known as *position-classification*. All the positions in a class are paid according to the salary range for that class. One class title covers all of these positions, and they are all tested by the same examination.

B. FOUR BASIC STEPS

1) Study the announcement

How, then, can you know what subjects to study? Our best answer is: "Learn as much as possible about the class of positions for which you've applied." The exam will test the knowledge, skills and abilities needed to do the work.

Your most valuable source of information about the position you want is the official exam announcement. This announcement lists the training and experience qualifications. Check these standards and apply only if you come reasonably close to meeting them.

The brief description of the position in the examination announcement offers some clues to the subjects which will be tested. Think about the job itself. Review the duties in your mind. Can you perform them, or are there some in which you are rusty? Fill in the blank spots in your preparation.

Many jurisdictions preview the written test in the exam announcement by including a section called "Knowledge and Abilities Required," "Scope of the Examination," or some similar heading. Here you will find out specifically what fields will be tested.

2) Review your own background

Once you learn in general what the position is all about, and what you need to know to do the work, ask yourself which subjects you already know fairly well and which need improvement. You may wonder whether to concentrate on improving your strong areas or on building some background in your fields of weakness. When the announcement has specified "some knowledge" or "considerable knowledge," or has used adjectives like "beginning principles of…" or "advanced … methods," you can get a clue as to the number and difficulty of questions to be asked in any given field. More questions, and hence broader coverage, would be included for those subjects which are more important in the work. Now weigh your strengths and weaknesses against the job requirements and prepare accordingly.

3) Determine the level of the position

Another way to tell how intensively you should prepare is to understand the level of the job for which you are applying. Is it the entering level? In other words, is this the position in which beginners in a field of work are hired? Or is it an intermediate or advanced level? Sometimes this is indicated by such words as "Junior" or "Senior" in the class title. Other jurisdictions use Roman numerals to designate the level – Clerk I, Clerk II, for example. The word "Supervisor" sometimes appears in the title. If the level is not indicated by the title, check the description of duties. Will you be working under very close supervision, or will you have responsibility for independent decisions in this work?

4) Choose appropriate study materials

Now that you know the subjects to be examined and the relative amount of each subject to be covered, you can choose suitable study materials. For beginning level jobs, or even advanced ones, if you have a pronounced weakness in some aspect of your training, read a modern, standard textbook in that field. Be sure it is up to date and has general coverage. Such books are normally available at your library, and the librarian will be glad to help you locate one. For entry-level positions, questions of appropriate difficulty are chosen – neither highly advanced questions, nor those too simple. Such questions require careful thought but not advanced training.

If the position for which you are applying is technical or advanced, you will read more advanced, specialized material. If you are already familiar with the basic principles of your field, elementary textbooks would waste your time. Concentrate on advanced textbooks and technical periodicals. Think through the concepts and review difficult problems in your field.

These are all general sources. You can get more ideas on your own initiative, following these leads. For example, training manuals and publications of the government agency which employs workers in your field can be useful, particularly for technical and professional positions. A letter or visit to the government department involved may result in more specific study suggestions, and certainly will provide you with a more definite idea of the exact nature of the position you are seeking.

III. KINDS OF TESTS

Tests are used for purposes other than measuring knowledge and ability to perform specified duties. For some positions, it is equally important to test ability to make adjustments to new situations or to profit from training. In others, basic mental abilities not dependent on information are essential. Questions which test these things may not appear as pertinent to the duties of the position as those which test for knowledge and information. Yet they are often highly important parts of a fair examination. For very general questions, it is almost impossible to help you direct your study efforts. What we can do is to point out some of the more common of these general abilities needed in public service positions and describe some typical questions.

1) General information

Broad, general information has been found useful for predicting job success in some kinds of work. This is tested in a variety of ways, from vocabulary lists to questions about current events. Basic background in some field of work, such as sociology or economics, may be sampled in a group of questions. Often these are principles which have become familiar to most persons through exposure rather than through formal training. It is difficult to advise you how to study for these questions; being alert to the world around you is our best suggestion.

2) Verbal ability

An example of an ability needed in many positions is verbal or language ability. Verbal ability is, in brief, the ability to use and understand words. Vocabulary and grammar tests are typical measures of this ability. Reading comprehension or paragraph interpretation questions are common in many kinds of civil service tests. You are given a paragraph of written material and asked to find its central meaning.

3) Numerical ability

Number skills can be tested by the familiar arithmetic problem, by checking paired lists of numbers to see which are alike and which are different, or by interpreting charts and graphs. In the latter test, a graph may be printed in the test booklet which you are asked to use as the basis for answering questions.

4) Observation

A popular test for law-enforcement positions is the observation test. A picture is shown to you for several minutes, then taken away. Questions about the picture test your ability to observe both details and larger elements.

5) Following directions

In many positions in the public service, the employee must be able to carry out written instructions dependably and accurately. You may be given a chart with several columns, each column listing a variety of information. The questions require you to carry out directions involving the information given in the chart.

6) Skills and aptitudes

Performance tests effectively measure some manual skills and aptitudes. When the skill is one in which you are trained, such as typing or shorthand, you can practice. These tests are often very much like those given in business school or high school courses. For many of the other skills and aptitudes, however, no short-time preparation can be made. Skills and abilities natural to you or that you have developed throughout your lifetime are being tested.

Many of the general questions just described provide all the data needed to answer the questions and ask you to use your reasoning ability to find the answers. Your best preparation for these tests, as well as for tests of facts and ideas, is to be at your physical and mental best. You, no doubt, have your own methods of getting into an exam-taking mood and keeping "in shape." The next section lists some ideas on this subject.

IV. KINDS OF QUESTIONS

Only rarely is the "essay" question, which you answer in narrative form, used in civil service tests. Civil service tests are usually of the short-answer type. Full instructions for answering these questions will be given to you at the examination. But in case this is your first experience with short-answer questions and separate answer sheets, here is what you need to know:

1) Multiple-choice Questions

Most popular of the short-answer questions is the "multiple choice" or "best answer" question. It can be used, for example, to test for factual knowledge, ability to solve problems or judgment in meeting situations found at work.

A multiple-choice question is normally one of three types—
- It can begin with an incomplete statement followed by several possible endings. You are to find the one ending which *best* completes the statement, although some of the others may not be entirely wrong.
- It can also be a complete statement in the form of a question which is answered by choosing one of the statements listed.

- It can be in the form of a problem – again you select the best answer.

Here is an example of a multiple-choice question with a discussion which should give you some clues as to the method for choosing the right answer:

When an employee has a complaint about his assignment, the action which will *best* help him overcome his difficulty is to
    A. discuss his difficulty with his coworkers
    B. take the problem to the head of the organization
    C. take the problem to the person who gave him the assignment
    D. say nothing to anyone about his complaint

In answering this question, you should study each of the choices to find which is best. Consider choice "A" – Certainly an employee may discuss his complaint with fellow employees, but no change or improvement can result, and the complaint remains unresolved. Choice "B" is a poor choice since the head of the organization probably does not know what assignment you have been given, and taking your problem to him is known as "going over the head" of the supervisor. The supervisor, or person who made the assignment, is the person who can clarify it or correct any injustice. Choice "C" is, therefore, correct. To say nothing, as in choice "D," is unwise. Supervisors have and interest in knowing the problems employees are facing, and the employee is seeking a solution to his problem.

2) True/False Questions

The "true/false" or "right/wrong" form of question is sometimes used. Here a complete statement is given. Your job is to decide whether the statement is right or wrong.

SAMPLE: A roaming cell-phone call to a nearby city costs less than a non-roaming call to a distant city.

This statement is wrong, or false, since roaming calls are more expensive.

This is not a complete list of all possible question forms, although most of the others are variations of these common types. You will always get complete directions for answering questions. Be sure you understand *how* to mark your answers – ask questions until you do.

V. RECORDING YOUR ANSWERS

Computer terminals are used more and more today for many different kinds of exams.
For an examination with very few applicants, you may be told to record your answers in the test booklet itself. Separate answer sheets are much more common. If this separate answer sheet is to be scored by machine – and this is often the case – it is highly important that you mark your answers correctly in order to get credit.
An electronic scoring machine is often used in civil service offices because of the speed with which papers can be scored. Machine-scored answer sheets must be marked with a pencil, which will be given to you. This pencil has a high graphite content which responds to the electronic scoring machine. As a matter of fact, stray dots may register as answers, so do not let your pencil rest on the answer sheet while you are pondering the correct answer. Also, if your pencil lead breaks or is otherwise defective, ask for another.

Since the answer sheet will be dropped in a slot in the scoring machine, be careful not to bend the corners or get the paper crumpled.

The answer sheet normally has five vertical columns of numbers, with 30 numbers to a column. These numbers correspond to the question numbers in your test booklet. After each number, going across the page are four or five pairs of dotted lines. These short dotted lines have small letters or numbers above them. The first two pairs may also have a "T" or "F" above the letters. This indicates that the first two pairs only are to be used if the questions are of the true-false type. If the questions are multiple choice, disregard the "T" and "F" and pay attention only to the small letters or numbers.

Answer your questions in the manner of the sample that follows:

32. The largest city in the United States is
    A. Washington, D.C.
    B. New York City
    C. Chicago
    D. Detroit
    E. San Francisco

1) Choose the answer you think is best. (New York City is the largest, so "B" is correct.)
2) Find the row of dotted lines numbered the same as the question you are answering. (Find row number 32)
3) Find the pair of dotted lines corresponding to the answer. (Find the pair of lines under the mark "B.")
4) Make a solid black mark between the dotted lines.

VI. BEFORE THE TEST

Common sense will help you find procedures to follow to get ready for an examination. Too many of us, however, overlook these sensible measures. Indeed, nervousness and fatigue have been found to be the most serious reasons why applicants fail to do their best on civil service tests. Here is a list of reminders:

- Begin your preparation early – Don't wait until the last minute to go scurrying around for books and materials or to find out what the position is all about.
- Prepare continuously – An hour a night for a week is better than an all-night cram session. This has been definitely established. What is more, a night a week for a month will return better dividends than crowding your study into a shorter period of time.
- Locate the place of the exam – You have been sent a notice telling you when and where to report for the examination. If the location is in a different town or otherwise unfamiliar to you, it would be well to inquire the best route and learn something about the building.
- Relax the night before the test – Allow your mind to rest. Do not study at all that night. Plan some mild recreation or diversion; then go to bed early and get a good night's sleep.
- Get up early enough to make a leisurely trip to the place for the test – This way unforeseen events, traffic snarls, unfamiliar buildings, etc. will not upset you.
- Dress comfortably – A written test is not a fashion show. You will be known by number and not by name, so wear something comfortable.

- Leave excess paraphernalia at home – Shopping bags and odd bundles will get in your way. You need bring only the items mentioned in the official notice you received; usually everything you need is provided. Do not bring reference books to the exam. They will only confuse those last minutes and be taken away from you when in the test room.
- Arrive somewhat ahead of time – If because of transportation schedules you must get there very early, bring a newspaper or magazine to take your mind off yourself while waiting.
- Locate the examination room – When you have found the proper room, you will be directed to the seat or part of the room where you will sit. Sometimes you are given a sheet of instructions to read while you are waiting. Do not fill out any forms until you are told to do so; just read them and be prepared.
- Relax and prepare to listen to the instructions
- If you have any physical problem that may keep you from doing your best, be sure to tell the test administrator. If you are sick or in poor health, you really cannot do your best on the exam. You can come back and take the test some other time.

VII. AT THE TEST

The day of the test is here and you have the test booklet in your hand. The temptation to get going is very strong. Caution! There is more to success than knowing the right answers. You must know how to identify your papers and understand variations in the type of short-answer question used in this particular examination. Follow these suggestions for maximum results from your efforts:

1) Cooperate with the monitor

The test administrator has a duty to create a situation in which you can be as much at ease as possible. He will give instructions, tell you when to begin, check to see that you are marking your answer sheet correctly, and so on. He is not there to guard you, although he will see that your competitors do not take unfair advantage. He wants to help you do your best.

2) Listen to all instructions

Don't jump the gun! Wait until you understand all directions. In most civil service tests you get more time than you need to answer the questions. So don't be in a hurry. Read each word of instructions until you clearly understand the meaning. Study the examples, listen to all announcements and follow directions. Ask questions if you do not understand what to do.

3) Identify your papers

Civil service exams are usually identified by number only. You will be assigned a number; you must not put your name on your test papers. Be sure to copy your number correctly. Since more than one exam may be given, copy your exact examination title.

4) Plan your time

Unless you are told that a test is a "speed" or "rate of work" test, speed itself is usually not important. Time enough to answer all the questions will be provided, but this does not mean that you have all day. An overall time limit has been set. Divide the total time (in minutes) by the number of questions to determine the approximate time you have for each question.

5) Do not linger over difficult questions

If you come across a difficult question, mark it with a paper clip (useful to have along) and come back to it when you have been through the booklet. One caution if you do this – be sure to skip a number on your answer sheet as well. Check often to be sure that you have not lost your place and that you are marking in the row numbered the same as the question you are answering.

6) Read the questions

Be sure you know what the question asks! Many capable people are unsuccessful because they failed to *read* the questions correctly.

7) Answer all questions

Unless you have been instructed that a penalty will be deducted for incorrect answers, it is better to guess than to omit a question.

8) Speed tests

It is often better NOT to guess on speed tests. It has been found that on timed tests people are tempted to spend the last few seconds before time is called in marking answers at random – without even reading them – in the hope of picking up a few extra points. To discourage this practice, the instructions may warn you that your score will be "corrected" for guessing. That is, a penalty will be applied. The incorrect answers will be deducted from the correct ones, or some other penalty formula will be used.

9) Review your answers

If you finish before time is called, go back to the questions you guessed or omitted to give them further thought. Review other answers if you have time.

10) Return your test materials

If you are ready to leave before others have finished or time is called, take ALL your materials to the monitor and leave quietly. Never take any test material with you. The monitor can discover whose papers are not complete, and taking a test booklet may be grounds for disqualification.

VIII. EXAMINATION TECHNIQUES

1) Read the general instructions carefully. These are usually printed on the first page of the exam booklet. As a rule, these instructions refer to the timing of the examination; the fact that you should not start work until the signal and must stop work at a signal, etc. If there are any *special* instructions, such as a choice of questions to be answered, make sure that you note this instruction carefully.

2) When you are ready to start work on the examination, that is as soon as the signal has been given, read the instructions to each question booklet, underline any key words or phrases, such as *least, best, outline, describe* and the like. In this way you will tend to answer as requested rather than discover on reviewing your paper that you *listed without describing*, that you selected the *worst* choice rather than the *best* choice, etc.

3) If the examination is of the objective or multiple-choice type – that is, each question will also give a series of possible answers: A, B, C or D, and you are called upon to select the best answer and write the letter next to that answer on your answer paper – it is advisable to start answering each question in turn. There may be anywhere from 50 to 100 such questions in the three or four hours allotted and you can see how much time would be taken if you read through all the questions before beginning to answer any. Furthermore, if you come across a question or group of questions which you know would be difficult to answer, it would undoubtedly affect your handling of all the other questions.

4) If the examination is of the essay type and contains but a few questions, it is a moot point as to whether you should read all the questions before starting to answer any one. Of course, if you are given a choice – say five out of seven and the like – then it is essential to read all the questions so you can eliminate the two that are most difficult. If, however, you are asked to answer all the questions, there may be danger in trying to answer the easiest one first because you may find that you will spend too much time on it. The best technique is to answer the first question, then proceed to the second, etc.

5) Time your answers. Before the exam begins, write down the time it started, then add the time allowed for the examination and write down the time it must be completed, then divide the time available somewhat as follows:
    - If 3-1/2 hours are allowed, that would be 210 minutes. If you have 80 objective-type questions, that would be an average of 2-1/2 minutes per question. Allow yourself no more than 2 minutes per question, or a total of 160 minutes, which will permit about 50 minutes to review.
    - If for the time allotment of 210 minutes there are 7 essay questions to answer, that would average about 30 minutes a question. Give yourself only 25 minutes per question so that you have about 35 minutes to review.

6) The most important instruction is to *read each question* and make sure you know what is wanted. The second most important instruction is to *time yourself properly* so that you answer every question. The third most important instruction is to *answer every question*. Guess if you have to but include something for each question. Remember that you will receive no credit for a blank and will probably receive some credit if you write something in answer to an essay question. If you guess a letter – say "B" for a multiple-choice question – you may have guessed right. If you leave a blank as an answer to a multiple-choice question, the examiners may respect your feelings but it will not add a point to your score. Some exams may penalize you for wrong answers, so in such cases *only*, you may not want to guess unless you have some basis for your answer.

7) Suggestions
    a. Objective-type questions
        1. Examine the question booklet for proper sequence of pages and questions
        2. Read all instructions carefully
        3. Skip any question which seems too difficult; return to it after all other questions have been answered
        4. Apportion your time properly; do not spend too much time on any single question or group of questions

5. Note and underline key words – *all, most, fewest, least, best, worst, same, opposite,* etc.
6. Pay particular attention to negatives
7. Note unusual option, e.g., unduly long, short, complex, different or similar in content to the body of the question
8. Observe the use of "hedging" words – *probably, may, most likely,* etc.
9. Make sure that your answer is put next to the same number as the question
10. Do not second-guess unless you have good reason to believe the second answer is definitely more correct
11. Cross out original answer if you decide another answer is more accurate; do not erase until you are ready to hand your paper in
12. Answer all questions; guess unless instructed otherwise
13. Leave time for review

b. Essay questions
1. Read each question carefully
2. Determine exactly what is wanted. Underline key words or phrases.
3. Decide on outline or paragraph answer
4. Include many different points and elements unless asked to develop any one or two points or elements
5. Show impartiality by giving pros and cons unless directed to select one side only
6. Make and write down any assumptions you find necessary to answer the questions
7. Watch your English, grammar, punctuation and choice of words
8. Time your answers; don't crowd material

8) Answering the essay question

Most essay questions can be answered by framing the specific response around several key words or ideas. Here are a few such key words or ideas:

M's: manpower, materials, methods, money, management
P's: purpose, program, policy, plan, procedure, practice, problems, pitfalls, personnel, public relations

a. Six basic steps in handling problems:
1. Preliminary plan and background development
2. Collect information, data and facts
3. Analyze and interpret information, data and facts
4. Analyze and develop solutions as well as make recommendations
5. Prepare report and sell recommendations
6. Install recommendations and follow up effectiveness

b. Pitfalls to avoid
1. *Taking things for granted* – A statement of the situation does not necessarily imply that each of the elements is necessarily true; for example, a complaint may be invalid and biased so that all that can be taken for granted is that a complaint has been registered

2. *Considering only one side of a situation* – Wherever possible, indicate several alternatives and then point out the reasons you selected the best one
3. *Failing to indicate follow up* – Whenever your answer indicates action on your part, make certain that you will take proper follow-up action to see how successful your recommendations, procedures or actions turn out to be
4. *Taking too long in answering any single question* – Remember to time your answers properly

IX. AFTER THE TEST

Scoring procedures differ in detail among civil service jurisdictions although the general principles are the same. Whether the papers are hand-scored or graded by machine we have described, they are nearly always graded by number. That is, the person who marks the paper knows only the number – never the name – of the applicant. Not until all the papers have been graded will they be matched with names. If other tests, such as training and experience or oral interview ratings have been given, scores will be combined. Different parts of the examination usually have different weights. For example, the written test might count 60 percent of the final grade, and a rating of training and experience 40 percent. In many jurisdictions, veterans will have a certain number of points added to their grades.

After the final grade has been determined, the names are placed in grade order and an eligible list is established. There are various methods for resolving ties between those who get the same final grade – probably the most common is to place first the name of the person whose application was received first. Job offers are made from the eligible list in the order the names appear on it. You will be notified of your grade and your rank as soon as all these computations have been made. This will be done as rapidly as possible.

People who are found to meet the requirements in the announcement are called "eligibles." Their names are put on a list of eligible candidates. An eligible's chances of getting a job depend on how high he stands on this list and how fast agencies are filling jobs from the list.

When a job is to be filled from a list of eligibles, the agency asks for the names of people on the list of eligibles for that job. When the civil service commission receives this request, it sends to the agency the names of the three people highest on this list. Or, if the job to be filled has specialized requirements, the office sends the agency the names of the top three persons who meet these requirements from the general list.

The appointing officer makes a choice from among the three people whose names were sent to him. If the selected person accepts the appointment, the names of the others are put back on the list to be considered for future openings.

That is the rule in hiring from all kinds of eligible lists, whether they are for typist, carpenter, chemist, or something else. For every vacancy, the appointing officer has his choice of any one of the top three eligibles on the list. This explains why the person whose name is on top of the list sometimes does not get an appointment when some of the persons lower on the list do. If the appointing officer chooses the second or third eligible, the No. 1 eligible does not get a job at once, but stays on the list until he is appointed or the list is terminated.

X. HOW TO PASS THE INTERVIEW TEST

The examination for which you applied requires an oral interview test. You have already taken the written test and you are now being called for the interview test – the final part of the formal examination.

You may think that it is not possible to prepare for an interview test and that there are no procedures to follow during an interview. Our purpose is to point out some things you can do in advance that will help you and some good rules to follow and pitfalls to avoid while you are being interviewed.

What is an interview supposed to test?

The written examination is designed to test the technical knowledge and competence of the candidate; the oral is designed to evaluate intangible qualities, not readily measured otherwise, and to establish a list showing the relative fitness of each candidate – as measured against his competitors – for the position sought. Scoring is not on the basis of "right" and "wrong," but on a sliding scale of values ranging from "not passable" to "outstanding." As a matter of fact, it is possible to achieve a relatively low score without a single "incorrect" answer because of evident weakness in the qualities being measured.

Occasionally, an examination may consist entirely of an oral test – either an individual or a group oral. In such cases, information is sought concerning the technical knowledges and abilities of the candidate, since there has been no written examination for this purpose. More commonly, however, an oral test is used to supplement a written examination.

Who conducts interviews?

The composition of oral boards varies among different jurisdictions. In nearly all, a representative of the personnel department serves as chairman. One of the members of the board may be a representative of the department in which the candidate would work. In some cases, "outside experts" are used, and, frequently, a businessman or some other representative of the general public is asked to serve. Labor and management or other special groups may be represented. The aim is to secure the services of experts in the appropriate field.

However the board is composed, it is a good idea (and not at all improper or unethical) to ascertain in advance of the interview who the members are and what groups they represent. When you are introduced to them, you will have some idea of their backgrounds and interests, and at least you will not stutter and stammer over their names.

What should be done before the interview?

While knowledge about the board members is useful and takes some of the surprise element out of the interview, there is other preparation which is more substantive. It *is* possible to prepare for an oral interview – in several ways:

1) Keep a copy of your application and review it carefully before the interview

This may be the only document before the oral board, and the starting point of the interview. Know what education and experience you have listed there, and the sequence and dates of all of it. Sometimes the board will ask you to review the highlights of your experience for them; you should not have to hem and haw doing it.

2) Study the class specification and the examination announcement

Usually, the oral board has one or both of these to guide them. The qualities, characteristics or knowledges required by the position sought are stated in these documents. They offer valuable clues as to the nature of the oral interview. For example, if the job involves supervisory responsibilities, the announcement will usually indicate that knowledge of modern supervisory methods and the qualifications of the candidate as a supervisor will be tested. If so, you can expect such questions, frequently in the form of a hypothetical situation which you are expected to solve. NEVER go into an oral without knowledge of the duties and responsibilities of the job you seek.

3) Think through each qualification required

Try to visualize the kind of questions you would ask if you were a board member. How well could you answer them? Try especially to appraise your own knowledge and background in each area, *measured against the job sought*, and identify any areas in which you are weak. Be critical and realistic – do not flatter yourself.

4) Do some general reading in areas in which you feel you may be weak

For example, if the job involves supervision and your past experience has NOT, some general reading in supervisory methods and practices, particularly in the field of human relations, might be useful. Do NOT study agency procedures or detailed manuals. The oral board will be testing your understanding and capacity, not your memory.

5) Get a good night's sleep and watch your general health and mental attitude

You will want a clear head at the interview. Take care of a cold or any other minor ailment, and of course, no hangovers.

What should be done on the day of the interview?

Now comes the day of the interview itself. Give yourself plenty of time to get there. Plan to arrive somewhat ahead of the scheduled time, particularly if your appointment is in the fore part of the day. If a previous candidate fails to appear, the board might be ready for you a bit early. By early afternoon an oral board is almost invariably behind schedule if there are many candidates, and you may have to wait. Take along a book or magazine to read, or your application to review, but leave any extraneous material in the waiting room when you go in for your interview. In any event, relax and compose yourself.

The matter of dress is important. The board is forming impressions about you – from your experience, your manners, your attitude, and your appearance. Give your personal appearance careful attention. Dress your best, but not your flashiest. Choose conservative, appropriate clothing, and be sure it is immaculate. This is a business interview, and your appearance should indicate that you regard it as such. Besides, being well groomed and properly dressed will help boost your confidence.

Sooner or later, someone will call your name and escort you into the interview room. *This is it.* From here on you are on your own. It is too late for any more preparation. But remember, you asked for this opportunity to prove your fitness, and you are here because your request was granted.

What happens when you go in?

The usual sequence of events will be as follows: The clerk (who is often the board stenographer) will introduce you to the chairman of the oral board, who will introduce you to the other members of the board. Acknowledge the introductions before you sit down. Do not be surprised if you find a microphone facing you or a stenotypist sitting by. Oral interviews are usually recorded in the event of an appeal or other review.

Usually the chairman of the board will open the interview by reviewing the highlights of your education and work experience from your application – primarily for the benefit of the other members of the board, as well as to get the material into the record. Do not interrupt or comment unless there is an error or significant misinterpretation; if that is the case, do not hesitate. But do not quibble about insignificant matters. Also, he will usually ask you some question about your education, experience or your present job – partly to get you to start talking and to establish the interviewing "rapport." He may start the actual questioning, or turn it over to one of the other members. Frequently, each member undertakes the questioning on a particular area, one in which he is perhaps most competent, so you can expect each member to participate in the examination. Because time is limited, you may also expect some rather abrupt switches in the direction the questioning takes, so do not be upset by it. Normally, a board member will not pursue a single line of questioning unless he discovers a particular strength or weakness.

After each member has participated, the chairman will usually ask whether any member has any further questions, then will ask you if you have anything you wish to add. Unless you are expecting this question, it may floor you. Worse, it may start you off on an extended, extemporaneous speech. The board is not usually seeking more information. The question is principally to offer you a last opportunity to present further qualifications or to indicate that you have nothing to add. So, if you feel that a significant qualification or characteristic has been overlooked, it is proper to point it out in a sentence or so. Do not compliment the board on the thoroughness of their examination – they have been sketchy, and you know it. If you wish, merely say, "No thank you, I have nothing further to add." This is a point where you can "talk yourself out" of a good impression or fail to present an important bit of information. Remember, *you close the interview yourself*.

The chairman will then say, "That is all, Mr. _____, thank you." Do not be startled; the interview is over, and quicker than you think. Thank him, gather your belongings and take your leave. Save your sigh of relief for the other side of the door.

How to put your best foot forward

Throughout this entire process, you may feel that the board individually and collectively is trying to pierce your defenses, seek out your hidden weaknesses and embarrass and confuse you. Actually, this is not true. They are obliged to make an appraisal of your qualifications for the job you are seeking, and they want to see you in your best light. Remember, they must interview all candidates and a non-cooperative candidate may become a failure in spite of their best efforts to bring out his qualifications. Here are 15 suggestions that will help you:

1) Be natural – Keep your attitude confident, not cocky

If you are not confident that you can do the job, do not expect the board to be. Do not apologize for your weaknesses, try to bring out your strong points. The board is interested in a positive, not negative, presentation. Cockiness will antagonize any board member and make him wonder if you are covering up a weakness by a false show of strength.

2) Get comfortable, but don't lounge or sprawl

Sit erectly but not stiffly. A careless posture may lead the board to conclude that you are careless in other things, or at least that you are not impressed by the importance of the occasion. Either conclusion is natural, even if incorrect. Do not fuss with your clothing, a pencil or an ashtray. Your hands may occasionally be useful to emphasize a point; do not let them become a point of distraction.

3) Do not wisecrack or make small talk

This is a serious situation, and your attitude should show that you consider it as such. Further, the time of the board is limited – they do not want to waste it, and neither should you.

4) Do not exaggerate your experience or abilities

In the first place, from information in the application or other interviews and sources, the board may know more about you than you think. Secondly, you probably will not get away with it. An experienced board is rather adept at spotting such a situation, so do not take the chance.

5) If you know a board member, do not make a point of it, yet do not hide it

Certainly you are not fooling him, and probably not the other members of the board. Do not try to take advantage of your acquaintanceship – it will probably do you little good.

6) Do not dominate the interview

Let the board do that. They will give you the clues – do not assume that you have to do all the talking. Realize that the board has a number of questions to ask you, and do not try to take up all the interview time by showing off your extensive knowledge of the answer to the first one.

7) Be attentive

You only have 20 minutes or so, and you should keep your attention at its sharpest throughout. When a member is addressing a problem or question to you, give him your undivided attention. Address your reply principally to him, but do not exclude the other board members.

8) Do not interrupt

A board member may be stating a problem for you to analyze. He will ask you a question when the time comes. Let him state the problem, and wait for the question.

9) Make sure you understand the question

Do not try to answer until you are sure what the question is. If it is not clear, restate it in your own words or ask the board member to clarify it for you. However, do not haggle about minor elements.

10) Reply promptly but not hastily

A common entry on oral board rating sheets is "candidate responded readily," or "candidate hesitated in replies." Respond as promptly and quickly as you can, but do not jump to a hasty, ill-considered answer.

11) Do not be peremptory in your answers

A brief answer is proper – but do not fire your answer back. That is a losing game from your point of view. The board member can probably ask questions much faster than you can answer them.

12) Do not try to create the answer you think the board member wants

He is interested in what kind of mind you have and how it works – not in playing games. Furthermore, he can usually spot this practice and will actually grade you down on it.

13) Do not switch sides in your reply merely to agree with a board member

Frequently, a member will take a contrary position merely to draw you out and to see if you are willing and able to defend your point of view. Do not start a debate, yet do not surrender a good position. If a position is worth taking, it is worth defending.

14) Do not be afraid to admit an error in judgment if you are shown to be wrong

The board knows that you are forced to reply without any opportunity for careful consideration. Your answer may be demonstrably wrong. If so, admit it and get on with the interview.

15) Do not dwell at length on your present job

The opening question may relate to your present assignment. Answer the question but do not go into an extended discussion. You are being examined for a *new* job, not your present one. As a matter of fact, try to phrase ALL your answers in terms of the job for which you are being examined.

Basis of Rating

Probably you will forget most of these "do's" and "don'ts" when you walk into the oral interview room. Even remembering them all will not ensure you a passing grade. Perhaps you did not have the qualifications in the first place. But remembering them will help you to put your best foot forward, without treading on the toes of the board members.

Rumor and popular opinion to the contrary notwithstanding, an oral board wants you to make the best appearance possible. They know you are under pressure – but they also want to see how you respond to it as a guide to what your reaction would be under the pressures of the job you seek. They will be influenced by the degree of poise you display, the personal traits you show and the manner in which you respond.

ABOUT THIS BOOK

This book contains tests divided into Examination Sections. Go through each test, answering every question in the margin. We have also attached a sample answer sheet at the back of the book that can be removed and used. At the end of each test look at the answer key and check your answers. On the ones you got wrong, look at the right answer choice and learn. Do not fill in the answers first. Do not memorize the questions and answers, but understand the answer and principles involved. On your test, the questions will likely be different from the samples. Questions are changed and new ones added. If you understand these past questions you should have success with any changes that arise. Tests may consist of several types of questions. We have additional books on each subject should more study be advisable or necessary for you. Finally, the more you study, the better prepared you will be. This book is intended to be the last thing you study before you walk into the examination room. Prior study of relevant texts is also recommended. NLC publishes some of these in our Fundamental Series. Knowledge and good sense are important factors in passing your exam. Good luck also helps. So now study this Passbook, absorb the material contained within and take that knowledge into the examination. Then do your best to pass that exam.

EXAMINATION SECTION

EXAMINATION SECTION
TEST 1

DIRECTIONS: Each question or incomplete statement is followed by several suggested answers or completions. Select the one that BEST answers the question or completes the statement. *PRINT THE LETTER OF THE CORRECT ANSWER IN THE SPACE AT THE RIGHT.*

1. The basis of differentiating between a *Class A* and a *Class B* multiple dwelling is   1.____

    A. the date when the building was erected
    B. the size of the building
    C. whether residents are permanent or transient
    D. the number of families living in the building

2. The basis of differentiating between a *cellar* and a *basement* is   2.____

    A. whether or not there are windows
    B. the relationship of its height to curb level
    C. the ventilation available
    D. the number of exists provided

3. The MINIMUM horizontal dimension permitted for a living room in an apartment house erected after 1929 is   3.____

    A. 8'0"   B. 8'6"   C. 9'0"   D. 9'6"

4. It is proposed to build a garage for two cars for use by the tenants in a three-family dwelling. The garage will be on the same lot as the dwelling.   4.____
Of the following, the statement that MOST completely gives the type or types of construction that would be permitted for the garage is _____ with concrete roof.

    A. frame or block walls with flat wood roof or block walls with wood peak roof, or block walls
    B. block walls with flat wood roof or block walls with wood peak roof or block walls
    C. block walls with wood peak roof or block walls
    D. block walls

5. A restaurant is permitted in a hotel of non-fireproof construction providing that   5.____

    A. there are automatic sprinkler heads in the kitchen
    B. there are two means of egress from the kitchen
    C. the kitchen has windows opening to a required yard
    D. the walls of the kitchen have one hour fire rating

6. The one of the following that is considered a *living room* is a   6.____

    A. bathroom   B. foyer
    C. public room   D. kitchen

7. In certain types of occupancies, gas-fueled space heaters may be used instead of a central heating system. One of the requirements that MUST be met in order that space heaters be permitted in an apartment is that the   7.____

1

A. building be of fireproof construction
B. apartment must consist of two or more living rooms
C. building is not a tenement
D. apartment has two means of egress

8. Where a parapet wall is required, the MINIMUM height permitted is

A. 3'0"   B. 3'6"   C. 4'0"   D. 4'6"

9. Ceilings over boilers in converted dwellings MUST be fire-retarded with

A. two layers of 3/8" sheet rock
B. wire lath and 3/4" cement mortar
C. 3/8" rock lath and 1/2" gypsum mortar
D. 3/8" sheet rock with #26 U.S. gage stamped metal

10. A fire alarm signal is required in all multiple dwellings which have the following type of occupancy:

A. tenement   B. hotel
C. converted dwelling   D. single room

11. The multiple dwelling law requires that every living room be ventilated by windows having an area of at least 10% of the floor surface of the room. Assume that a certain living room is 10'6" long by 9'6" wide.
Of the following, the MINIMUM window size that would be acceptable is

A. 3'2" x 3'6"   B. 3'4" x 3'6"
C. 3'4" x 3'8"   D. 3'6" x 3'8"

12. The multiple dwelling law specifies the minimum area and height of living rooms. The PRINCIPAL reason for this is to

A. insure adequate light and air
B. make inspections easier
C. reduce possibility of serious fires
D. control the number of occupants

13. The one of the following that is considered a multiple dwelling when located in a building separate from other buildings is a

A. jail   B. monastery
C. nurses' residence D. asylum

14. When any part of a building is to be fire-retarded, that part of the building MUST be protected by materials having a fire rating of at least _____ hour(s).

A. 1   B. 2   C. 3   D. 4

15. A *fire damper* is necessary to

A. adjust the draft in a chimney
B. wet down combustible material in case of fire
C. prevent the passage of heat and smoke through an air duct
D. control the flame in an incinerator

Questions 16-18.

DIRECTIONS: Questions 16 through 18 must be answered in accordance with the following paragraph.

When constructed within a multiple dwelling, such storage space shall be equipped with a sprinkler system and also with a system of mechanical ventilation in no way connected with any other ventilating system. Such storage space shall have no opening into any other part of the dwelling except through a fireproof vestibule. Any such vestibule shall have a minimum superficial floor area of fifty square feet and its maximum area shall not exceed seventy-five square feet. It shall be enclosed with incombustible partitions having a fire-resistive rating of three hours. The floor and ceiling of such vestibule shall also be of incombustible material having a fire-resistive rating of at least three hours. There shall be two doors to provide access from the dwelling to the car storage space. Each such door shall have a fire-resistive rating of one and one-half hours and shall be provided with a device to prevent the opening of one door until the other door is entirely closed.

16. According to the above paragraph, the one of the following that is REQUIRED in order for cars to be permitted to be stored in a multiple dwelling is a(n)

    A. fireproof vestibule
    B. elevator from the garage
    C. approved heating system
    D. sprinkler system

17. According to the above paragraph, the one of the following materials that would NOT be acceptable for the walls of a vestibule connecting a garage to the dwelling portion of a building is

    A. 3" solid gypsum blocks
    B. 4" brick
    C. 4" hollow gypsum blocks, plastered both sides
    D. 6" solid cinder concrete blocks

18. According to the above paragraph, the one of the following that would be ACCEPTABLE for the width and length of a vestibule connecting a garage that is within a multiple dwelling to the dwelling portion of the building is

    A. 3'8" x 13'0"   B. 4'6" x 18'6"
    C. 4'9" x 14'6"   D. 4'3" x 19'3"

Questions 19-20.

DIRECTIONS: Questions 19 and 20 must be answered in accordance with the following paragraph.

It shall be unlawful to place, use, or to maintain in a condition intended, arranged or designed for use, any gas-fired cooking appliance, laundry stove, heating stove, range or water heater or combination of such appliances in any room or space used for living or sleeping in any new or existing multiple dwelling unless such room or space has a window opening to the outer air or such gas appliance is vented to the outer air. All automatically operated gas appliances shall be equipped with a device which shall shut off automatically the gas supply to the main burners when the pilot light in such appliance is extinguished. A gas range or the cooking portion of a gas appliance incorporating a room heater shall not be deemed an automatically operated gas appliance. However, burners in gas ovens and broilers which can be turned on and off or ignited by non-manual means shall be equipped with a device which shall shut off automatically the gas supply to those burners when the operation of such non-manual means fails.

19. According to the above paragraph, an automatic shut-off device is NOT required on a gas

    A. hot water heater
    B. laundry drier
    C. space heater
    D. range

20. According to the above paragraph, a gas-fired water heater is permitted

    A. only in kitchens
    B. only in bathrooms
    C. only in living rooms
    D. in any type of room

21. A tenant tells an inspector that the spring on the entrance door to his apartment is broken and the door remains open.
    Of the following, the BEST action for the inspector to take, after verifying the facts, is to

    A. tell the tenant to get the janitor to fix it
    B. tell the janitor to get it fixed
    C. tell the landlord to hire someone to fix it
    D. report it as a violation and tell the janitor to get it fixed

22. An owner of a two-family house tells you, an inspector, that he wants to convert his house to a three-family dwelling. He asks you for your advice as to the requirements that must be met for this change.
    You should

    A. inspect the building so that you can give him all the necessary information
    B. refer him to your supervisor for fuller advice
    C. tell him to consult a competent architect
    D. tell him you can't give him the information unless he gives you the plans of the building to check

23. An inspector receiving a complaint from a tenant should consider it as

    A. most likely the result of a quarrel with the landlord
    B. usually an exaggerated statement of the facts
    C. a matter which should be investigated
    D. something to be checked after all other work has been completed

24. In a dispute about a matter covered by the multiple dwelling law, an inspector should carefully AVOID

    A. taking the attitude that the landlord is always wrong
    B. sounding out both the landlord and the tenant when both sides disagree
    C. investigating the basis of the disagreement
    D. getting involved in the matter until both the landlord and the tenant agree on the facts

25. If an inspector does not clearly understand one of the provisions of the multiple dwelling law, he should

   A. interpret it as best he can
   B. get his superior to explain it to him
   C. avoid having to enforce this provision
   D. consider this provision unimportant

26. If a tenant continues to ask an inspector a great many questions, the inspector should

   A. tell the tenant not to ask so many questions because the inspector has too many other things to do
   B. pretend he does not hear the tenant unless the tenant persists
   C. tell the tenant that all questions should be referred to the main office
   D. answer the questions as briefly as he can without creating the impression he is trying to *brush off* the tenant

27. If an inspector is dissatisfied with his assignment, he should

   A. demand that he be re-assigned to another task
   B. slow down his work so that his superior knows he is dissatisfied
   C. continue doing his work as well as he can but request a reassignment at the earliest opportunity
   D. make sure his fellow inspectors know his feelings

28. The MAIN reason why an inspector should know the value of his work is that

   A. he will have more of an incentive to do a better job
   B. he can better explain his job to the public
   C. it will be easier for him to get a promotion
   D. he will be able to ignore minor inspections

29. A landlord has made an unjustified complaint about an inspector to the inspector's superiors.
   In future contacts with this landlord, the inspector should be

   A. cool and distant to avoid more trouble
   B. smiling and friendly to ease matters
   C. courteous and fair in enforcing the law
   D. strict so that the landlord knows he must comply with his orders

30. Assume that an inspector believes that one of the provisions of the multiple dwelling law is unfair.
   The inspector should

   A. refuse to enforce this provision because it is unfair
   B. enforce this provision because it does not matter whether the law is fair or not
   C. refuse to enforce this provision because it is impossible to make the public comply with this provision
   D. enforce the provision because it is the law

31. In wood frame construction, mortise and tenon joints may be illegal. The basis for determining whether or not such a joint is legal is

   A. type of wood
   B. size of members
   C. load carried by the members
   D. age of wood

32. Of the following terms, the one LEAST related to the others is

   A. scuttle B. buttress C. bulkhead D. parapet

33. Of the following terms, the one LEAST related to the others is

   A. egress B. fire tower
   C. fire wall D. fire escape

34. A deformed bar would MOST likely be used in

   A. masonry work
   B. steel construction
   C. wood construction
   D. reinforced concrete construction

35. A party wall is a(n)

   A. wall serving two structures
   B. interior wall
   C. retaining wall
   D. wall without openings

36. Of the following types of walls, the one LEAST related to the others is

   A. faced B. spandrel C. apron D. panel

37. A bar bending table would MOST likely be used in the following type of construction:

   A. steel B. reinforced concrete
   C. wood D. masonry

38. Of the following terms, the one which is LEAST related to the others is

   A. down-spout B. ground seat
   C. gutter D. leader

39. Of the following terms, the one which is LEAST related to the others is

   A. ball-peen B. doublecut flat
   C. file card D. rat tail

40. Of the following, the one which is LEAST related to the others is

   A. chase B. footing C. pier D. pile

Questions 41-45.

DIRECTIONS: Questions 41 through 45 are to be answered in accordance with the floor plan of one floor of a converted dwelling shown on the last page of this test.

41. The depth of the linen closet, indicated by the letter S, is 41.____

    A. 1'4"   B. 1'5"   C. 1'6"   D. 1'7"

42. The door that should have a fire rating is indicated by the letter 42.____

    A. G   B. H   C. J   D. K

43. The walls of the building are of 43.____

    A. frame construction   B. solid brick
    C. brick and block   D. solid block

44. Of the following types of steel sections, the one that MOST closely resembles, in appearance, the steel beams used to support the floor joists is 44.____

    A. ⊔   B. ST   C. L   D. WF

45. The grade of lumber indicated for joists FORMERLY was called # 45.____

    A. 1 common   B. 1 select   C. 2 common   D. 2 select

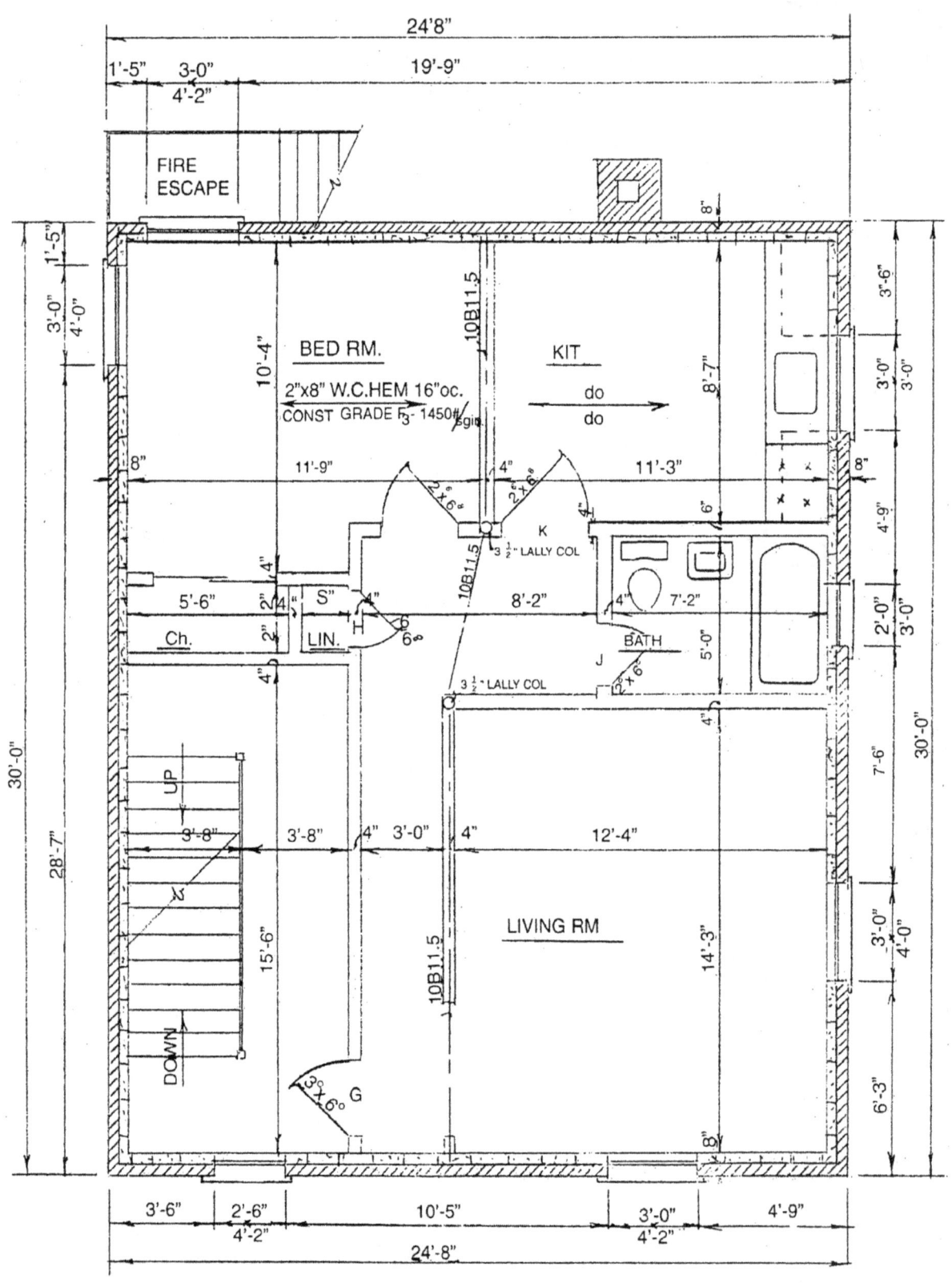

FLOOR PLAN

KEY (CORRECT ANSWERS)

1. C	11. A	21. D	31. B	41. C
2. B	12. A	22. C	32. B	42. A
3. A	13. C	23. C	33. C	43. C
4. D	14. A	24. A	34. D	44. D
5. A	15. C	25. B	35. A	45. A
6. D	16. D	26. D	36. A	
7. B	17. B	27. C	37. B	
8. B	18. C	28. A	38. B	
9. B	19. D	29. C	39. A	
10. D	20. D	30. D	40. A	

EXAMINATION SECTION
TEST 1

DIRECTIONS: Each question or incomplete statement is followed by several suggested answers or completions. Select the one that BEST answers the question or completes the statement. *PRINT THE LETTER OF THE CORRECT ANSWER IN THE SPACE AT THE RIGHT.*

1. A kitchenette is defined as a cooking space having a floor area of LESS than _____ square feet.

    A. 57   B. 58   C. 59   D. 60

2. The one of the following that is classed as a converted dwelling is a(n)

    A. apartment house erected prior to 1929, now used as a hotel
    B. lodging house erected prior to 1913, now used as a multiple dwelling
    C. one-family house erected prior to 1929, now used as a multiple dwelling
    D. rooming house erected prior to 1913, now used as a hotel

3. A *fire-retarded* partition must have a fire-resistive rating of AT LEAST _____ hour(s).

    A. 1   B. 2   C. 3   D. 4

4. The multiple dwelling law states that the total window area of a room must be at least one-tenth of the floor surface area of the room.
The one of the following types of rooms that is exempted from this provision is a

    A. bedroom   B. kitchen
    C. recreation room   D. bathroom

5. In a non-fireproof multiple dwelling, the HIGHEST story in which a factory may be operated is the

    A. 1st   B. 2nd   C. 3rd   D. 4th

6. In a multiple dwelling under construction, the MINIMUM required width of an entrance hall, from the entrance to the first stair, is

    A. 3'4"   B. 3'8"   C. 4'0"   D. 4'4"

7. Access to a required fire escape, used as a legal second means of egress from an apartment, may be from a

    A. public hall   B. kitchen
    C. bathroom   D. closet

8. The basis for differentiating between a *tenement* and any other *Class A multiple dwelling* is

    A. the year in which it was built
    B. the number of families now residing therein
    C. whether residents are permanent or transient
    D. classification of construction

9. In a 6-story multiple dwelling under construction, wood floor joists would NOT be used for

   A. apartments
   B. recreation rooms
   C. toilets
   D. public halls

10. If plans were to be filed now for a change of occupancy, the type of occupancy for which a fire escape is NOT acceptable as a second means of egress is

    A. club house
    B. single room
    C. tenement
    D. garden type maisonette

11. The multiple dwelling law requires self-closing doors between apartments and halls in all Class A multiple dwellings.
    The PRINCIPAL reason for this is to

    A. insure privacy of the tenants
    B. protect other tenants from excessive noise
    C. reduce heat loss
    D. prevent the spread of fire

12. The multiple dwelling law prohibits the erection of a building the height of which is in excess of one and one-half times the width of the widest street on which it faces.
    The MAIN reason for this prohibition is to

    A. insure that tenants will not have to travel too far to the street in case of fire
    B. provide adequate light and air
    C. prevent excessive loadings on the footings
    D. provide adequate water pressure on the top floor

13. The multiple dwelling law requires that the walls of all interior courts shall be built with a light-colored brick. The PRINCIPAL reason for this is that

    A. light-colored brick is easier to clean
    B. more light will be reflected into the apartments
    C. light-colored brick is usually stronger
    D. rain will not penetrate light-colored brick readily

14. The multiple dwelling law requires that every fire escape constructed of material subject to rusting shall be painted with two or more coats of paint of contrasting colors.
    The reason that each coat is required to be of a different color is that

    A. the different pigments in the two coats will better protect the steel from rust
    B. when two colors are used, the sun will not bleach the top color as rapidly as when only one color is used
    C. the contrasting colors make inspection easier
    D. a better bond is obtained between paint of different color

15. The multiple dwelling law requires that every fire escape at the top story of a building shall be provided with a stairway or ladder to the roof, except where the roof is a peak roof with a pitch in excess of twenty degrees. The reason that access to the roof from the fire escape is NOT required where the pitch of the roof is in excess of twenty degrees is that

    A. it would be difficult to walk on a roof with such a slope
    B. a steep roof would tend to catch fire quicker, so people should not be on the roof

C. sparks from a fire would tend to roll down the roof toward any person climbing up the ladder
D. it is almost impossible to anchor a ladder to a steep roof

16. The multiple dwelling law states that for stairs, each tread shall be not less than nine and one-half inches wide; each riser shall not exceed seven and three-quarters inches in height; and the product of the number of inches in the width of the tread and the number of inches in the height of the riser shall be at least seventy and at most seventy-five. The one of the following sets of dimensions that is acceptable for the stairs of a multiple dwelling is tread _____, riser _____.

   A. 9 3/4"; 7 1/8"
   B. 9 1/4"; 8"
   C. 10 1/4"; 7 1/8"
   D. 10 1/2"; 7 1/2"

17. The multiple dwelling law prohibits construction of a frame multiple dwelling. The PRINCIPAL reason for this is that

   A. frame buildings are more susceptible to vermin infection
   B. the heavier loads occurring in multiple dwellings can not be supported in frame buildings
   C. frame buildings, used as multiple dwellings, tend to become slums
   D. fire in a frame building is more dangerous than in other types of buildings

18. The multiple dwelling law states that no radio or other wires shall be attached to any vent line extending above the roof.
The PRINCIPAL reason for this prohibition is that

   A. vent lines are relatively weak structures
   B. wires increase the danger of electric shock due to lightning
   C. low wires are a safety hazard
   D. ventilation will be blocked

19. In a non-fireproof building, the multiple dwelling law requires that certain partitions shall be fire-stopped. This means that

   A. fireproof doors must be used
   B. the partitions must be constructed of incombustible material
   C. the covering of the studs must be of incombustible material
   D. the spaces between the top of a partition and the ceiling and floors above must be filled with incombustible material

20. The building code states that the floor of a multiple dwelling shall be designed for a live load of 40 pounds per square foot.
Live load means weight of

   A. floor joists, beams, and girders
   B. tenants only
   C. tenants and their furniture
   D. floor joists, beams, girders, tenants, and furniture

21. An anonymous complaint is made to the Department of Buildings. 21.___
This complaint should be

    A. ignored because it is not signed
    B. investigated because it may be valid
    C. filed to see if further complaints of a like nature are made
    D. ignored because only troublemakers make anonymous complaints

22. In order to make certain emergency repairs to an occupied multiple dwelling, a fire 22.___
escape must be removed. The owner asks you, an inspector, for permission to do this.
You should

    A. grant the request, since the only way to make the repair is to remove the fire escape
    B. tell the owner to find another method of making the repair since a fire escape may not be removed
    C. refer the owner to your superiors, since you do not have the authority to grant the request
    D. grant the request only if fire extinguishers are provided to prevent danger of fire

23. The cellar ceiling of a converted multiple dwelling is to be fire-retarded by applying two 23.___
layers of 1/2" plaster boards to the existing ceiling. The owner tells you that the existing lath is too weak to support the weight of the additional plaster boards.
You should

    A. insist that the plaster boards shall be applied on the existing ceiling
    B. tell the owner that the plaster boards will not be necessary since their application would be dangerous
    C. permit installation of only one layer of plaster boards in order to reduce the load on the lath
    D. require that the lath be strengthened first and then that the two layers of plaster boards be applied

24. A tenant has made a complaint that water leaking from a pipe in the apartment above 24.___
has damaged the ceiling of the tenant's apartment. While the premises are being inspected, the tenant mentions other complaints to you. You should

    A. tell the tenant you are there to inspect the original complaint only
    B. listen courteously to the tenant, but discourage further complaints
    C. check each of the complaints to determine their validity
    D. place a violation on the landlord for all the complaints

25. The public halls of a multiple dwelling were painted two months ago. A tenant has filed a 25.___
complaint stating that the walls are now peeling and are in a dirty, deteriorated condition.
When investigating this complaint, you find that it is justified.
You should

    A. test the paint to find out why it peeled so rapidly
    B. notify the landlord to repaint the walls properly
    C. tell the tenant that since the walls were painted within three years, nothing further can be done
    D. refer the complaint to the legal department so that court action may be taken

26. A multiple dwelling is being erected with one wall on a lot line. On the adjoining lot is a two-family house. The owner of this house complaints that the new building is cutting off light and ventilation from the two-family house.
You should

    A. tell the small home owner that nothing can be done since the law permits such construction
    B. tell the small home owner that nothing can be done since two-family houses are not within your jurisdiction
    C. stop construction of the multiple dwelling since it is illegal to block ventilation of another house
    D. tell the small home owner to sue the city for the decrease in the value of his property

27. The approved plans for a converted multiple dwelling call for fireproofing the stair enclosure with metal lath and cement plaster. The contractor would like to substitute two layers of 1/2 inch plaster board since this has the same fire-resistive rating as the lath and plaster.
The inspector should

    A. permit this, since the fire ratings are the same
    B. deny this, since the structural strengths may not be the same
    C. permit this only if an amended plan showing the substitution is approved
    D. permit this only if the structural strengths and the fire-resistive ratings are the same

28. During a routine inspection of a multiple dwelling, an inspector discovers that a fire door has been blocked open.
The FIRST action of the inspector should be to

    A. order the owner or his representative to remove the blocking immediately
    B. notify the owner in writing that a violation of the law exists on the premises
    C. warn the tenants that a fire hazard exists
    D. remove the blocking himself

29. When writing a report of an investigation of a tenant's complaint, the item that you should consider LEAST important for inclusion in the report is the

    A. name of tenant   B. apartment number
    C. age of building   D. location of building

30. A tenant asks you about the procedures the Department of Buildings uses in processing a violation complaint.
You should

    A. refer the tenant to your superiors since they are the only ones permitted to give official information
    B. tell the tenant that such information is none of his business
    C. give the tenant the information in as concise a manner as possible
    D. explain completely and in detail all the ramifications of departmental procedure

31. In investigating the adequacy of the exits of a multiple dwelling, the LEAST important item to check is the

    A. location of exits
    B. width of stairs
    C. size of stair platforms
    D. number of treads and risers

32. In a 8-story fireproof multiple dwelling of skeleton steel construction, the one of the following members that would be LEAST likely to have a fire-resistive enclosure is a

    A. beam   B. column   C. joist   D. lintel

33. The one of the following that is LEAST related to the others is

    A. pile   B. footing   C. caisson   D. pilaster

34. A pit at the low point of a cellar floor is known as a(n)

    A. sump   B. well
    C. accumulator   D. drain

35. The structure above the roof of a building that encloses a stairway is called a

    A. bulkhead   B. penthouse
    C. mezzanine   D. stairwell

36. To prevent flying sparks, incinerator chimneys in multiple dwellings are frequently covered with

    A. cement copings   B. draft hoods
    C. goosenecks   D. wire mesh

37. A valve used to prevent boiler explosions due to excessive pressure is a _____ valve.

    A. check   B. gate   C. relief   D. fuller

38. The one of the following that is acceptable according to the building code for a 3-hour fire partition is 6"

    A. solid brick
    B. solid stone concrete blocks
    C. solid cinder concrete blocks
    D. plain concrete

39. A fire tower is a

    A. means of egress from a building
    B. water tank on the roof of a building
    C. piece of Fire Department equipment
    D. draft space through which fire will spread

Questions 40-45.

DIRECTIONS: Questions 40 through 45, inclusive, refer to the sketch of an apartment building shown on the last page. All questions are to be answered on the basis of this sketch.

40. The dimension of the bedroom indicated by the letter Y is

    A. 9'1 5/16"
    B. 9'1 13/16"
    C. 9'2 3/16"
    D. 9'2 11/16"

41. Following is an abstract of the multiple dwelling law:
    1. Every living room (including bedrooms) shall contain at least 80 square feet of floor space.
    2. Every living room shall be at least eight feet in least horizontal dimension except that any number of bedrooms up to one-half the total number in any apartment containing three or more bedrooms may have a least horizontal dimension of seven feet or more.

    In order to increase the width of the hall, it is necessary to decrease the width of the bedroom indicated by the letter Y.
    The one of the following that is the smallest acceptable width of this room is

    A. 7'0"   B. 7'6"   C. 8'0"   D. 8'6"

42. The columns shown are

    A. wood posts
    B. concrete filled pipes
    C. I beams
    D. built up channels

43. The letter indicating the partition that is MOST likely to be a bearing partition is

    A. M
    B. W
    C. X
    D. There are no bearing partitions

44. The exit door

    A. does not swing in the direction of egress
    B. is too large
    C. will block the stairs
    D. is not fireproof

45. The one of the following general notes that is MOST likely to appear in connection with this plan is:

    A. Masonry walls shall be braced horizontally at maximum intervals of twenty times the wall thickness
    B. Buttresses shall be bonded into the wall by masonry in the same manner as employed in the construction of the wall
    C. Masonry walls shall be anchored at maximum intervals of four feet, to each tier of joists bearing on such walls, by metal anchors
    D. Openings in the masonry wall shall be spanned by a lintel or arch of incombustible materia

8 (#1)

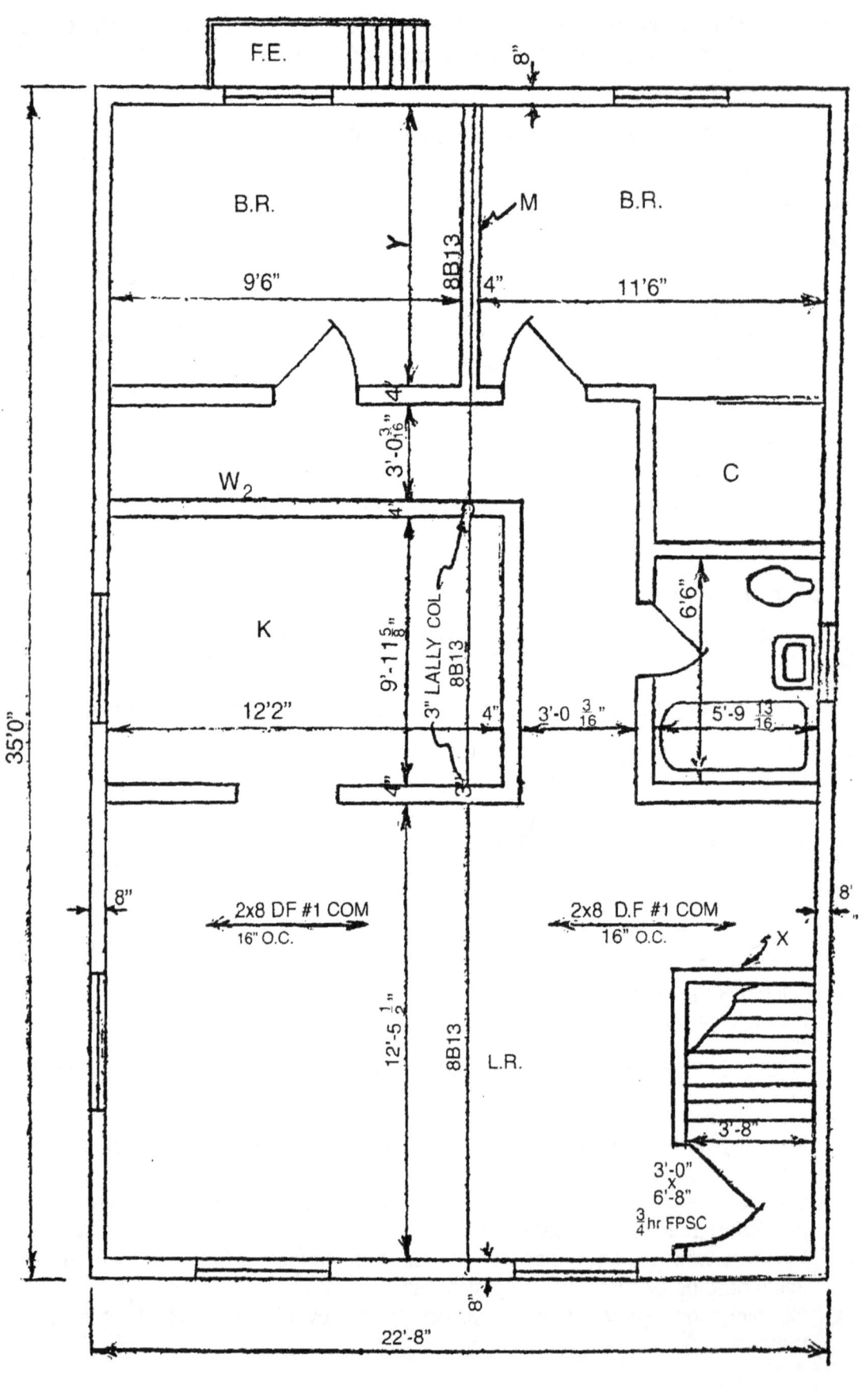

KEY (CORRECT ANSWERS)

1. C	11. D	21. B	31. D	41. D
2. C	12. B	22. C	32. D	42. B
3. A	13. B	23. D	33. D	43. D
4. D	14. C	24. C	34. A	44. C
5. B	15. A	25. B	35. A	45. C
6. C	16. C	26. A	36. D	
7. B	17. D	27. C	37. C	
8. A	18. A	28. A	38. C	
9. D	19. D	29. C	39. A	
10. B	20. C	30. C	40. D	

EXAMINATION SECTION
TEST 1

DIRECTIONS: Each question or incomplete statement is followed by several suggested answers or completions. Select the one that BEST answers the question or completes the statement. *PRINT THE LETTER OF THE CORRECT ANSWER IN THE SPACE AT THE RIGHT.*

Questions 1-5.

DIRECTIONS: Questions 1 through 5 are to be answered on the basis of the following statement. Use ONLY the information contained in this statement in answering these questions.

No multiple dwelling shall be erected to a height in excess of one and one-half times the width of the widest street on which it faces, except that above the level of such height, for each one foot that the front wall of such dwelling sets back from the street line, three feet shall be added to the height limit of such dwelling, but such dwelling shall not exceed in maximum height three feet plus one and three-quarter times the width of the widest street on which it faces.
Any such dwelling facing a street more than one hundred feet in width shall be subject to the same height limitations as though such dwelling faced a street one hundred feet in width.

1. The MAXIMUM height of a multiple dwelling set back five feet from the street line and facing a 60 foot wide street is _____ feet.

    A. 60   B. 90   C. 105   D. 165

2. The MAXIMUM height of a multiple dwelling set back six feet from the street line and facing a 120 foot wide street is _____ feet.

    A. 198   B. 168   C. 120   D. 105

3. The MAXIMUM height of a multiple dwelling is

    A. 100 ft.   B. 150 ft.   C. 178 ft.   D. unlimited

4. The MAXIMUM height of a multiple dwelling set back 10 feet from the street line and facing a 110 foot wide street is _____ feet.

    A. 178   B. 180   C. 195   D. 205

5. The MAXIMUM height of a multiple dwelling set back eight feet from the street line and facing a 90 foot wide street is _____ feet.

    A. 135   B. 147   C. 178   D. 159

Questions 6-10.

DIRECTIONS: Questions 6 through 10 are to be answered on the basis of the following statement. Use ONLY the information contained in this statement in answering these questions.

The number of persons accommodated on any story in a lodging house shall not be greater than the sum of the following components.
    a. 22 persons for each full multiple of 22 inches in the smallest clear width for each means of egress approved by the department, other than fire escapes.
    b. 20 persons for each lawful fire escape accessible from such story.

6. The MAXIMUM number of persons that may be accommodated on a story in a lodging house depends on the

    A. number of lawful fire escapes *only*
    B. number of approved means of egress *only*
    C. smallest clear width in each approved means of egress *only*
    D. number of lawful fire escapes and sum total of smallest clear widths in each approved means of egress

7. The MAXIMUM number of persons that may be accommodated on a story of a lodging house having one lawful fire escape and a sum total of 44 inches in the smallest clear widths of the two approved means of egress is

    A. 20   B. 22   C. 42   D. 64

8. The MAXIMUM number of persons that may be accommodated on a story of a lodging house having two lawful fire escapes and a sum total of 60 inches in the smallest clear width of the approved means of egress is

    A. 64   B. 84   C. 100   D. 106

9. The MAXIMUM number of persons that may be accommodated on a story of a lodging house having one lawful fire escape and a sum total of 33 inches in the smallest clear width of the approved means of egress is

    A. 42   B. 53   C. 64   D. 73

10. The MAXIMUM number of persons that may be accommodated on a story of a lodging house having two lawful fire escapes and two approved means of egress, with 40 inches and 44 inches in the smallest clear widths, respectively, is

    A. 84   B. 104   C. 106   D. 108

11. An employee of the Department of Housing and Buildings may take outside employment in private industry as a(n)

    A. architect   B. mason
    C. plumber   D. none of the above

12. The one of the following that is NOT a multiple dwelling is a

    A. college dormitory
    B. dwelling occupied by three families
    C. hospital
    D. lodging house

13. The one of the following that is a Class A multiple dwelling is a

    A. commercial building containing a janitor's apartment
    B. furnished room house

C. hotel
D. tenement

14. A dwelling occupied by one family with five transient roomers is a _____ dwelling.

    A. Class A multiple
    B. Class B multiple
    C. single family private
    D. two-family private

15. The one of the following that is deemed a living room by the multiple dwelling law is a

    A. bathroom
    B. bedroom
    C. dinette, 45 sq. ft. in area
    D. kitchenette, 45 sq. ft. in area

16. The MAXIMUM number of stories to which a new multiple dwelling may be erected without having a passenger elevator is

    A. 4   B. 5   C. 6   D. 7

17. In a new multiple dwelling, which of the following rooms are required to have windows?

    A. Bathroom
    B. Kitchen
    C. Water-closet compartment
    D. All of the above

18. New multiple dwellings three stories or more in height must have hot water supplied during

    A. the hours between 6 A.M. and Midnight *only*
    B. the hours between 8 A.M. and 8 P.M. *only*
    C. the hours between 6 A.M. and Noon and 6 P.M. and Midnight *only*
    D. all hours

19. A winding stair in a new multiple dwelling is

    A. not permitted under any circumstances
    B. permitted under all circumstances
    C. permitted only when the building is more than 6 stories high
    D. permitted only when the building is less than 6 stories high

20. All elevator shaft walls in new multiple dwellings MUST be

    A. at least 4 inches thick
    B. fireproof
    C. hollow
    D. made of gypsum plaster

21. The one of the following statements about new multiple dwellings that is NOT true is:

    A. Boiler rooms in multiple dwellings four stories or more in height must have fireproof doors
    B. Every open roof area must have a guard rail or parapet wall at least 3'6" high
    C. A new multiple dwelling may be placed on the same lot with a frame building
    D. A new multiple dwelling may be used for parking of passenger motor vehicles

22. A tenement within the meaning of the multiple dwelling law is a building erected BEFORE

    A. April 18, 1929
    B. April 6, 1948
    C. April 12, 1949
    D. March 25, 1952

23. Every entrance hall in a multiple dwelling must be provided with a light of AT LEAST _____ watts.

    A. 5
    B. 10
    C. 15
    D. 40

24. From the entrance to the first stair, every entrance hall in a new multiple dwelling must be, in clear width, AT LEAST

    A. 3'8"
    B. 4'
    C. 6'
    D. 8'

25. A basement in a new multiple dwelling exceeding seven stories in height MUST have AT LEAST one-half of its height _____ curb level and is _____ as a story.

    A. above; counted
    B. above; not counted
    C. below; counted
    D. below; not counted

26. The lower ends of mitred cross bridging should be nailed to the beams

    A. at the same time that the top ends are nailed
    B. before the rough flooring is placed
    C. after the plastering is complete
    D. after the flooring is placed

27. The maximum distance between lines of bridging should NOT exceed

    A. 10'0"
    B. 8'0"
    C. 6'6"
    D. 4'6"

28. The building code states that it shall be unlawful to corbel walls less than twelve inches thick, except for fire-stopping.
    From this, it may be concluded that

    A. walls 12 inches or more in thickness shall not be corbelled
    B. if a wall is less than 12 inches thick, it is permissible to corbel provided some of the corbelling is used for fire-stopping
    C. fire-stopping shall not be considered to be corbelling
    D. corbelling and fire-stopping are the same

29. The building code states that curtain walls of solid masonry shall be at least eight inches thick for the uppermost thirteen feet and at least twelve inches thick for the next fifty-two feet or fraction thereof below and shall be increased four inches in thickness for each succeeding sixty feet or fraction thereof below.
    This means that the thickness of a solid masonry curtain wall 126 feet high should be AT LEAST

    A. 20 inches throughout its height
    B. 20 inches at the base
    C. 16 inches throughout its height
    D. 16 inches at the base

30. The term *curb cut* refers to

    A. openings in a curb
    B. tire cuts made while parking
    C. surveying marks chiseled in a curb
    D. rental for sidewalk stands

31. A bearing wall is a wall which

    A. carries its own weight *only*
    B. carries load other than its own weight
    C. bears on structural supports at each story
    D. is more than 12 feet high

32. A column is an _____ member.

    A. upright compression
    B. inclined compression
    C. upright tension
    D. inclined tension

33. A lintel could be broadly classified as a

    A. beam   B. column   C. footing   D. strut

34. A flat slab is MOST commonly used in _____ construction.

    A. sidewalk   B. roadway   C. conduit   D. building

35. Of the following, the member which would MOST likely be supported on a footing is the

    A. beam   B. girder   C. column   D. joist

36. A parapet wall would MOST likely support

    A. a coping
    B. roof joists
    C. floor joists
    D. partitions

37. Jack arches are used

    A. in ornamental iron work
    B. in fancy stairways
    C. when lintels are omitted
    D. in foundations

38. If green lumber is used for joists, shrinkage will have its MOST serious effect in _____ of joists.

    A. length   B. width   C. depth   D. weight

39. The phrase *concealed draft openings* is MOST likely to be used in connection with

    A. fireplaces
    B. flues
    C. fire-stopping
    D. automatic dampers

40. Of the following terms, the one which is LEAST related to the others is the

    A. jamb
    B. strike plate
    C. latch bolt
    D. pulley stile

Questions 41-45.

DIRECTIONS: Questions 41 through 45 are to be answered in accordance with the following sketch.

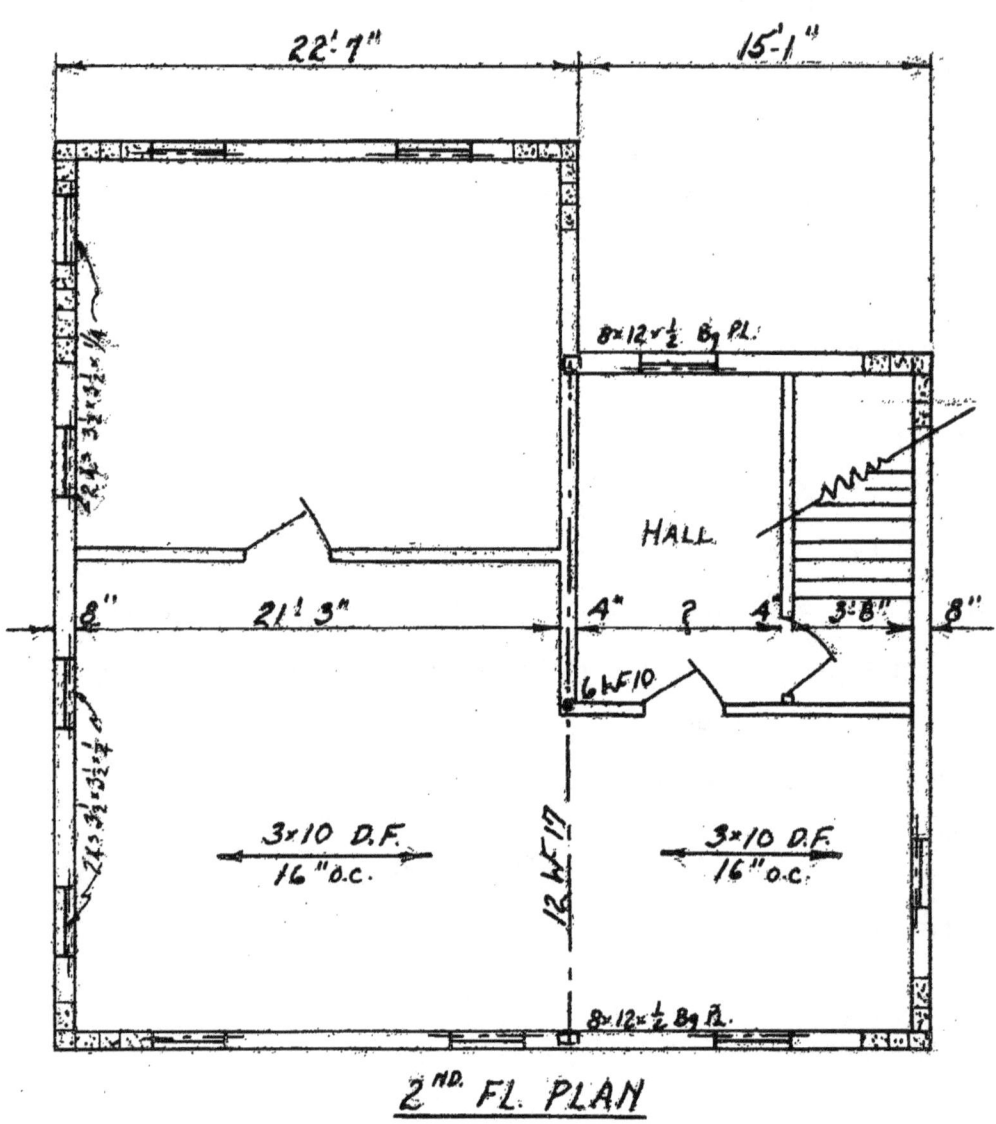

2ND. FL. PLAN

41. The one of the following statements that is CORRECT is: The building

    A. is of fireproof construction
    B. has masonry walls, with wood joists
    C. is of wood frame construction
    D. has timber posts and girders

42. The one of the following statements that is CORRECT is:

    A. The stairway from the ground floor continues through the roof
    B. There are two means of egress from the second floor of this building
    C. The door on the second floor stair landing opens in the direction of egress
    D. The entire stair is shown on this plan

43. The width of the hall is

    A. 10'3" B. 10'5" C. 10'7" D. 10'9"

44. The lintels shown are

    A. angles
    B. a channel and an angle
    C. an I-beam
    D. precast concrete

45. The one of the following statements that is CORRECT is: The steel beam is

    A. supported by columns at the center and at the ends
    B. entirely supported by the walls
    C. supported on columns at the ends only
    D. supported at the center by a column and at the ends by the walls

KEY (CORRECT ANSWERS)

1. C	11. D	21. C	31. B	41. B
2. B	12. C	22. A	32. A	42. C
3. C	13. D	23. C	33. A	43. D
4. A	14. B	24. B	34. D	44. A
5. D	15. B	25. A	35. C	45. D
6. D	16. C	26. D	36. A	
7. D	17. D	27. B	37. C	
8. B	18. A	28. C	38. C	
9. A	19. A	29. B	39. C	
10. C	20. B	30. A	40. D	

EXAMINATION SECTION

DIRECTIONS: Each question or incomplete statement is followed by several suggested answers or completions. Select the one that BEST answers the question or or completes the statement. *PRINT THE LETTER OF THE CORRECT ANSWER IN THE SPACE AT THE RIGHT.*

1. A lintel is MOST CLOSELY associated with a
   A. wall opening
   B. floor opening
   C. roof opening
   D. fire escape

   1.____

2. An apron is MOST CLOSELY associated with a
   A. door
   B. window
   C. yard
   D. bulkhead

   2.____

3. In remodeling a multiple dwelling, brickwork has been removed from an interior steel column and replaced with 3/4" plaster. The MOST SERIOUS consequence of this alteration relates to
   A. strength
   B. corrosion
   C. fire
   D. accidental damage

   3.____

4. In multiple dwellings, hand-rails must be provided on each side of a stairway if the stairway exceeds CERTAIN
   A. height
   B. width
   C. steepness
   D. tread-riser ratio

   4.____

5. A rectangular court is 16'0" wide by 20'0" long. The length of a diagonal is, in feet, most nearly,
   A. 25.2
   B. 25.4
   C. 25.6
   D. 25.8

   5.____

6. If concrete weighs 4000 pounds per cubic yard, the weight of a slab of concrete 2'6" by 6'9" by 3'2" is, in pounds, most nearly,
   A. 7920
   B. 7830
   C. 7740
   D. 7650

   6.____

7. In the case of new construction, a certificate of occupancy is required for
   A. class A multiple dwellings
   B. class A and class B multiple dwellings
   C. all dwellings
   D. all buildings

   7.____

8. A sewer which carries BOTH sewage and storm water is known as a _____ sewer.
   A. sanitary
   B. combined
   C. separate
   D. storm

   8.____

9. A fire-restrictive rating of an assembly indicates that the assembly
   A. is incombustible
   B. is non-flammable
   C. can withstand a fire of given duration without serious failure
   D. prevents the passage of heat

   9.____

10. Major classifications of districts established by the Zoning Resolution do NOT   10.____
    Include _____ districts.
    A. Use   B. Height   C. Residence   D. Area

11. The distinction between a Business District and a Business-1 District relates to   11.____
    A. types of businesses
    B. size of businesses
    C. types of business signs
    D. area allowed for manufacturing

12. The MAXIMUM hight to which a multiple dwelling fronting on a 100-foot street   12.____
    may be erected in a class one and on-half district is
    A. 178 ft.   B. 175 ft.   C. 150 ft.   D. 125 ft.

13. As a senior supervisor of Housing, you are directed to interview several men   13.____
    whom the department is considering for provisional employment as a supervisor of
    Housing. During the course of your interview with one of these men, you learn that he
    has good building construction experience, owns his home outright in the City for the
    past four years, and even owns the patent rights on certain items now being used in
    building construction work. With respect to this man, you should recommend that he
    A. be employed for a trial period of 30 days
    B. be employed for a provisional period of 90 days
    C. should not be employed unless further questioning shows that he complies with the
       Residence Law
    D. should not be employed unless he divests himself of certain properties

14. Multiple dwellings of non-fireproof construction may NOT exceed   14.____
    A. 75 feet in height
    B. 6 stories in height unless provided with elevators
    C. 5 stories in height
    D. 60 feet in height

15. Construction in a non-fireproof multiple dwelling more than three stories high must be   15.____
    fireproof in all of the following locations EXCEPT
    A. first floor
    B. stairs
    C. elevator shaft below first floor
    D. roof

16. Flue or chimney connections for every apartment are MOST LIKELY to be required in   16.____
    A. tenements
    B. class A multiple dwellings
    C. class B multiple dwellings
    D. buildings used for single-room occupancy

17. In a 6-story multiple dwelling, the required access to the yard form a street may   17.____
    NOT be provided by a
    A. court
    B. fire proof passage
    C. fire-retarded passage
    D. direct passage 3'6" clear width by 7'0" high

18. The required area a function of the of windows in a living room is
    A. floor area
    B. room volume
    C. wall area
    D. number of occupants

19. A living room in a class A multiple dwelling is 8'0" wide by 9'6" long by 8'6" high. This room fails to meet requirements of the Multiple Dwelling Law with respect to
    A. height
    B. volume
    C. area
    D. least horizontal dimension

20. A tenant complains to an inspector that the interior lock on his dumbwaiter door is faulty and that the door is continually coming open. The inspector should, after verifying the facts,
    A. tell the tenant to notify the landlord
    B. notify the janitor and report a violation to the Department
    C. tell the tenant to fix it himself
    D. tell the janitor to fix this lock

21. Fire escapes constructed of material subject to rusting should be painted
    A. every year
    B. every two years
    C. whenever they become rusty
    D. twice a year

22. A building fronts on an unpaved street without curbs or sidewalk. The legal height of the building
    A. can not be established
    B. is established by the architect
    C. may be established from the equivalent curb level
    D. is established by the owner

23. The story heights of a class B multiple dwelling are as follows: cellar, 12 ft.; first floor, 20 ft.; second floor, 15 ft.; third through sixth floors, 12 ft. The story height of the building is
    A. 6   B. 7   C. 8   D. 9

24. The distinction between "cellar" and "basement" is concerned with
    A. relative position with respect to curb elevation
    B. use
    C. height
    D. area

25. The distinction between fire-tower and fire-stair is based upon
    A. position with respect to building walls
    B. degree of fire-proofing
    C. height
    D. use of self-closing fireproof doors

26. Yards may NOT be omitted under any circumstances when a multiple dwelling occupies
    A. two or more entire blocks
    B. an interior lot
    C. an interior lot running through from street to street
    D. an entire block

27. A multiple dwelling is one which is occupied by at least
    A. 2 families   B. 3 families   C. 4 families   D. 5 familles

28. The distinction between class A and class B multiple dwellings relates to
    A. size   B. quality   C. fireproofing   D. residence

29. A portion of a multiple dwelling which is considered to be an apartment contains
    A. more than one room
    B. a kitchen
    C. a bathroom
    D. a water-closet compartment

30. Living rooms include
    A. water-closet compartments
    B. bathrooms
    C. kitchens
    D. foyers

31. Of the following, the one which is NOT considered to be an alteration is
    A. replacing wainscoting with plaster
    B. moving a building from one lot to another
    C. replacing bearing wall to make one large room from two small ones
    D. increasing the height of a building without increasing the number of stories

32. A trimmer arch is used in connection with a
    A. fireplace   B. window   C. closet door   D. stairway

33. A sidewalk shed
    A. is never permitted
    B. is used-when demolishing buildings
    C. is allowed in front of public buildings
    D. must have an open roof

Questions 34-39.
Questions 34 through 39 refer to the two columns below. Each item in Column 1 is associated with an item in Column 2. Place the letter of the item in Column 2 after the number of the item in Column 1 with which it is most closely associated. Items in Column 2 may be used more than once or not at all.

Column 1

34. Scratch coat
35. Flashing
36. Louvre
37. Bond
38. Soil stack
39. Shoring

Column 2

A. Welding
B. Bricklaying
C. Plumbing
D. Plastering
E. Roofing
F. Flooring
G. Excavating
H. Ventilatin

34._____
35._____
36._____
37._____
38._____
39._____

40. Of the following terms, the one which LEAST relates to the other is
    A. soffit B. newel C. nosing D. trimmer
    40._____

41. Of the following terms, the one which LEAST relates to the others is
    A. muntin B. stop-bead C. jamb D. sill
    41._____

42. Fire-stopping is synonymous with
    A. fireproofing
    B. fire-retarding
    C. fire-treated
    D. none of the foregoing
    42._____

43. A two-story building 32'0" by 60'0" is erected on a lot 75'0" by 110'0". The floor area ratio is, most nearly,
    A. 0.46 B. 0.42 C. 0.38 D. 0.34
    43._____

44. A portion of a multiple dwelling, other than an apartment or suite of rooms, separated as a unit from the rest of the building by fireproof construction, is known as a
    A. section B. unit C. separate D. wing
    44._____

45. Records maintained by the Department for each building in the City should include all of the following EXCEPT
    A. number of persons living in each apartment
    B. diagram of building
    C. date of erection
    D. deaths occurring in building each year
    45._____

46. Hospitals are required to make a weekly report to the Department of cases of sickness received in such hospital. This report does NOT state
    A. patient's name
    B. patient's address
    C. patient's sickness
    D. whether patient is an adult or child

47. The Police Department is required to make a weekly report to the Department of arrests. The report does NOT contain
    A. name
    B. address
    C. offense
    D. disposition of case

48. Of the following City Departments, the one which must be furnished information by the Department is
    A. Hospitals
    B. Welfare
    C. Public Works
    D. Tax

49. In a new multiple dwelling, gas meters may be located in
    A. boiler rooms
    B. stair halls
    C. public halls above the cellar
    D. none of the foregoing

50. A required sink may be placed in a
    A. bathroom containing a water-closet
    B. water-closet compartment
    C. public hall
    D. none of the foregoing

(KEY (CORRECT ANSWERS)

1. A	11. C	21. C	31. A	41. C
2. B	12. A	22. C	32. A	42. D
3. C	13. D	23. C	33. B	43. A
4. B	14. A	24. A	34. D	44. A
5. C	15. D	25. A	35. E	45. A
6. A	16. A	26. B	36. H	46. A
7. D	17. C	27. B	37. B	47. D
8. B	18. A	28. D	38. C	48. D
9. C	19. C	29. C	39. G	49. D
10. C	20. B	30. C	40. D	50. D

EXAMINATION SECTION
TEST 1

DIRECTIONS: Each question or incomplete statement is followed by several suggested answers or completions. Select the one that BEST answers the question or completes the statement. *PRINT THE LETTER OF THE CORRECT ANSWER IN THE SPACE AT THE RIGHT.*

1. Assume that a two story building measures 21'6" x 53'7". It is in a district that calls for an open space ratio of .80. The required open space on this lot must be *most nearly* square feet.

    A. 922   B. 1152   C. 1843   D. 2880

    1._____

2. Assume that the elevation at the back of a lot is 127.36 ft. and the elevation at the front of the same lot is 125.49 ft.
    The difference in elevation between front and back of the lot is most nearly

    A. 1'10 1/8"   B. 1'10 1/4"   C. 1'10 3/8"   D. 1'10 1/2"

    2._____

3. The sketch below represents the lowest story of a new building. In order for this story to be considered a basement, the elevation of the first floor must be AT LEAST

    A. 131.09   B. 131.14   C. 131.19   D. 131.24

    3._____

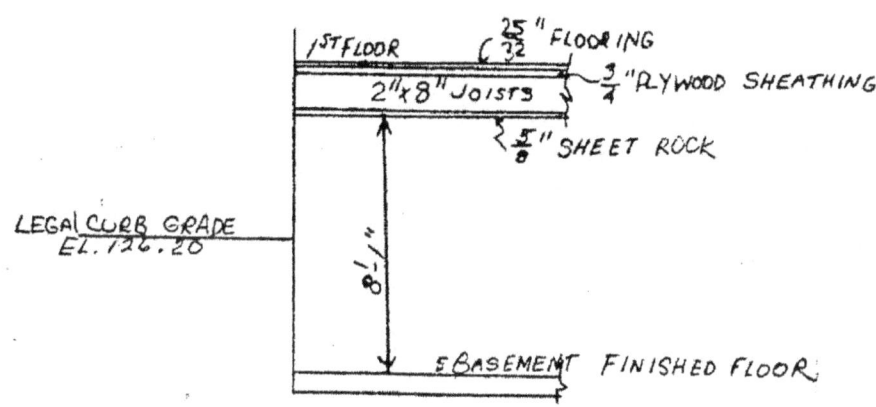

4. The MOST important requirement of a good report is that it should be

    A. properly addressed   B. clear and concise
    C. verbose   D. spelled correctly

    4._____

5. Of the following, in determining whether a violation should be referred for court action, the MOST important item that should be considered is

    A. the amount of available time you have to process the case
    B. the availability of the inspector
    C. whether or not the owner has indicated a desire to cooperate with the department
    D. whether or not the case is important enough to warrant court action

    5._____

35

6. In the Zoning Resolution, the size of required side yards would be found in the chapters on

   A. Use Groups
   B. Bulk Regulations
   C. Area Districts
   D. District Boundaries

7. According to the Zoning Resolution, the one of the following that is NOT considered part of the floor area of a building is a(n)

   A. basement
   B. stairwell at floor level
   C. penthouse
   D. attached garage on 1st floor

8. The one of the following that is permitted by the Zoning Resolution as a home occupation is

   A. veterinary medicine
   B. real estate broker
   C. teaching of music
   D. public relations agency

9. For the purpose of determining the number of rooms in a dwelling unit, the Zoning Resolution adds an arbitrary number to the number of *living rooms*.
   Where there are six or less living rooms, this arbitrary number is

   A. 1/2   B. 1   C. 1 1/2   D. 2

10. Assuming the following signs are all 10 square feet in area, the one that is NOT subject to the provisions of the Zoning Resolution is one indicating

    A. a freight entrance to a building
    B. a fund drive for a civic organization
    C. vacancies in an apartment building
    D. a parking area at the rear of a structure

11. On a plan, the symbol represents

    A. earth
    B. wood
    C. metal lath
    D. marble

12. On a plan, the symbol represents

    A. cinder
    B. brick
    C. plywood
    D. rock lath and plaster

13. On a plan, the symbol represents

    A. glass
    B. asphalt shingles
    C. concrete
    D. porcelain enamel

14. A corbel is a form of

    A. cricket
    B. crown molding
    C. cantilever
    D. curtain wall

15. In balloon type framing, the second floor joists rest on a

    A. sole plate
    B. ribband
    C. header
    D. sill

16. Condensation of moisture in inadequately ventilated attics or roof spaces is usually GREATEST in

    A. summer   B. autumn   C. winter   D. spring

17. Of the following combinations of tread and riser, the one that would be acceptable for required stairs in either a new office building or a multiple dwelling is

    A. 9 1/4", 7 1/2"
    B. 9 1/2", 7 1/4"
    C. 9 1/2", 7 3/4"
    D. 10", 8"

18. A meeting rail is a common part of a

    A. door frame
    B. window sash
    C. stairwell
    D. bulkhead

19. If doors in an old building do not close, it is MOST probably an indication that the

    A. frames have shrunk
    B. building has settled
    C. hinges were not set properly
    D. wood used for the doors are of inferior grade

20. Cracks in concrete are not necessarily caused by settlement of a structure. Sometimes they are caused by

    A. shrinkage
    B. curing
    C. hydration
    D. over-troweling

KEY (CORRECT ANSWERS)

1.	C	11.	A
2.	D	12.	B
3.	A	13.	A
4.	B	14.	C
5.	C	15.	B
6.	B	16.	C
7.	D	17.	C
8.	C	18.	B
9.	C	19.	B
10.	B	20.	A

TEST 2

DIRECTIONS: Each question or incomplete statement is followed by several suggested answers or completions. Select the one that BEST answers the question or completes the statement. *PRINT THE LETTER OF THE CORRECT ANSWER IN THE SPACE AT THE RIGHT.*

1. Required exit doors from a room must open in the direction of egress when the room is occupied by more than _____ persons.

    A. 15   B. 25   C. 35   D. 50

2. A window in a masonry wall on a lot line

    A. is not permitted
    B. must have a fire resistive rating of 3/4 hour
    C. must have a fire resistive rating of 1 hour
    D. must have a fire resistive rating of 1 1/2 hours

3. Air entrained concrete is required in all cases for

    A. garage floors   B. footings
    C. grade beams   D. columns

4. A parapet wall or railing would be required on new non-residential structures where the height of the structure is greater than (give lowest height specified by law) _____ feet.

    A. 15   B. 19   C. 22   D. 25

5. Of the following statements, the one that is CORRECT is that wood joists may

    A. not be supported on a fire wall
    B. be supported on a fire wall only if fireproofed wall is used
    C. be supported on a fire wall only if they are separated from each other by at least 4 inches of solid masonry
    D. be supported on a fire wall only if they are separated from each other by at least 12 inches of solid masonry

6. A foundation wall below grade may be of hollow block only if the building

    A. is a residence
    B. is no more than one story high
    C. is of frame construction
    D. has no cellar or basement

7. The Building Code specifies that lintels are required to be fire-proofed when the opening is more than _____ feet.

    A. 3   B. 4   C. 5   D. 6

8. In a 12-inch brick wall, the MAXIMUM permitted depth of a chase is

    A. none   B. 4"   C. 6"   D. 8"

9. Wood joists should clear flues and chimneys by at least

    A. 1"   B. 2"   C. 3"   D. 4"

10. Fire retarding or enclosure in shafts of all vent ducts are required when they

    A. go through more than one floor
    B. are used for intake as well as exhaust
    C. are more than 144 square inches in area
    D. are in rooms subdivided with wood partitions

11. Assume a builder is unable to complete the pour for a continuous concrete floor slab. The slab is supported by beams and girders.
    The construction joint should be made at a point

    A. over a beam
    B. one quarter of the span length from the beam
    C. one third of the span length from the beam
    D. midway between beams

12. Under required stairs in a Class 3 building,

    A. it is unlawful to locate a closet
    B. a closet is permitted provided that the stringers are fire retarded
    C. a closet is permitted provided that the closet is completely lined with incombustible material
    D. a closet is permitted provided that fireproof wood is used to frame out the closet

13. In New York City, the exit provisions of the State Labor Law apply

    A. only to factories
    B. to factories and warehouses
    C. to factories, warehouses, and restaurants
    D. to all types of uses

14. A Class 3 building, two stories high, may have required stairs enclosed with stud partitions fire retarded with gypsum boards unless the building is used for a

    A. factory
    B. storage warehouse
    C. bowling alley
    D. department store

15. The one of the following rooms in a *place of assembly* that is required to be sprinklered is a

    A. performer's dressing room
    B. kitchen
    C. service pantry
    D. waiting room

16. Of the following, the FIRST operation in the demolition of a building is the

    A. shoring of the adjoining buildings
    B. erection of railings around stairwells
    C. removal of windows
    D. venting of the roof

17. As used in the Building Code, *consistency* of concrete refers to

    A. composition
    B. water-cement ratio
    C. relative plasticity
    D. proportion of aggregates

18. One condition that is required for a building to be considered a *Special Occupancy Structure* is that the building is used for

    A. a theater
    B. a church
    C. a restaurant
    D. motor vehicle repairs

19. A wire glass vision panel on a door opening into a fire tower is

    A. not permitted
    B. permitted if the panel has a fire rating of 3/4 hour
    C. permitted if the panel has a fire rating of 3/4 hour and is less than 100 square inches in area
    D. permitted if the panel has a fire rating of 3/4 hour, is less than 100 square inches in area, and is glazed with two thicknesses of wire glass with an air space between

20. One of the requirements that must be met before untreated wood can be used as a subdividing partition in a Class 1 building is that the partition

    A. be no more than 8 feet high
    B. enclose an area less than 200 square feet in size
    C. enclose office space only
    D. be made of a single thickness of wood

KEY (CORRECT ANSWERS)

1.	D	11.	D
2.	B	12.	C
3.	A	13.	A
4.	C	14.	C
5.	C	15.	A
6.	D	16.	C
7.	B	17.	C
8.	B	18.	A
9.	D	19.	A
10.	A	20.	D

TEST 3

DIRECTIONS: Each question or incomplete statement is followed by several suggested answers or completions. Select the one that BEST answers the question or completes the statement. *PRINT THE LETTER OF THE CORRECT ANSWER IN THE SPACE AT THE RIGHT.*

1. There are two criteria required for determining whether a multiple dwelling shall be classified as a *converted dwelling*.
The FIRST is the number of families originally occupying the dwelling, and the second is the

    A. conjunctive uses
    B. date of erection of the building
    C. classification, whether Class A or B
    D. number of families now occupying the dwelling

2. According to the Multiple Dwelling Law, a *dinette* is NOT considered a living room if its area is _____ sq. ft. or less.

    A. 50   B. 55   C. 59   D. 64

3. Where a building faces only one street, the curb level used for measuring the height of the building is the

    A. lowest curb level in front of the building
    B. highest curb level in front of the building
    C. level of the curb at the center of the front of the building
    D. average of the levels of the lowest and highest curb level in front of the building

4. According to the Multiple Dwelling Code, one of the living rooms in each apartment of a newly created multiple dwelling shall have a MINIMUM floor area of _____ square feet.

    A. 59   B. 110   C. 150   D. 175

5. It is proposed to alter an old law tenement so as to increase the number of apartments. Of the following, the one that MOST completely gives the requirements to be met before the alteration can be approved is: Each new apartment must be provided a

    A. water closet
    B. water closet and a wash basin
    C. water closet, a wash basin, and a bath or shower
    D. water closet, a wash basin, a bath or shower, and centrally supplied heat

6. Gas fueled space heaters may be permitted in lieu of centrally supplied heat.
One of the following conditions required before the use of space heaters can be permitted is that

    A. each apartment has no more than two living rooms
    B. the building is a Class A multiple dwelling
    C. all apartments are used for single room occupancy
    D. D, the gas line supplying the heater be connected directly to the main so that the tenant cannot control the flow of gas

7. An incinerator is required in all multiple

   A. dwellings
   B. dwellings four or more stories in height
   C. dwellings four or more stories in height and occupied by more than twelve families
   D. dwellings four or more stories in height occupied by more than twelve families and erected after October 1, 1951

8. Tests of required sprinkler systems in a single room occupancy building must be made

   A. monthly
   B. quarterly
   C. semi-annually
   D. annually

9. An additional apartment may be created on the first floor of a Class A frame converted dwelling provided that no more than two families will occupy this floor and

   A. the entrance hall is sprinklered
   B. the building is brick veneered
   C. there is no basement occupancy
   D. all stairs are enclosed in one hour fire partitions

10. The MAIN feature differentiating a *five tower* from a *fire stair* is the

    A. fire rating of the enclosure walls
    B. use to which the fire tower is put
    C. method of entering the fire tower from the building
    D. height of the fire tower

11. A new elevator shaft is to be built into a non-fireproof multiple dwelling.
    Of the following materials, the one that has the lowest fire resistance that would be acceptable for the enclosure walls of this shaft is

    A. 3" solid gypsum block
    B. 2" x 4" studs with 5/8" fire code 60 each side
    C. steel studs, wire mesh and 3/4" P.C. plaster
    D. 4" hollow concrete blocks, plastered both sides

12. Of the following statements, the one that is MOST complete and accurate is that a frame extension 70 sq. ft. in area added to a frame multiple dwelling is

    A. not permitted
    B. permitted only if the walls of the extension are brick filled
    C. permitted only if the walls of the extension are brick filled and the extension is to be used solely for bathrooms
    D. permitted only if the walls of the extension are brick filled, the extension is to be used solely for bathrooms and the walls are at least 3 ft. from the side lot lines

13. Assume it is proposed to extend a business use in a non-fireproof multiple dwelling by erecting an extension at the rear of the building.
    The roof the extension is required to be fireproof

    A. in all cases
    B. when the business use requires a combustible occupancy permit
    C. when there are fire escapes above the extension
    D. if the business use is a factory

14. In a Class A dwelling, two water closets may

    A. be placed in one compartment only in old law tenements
    B. be placed in one compartment in either old law or new law tenements
    C. be placed in one compartment in all types of apartment houses
    D. not be placed in one compartment

15. According to the Multiple Dwelling Law, a janitor is NOT required when the maximum number of families occupying the dwelling is

    A. 6 B. 9 C. 12 D. 15

16. The first floor above the lowest cellar in a non-fireproof multiple dwelling does NOT have to be fireproof if

    A. the cellar is used only for incombustible storage
    B. there are two means of egress from the cellar
    C. the building is no more than three stories in height
    D. the dwelling is occupied by no more than nine families

17. In a converted multiple dwelling, ventilation of a room on the top story may be obtained by

    A. a skylight
    B. a duct with a wind blown hood
    C. a duct with an electrically operated fan
    D. by a window only and no other method is acceptable

18. *It* is proposed to build a closet under the stairs leading to the second floor in a non-fire-proof *new law* tenement. This is

    A. not permitted
    B. permitted only if the entire closet is built of non-combustible materials
    C. permitted only if the closet is used for non-combustible storage
    D. permitted if the closet is built of fire-retarded partitions and the soffit of the stairs is also fire-retarded

19. For multiple dwellings erected after April 18, 1929, a ladder from a fire escape to a roof is NOT required when

    A. the building is three stories or less in height
    B. the roof is built of incombustible material
    C. the fire escape is on the front of the building
    D. there is no safe access from the roof to another building

20. It is proposed to convert a Class B multiple dwelling used for summer resort occupancy to year-round Class B use. This conversion is

    A. illegal
    B. legal provided the exits comply with the requirements for Class B use
    C. legal provided the exits and toilet facilities comply with the requirements for Class B use
    D. legal provided the exits, toilet facilities, and ventilation requirements comply with the requirements for Class B use

KEY (CORRECT ANSWERS)

1. B
2. B
3. C
4. C
5. D

6. B
7. D
8. D
9. B
10. C

11. A
12. A
13. C
14. A
15. C

16. C
17. A
18. A
19. C
20. A

EXAMINATION SECTION
TEST 1

DIRECTIONS: Each question or incomplete statement is followed by several suggested answers or completions. Select the one that BEST answers the question or completes the statement. *PRINT THE LETTER OF THE CORRECT ANSWER IN THE SPACE AT THE RIGHT.*

1. Concrete with a slump of 2 inches would *most likely* be used for

   A. floors
   B. thin wall sections
   C. columns
   D. deep beams

   1.____

2. The structure above the roof of a building which encloses a stairway is called a

   A. scuttle
   B. bulkhead
   C. penthouse
   D. shaft

   2.____

3. A #4 reinforcing bar has a diameter, in inches, of *approximately*

   A. 1/4   B. 3/8   C. 1/2   D. 5/8

   3.____

4. A spandrel beam will usually be found

   A. at the wall
   B. around stairs
   C. at the peak of a roof
   D. underneath a column

   4.____

5. Oil is applied to the inside surfaces of concrete forms to

   A. prevent loss of water from the concrete
   B. obtain smoother concrete surfaces
   C. make stripping easier
   D. prevent honeycombing

   5.____

6. A retaining wall is built with a batter.
   Of the following conditions, the one which *most likely* applies to the wall is

   A. it is out of plumb
   B. it is thinner at top than at bottom
   C. neither surface is vertical
   D. both surfaces are vertical

   6.____

7. Two cubic yards of sand and four cubic yards of broken stone are to be used to make 1:2:4 concrete.
   If all the aggregate is used, the number of bags of cement that would be required is

   A. 1   B. 9   C. 18   D. 27

   7.____

8. A rectangular plot is 30 feet wide by 60 feet long. The length of the diagonal, in feet, is *most nearly*

   A. 68   B. 67   C. 66   D. 65

   8.____

9. Wood floor joists are supported on masonry walls which have a clear spacing of 17'0". The number of rows of cross-bridging required is

   A. 4   B. 3   C. 2   D. 1

   9.____

10. When painting wood, the puttying of nail holes and cracks should be done

    A. *after* the priming coat is dry
    B. *before* the priming coat is applied
    C. *while* the priming coat is still wet
    D. *after* the finish coat is applied

11. The material that would normally be used to make a corbel in a brick wall is

    A. brick B. wood C. steel D. concrete

12. Headers and trimmers are used in the construction of

    A. footings B. walls C. floors D. arches

13. In the design of stairs, the designer should consider

    A. maximum height of riser only
    B. minimum width of tread only
    C. product of riser height by tread width only
    D. all of the above

14. A reduction in the required number of columns in a building can be made by using one of the following types of beam. Which one?

    A. floor B. girder C. cantilever D. jack

15. Doors sheathed in metal are known as _____ doors.

    A. kalamein B. tin-clad C. bethlehem D. flemish

16. A coat of plaster which is scratched deliberately would *most likely* be

    A. used in two-coat work only
    B. the first coat placed
    C. the second coat placed
    D. condemned by the inspector

17. A concealed draft opening is

    A. *good* because it improves the appearance of a room
    B. *bad* because it might be accidentally blocked up
    C. *good* because it can be used to regulate the flow of fresh air
    D. *bad* because it is a fire hazard

18. A groove is cut in the underside of a stone sill. This is done to

    A. keep rain water from running down the wall
    B. allow the insertion of dowels
    C. improve the mortar bond
    D. reduce the weight of the sill

19. Of the following, the one which would LEAST likely be used in conjunction with the others is

    A. rafter
    B. collar beam
    C. ridgeboard
    D. tail beam

20. The dimensions of a 2 x 4 when dressed are, *most nearly,*

    A. 2 x 4
    B. 1 1/2 x 3 1/2
    C. 1 5/8 x 3 5/8
    D. 1 3/4 x 3 1/2

21. The story heights of a building could be MOST readily determined from

    A. a plan view
    B. an elevation view
    C. a plot map
    D. all of the above

22. Honeycombing in concrete is *most likely* to occur

    A. if the forms are vibrated
    B. near the top of the forms
    C. if the mix is stiff
    D. if the concrete is well-spaded

23. A weather joint in brick work is one in which the mortar is

    A. flush with the face of the lower brick and slopes inward
    B. flush with the face of the upper brick and slopes inward
    C. recessed a fixed distance behind the face of the brick
    D. flush with the face of upper and lower brick but curves inward between the two bricks

24. A 12 inch brick wall is constructed using stretchers only.
    The PRINCIPAL objection to such a wall is with

    A. appearance
    B. construction difficulties
    C. bond
    D. dimensional problems

25. To prevent sagging joists from damaging a brick wall in the event of a fire, it is BEST to

    A. anchor the joists firmly in the wall
    B. make a bevel cut on the end of the joists
    C. use bridal irons to support the joists
    D. box out the wall for the joists

26. Flashing would *most likely* be found in a

    A. footing   B. floor   C. ceiling   D. parapet

27. Vermiculite is used in plaster to

    A. reduce weight
    B. permit easier cleaning
    C. give architectural effects
    D. reduce the mixing water required

28. The volume in cubic feet of a room 8'6" wide by 10'6" long by 8'8" high is *most nearly*

   A. 770   B. 774   C. 778   D. 782

29. A slab of concrete is 2'0" by 3'0" by 8" thick.
    The weight of the slab is, in pounds, *most nearly*

   A. 450   B. 500   C. 550   D. 600

30. Wainscoting is USUALLY found on

   A. floors   B. walls   C. ceilings   D. roofs

31. A piece of wood covering the plaster below the stool of a window is called a(n)

   A. apron   B. sill   C. coping   D. trimmer

32. English bond is used in

   A. plastering   B. papering   C. roofing   D. bricklaying

33. In plastering, coves would *most likely* be found where

   A. wall meets ceiling   B. one wall meets another
   C. wall meets floor   D. wall meets column

34. Fire stopping is usually accomplished by

   A. installing self-closing doors
   B. bricking up the space between furring at floors
   C. installing wire glass
   D. using fire resistive materials throughout the building

35. A Class 1 (fireproof structure) building has floor sleepers of wood. This is

   A. *not permitted*
   B. *permitted*
   C. *permitted* if the space between sleepers is filled with incombustible material
   D. *permitted* if a wearing surface similar to asphalt tile is applied to the wooden flooring

KEY (CORRECT ANSWERS)

1.	A	16.	B
2.	B	17.	D
3.	C	18.	A
4.	A	19.	D
5.	C	20.	C
6.	B	21.	B
7.	D	22.	C
8.	B	23.	A
9.	C	24.	C
10.	A	25.	B
11.	A	26.	D
12.	C	27.	A
13.	D	28.	B
14.	C	29.	D
15.	A	30.	B

31. A
32. D
33. A
34. B
35. C

TEST 2

DIRECTIONS: Each question or incomplete statement is followed by several suggested answers or completions. Select the one that BEST answers the question or completes the statement. *PRINT THE LETTER OF THE CORRECT ANSWER IN THE SPACE AT THE RIGHT.*

1. Joints on interior surfaces of brick walls are usually flush joints EXCEPT when the walls are to be
    A. painted
    B. plastered
    C. waterproofed
    D. dampproofed

2. The headers in a brick veneer wall serve
    A. both a structural and an architectural purpose
    B. a structural purpose only
    C. an architectural purpose only
    D. NO structural or architectural purpose

3. Of the following, the one which is NOT usually classified as interior wood trim is
    A. apron
    B. ribbon
    C. jamb
    D. base mold

4. Single-strength glass would *most likely* be found in
    A. single light sash
    B. doors in fire walls
    C. doors in fire partitions
    D. multi-light sash

5. The one of the following items that is LEAST related to the others is
    A. newel
    B. riser
    C. nosing
    D. sill

6. In a plastered room, grounds for plaster are LEAST likely to be used
    A. at baseboards
    B. around windows
    C. around doors
    D. at the top of wainscoting

7. Of the following types of walls, the type which is *most likely* an interior wall is _____ wall.
    A. curtain
    B. faced
    C. panel
    D. fire

8. *Boxing* is *most likely* to be performed by a
    A. mason
    B. plasterer
    C. plumber
    D. painter

9. Linseed oil is classified as a
    A. vehicle
    B. thinner
    C. drying oil
    D. pigment

10. Curing of concrete would be MOST critical when the temperature and humidity are, respectively,

    A. 75° and 80%
    B. 80° and 90%
    C. 85° and 10%
    D. 90° and 95%

11. Of the following items, the item which is LEAST related to the others is

    A. putty
    B. sash weight
    C. glazier's points
    D. lights

12. Assume that a wood-frame house has studs of 2 x 4's.
    Placing the studs so that the wider dimension is parallel to the wall is

    A. *good* because it provides a wider nailing surface for sheathing and lathing
    B. *bad* because it reduces the open space available for windows
    C. *good* because it stiffens the frame
    D. *bad* because it reduces the load-carrying capacity of the studs

13. Government anchors are used in one of the following types of construction. Which one?

    A. Wood frame
    B. Steel beams supported on masonry bearing walls
    C. Wooden joists on masonry bearing walls
    D. Steel frame with steel joists

14. When rivet holes in structural steel fail to match up by an eighth of an inch, the BEST thing to do is

    A. ignore the mismatch and force the rivet into the hole
    B. enlarge the holes with a drift pin
    C. ream the holes to a larger diameter
    D. use a smaller sized rivet

15. The BEST way to use two angles to make a lintel is

16. A single channel section would *most likely* be used for a

    A. floor beam
    B. girder
    C. spandrel beam
    D. column

17. An oil-base paint is usually thinned with

    A. linseed oil
    B. turpentine
    C. a drying oil
    D. a resin

18. Red lead is often used as a pigment in metal priming paints PRIMARILY because it

    A. provides good coverage
    B. presents a good appearance
    C. makes painting easier
    D. is a rust inhibitor

19. Knots in wood that is to be painted

    A. require no special treatment
    B. should be painted with the priming paint before the priming paint is applied to the rest of the wood
    C. should be coated with linseed oil before any painting is done
    D. should be coated with shellac before any painting is done

20. A dove-tail anchor would *most likely* be used to bond brick veneer with a _____ wall.

    A. brick   B. concrete   C. wood frame   D. concrete block

21. A rafter is MOST similar in function to a

    A. joist   B. stud   C. sill   D. girder

22. In steel construction, it is usually MOST important to mill the ends of

    A. beams   B. girders   C. columns   D. lintels

23. Furring tile is usually set so that the air spaces in the tile are

    A. continuous in a vertical direction
    B. continuous in a horizontal direction
    C. closed off at the ends of each tile
    D. set at random

24. When plastering a wall surface of glazed tile, it is MOST important that the tile

    A. be wet   B. be dry
    C. be scored   D. joints be raked

25. In a peaked roof, the run of a rafter is

    A. less than the length of the rafter
    B. greater than the length of the rafter
    C. equal to the length of the rafter
    D. dependent upon the slope of the rafter

26. Construction of a dormer window does NOT usually involve

    A. cut rafters   B. rafter headers
    C. trimmer rafters   D. hip rafters

27. In a four-ply slag roof,

    A. there is no overlap of the roofing felt
    B. a uniform coating of pitch or asphalt is placed on top of the top layer of felt
    C. slag is placed between the layers of felt
    D. there is no need to use flashing

28. Copper wire basket strainers would *most likely* be used by a

    A. carpenter   B. plumber   C. painter   D. roofer

29. Splices of columns in steel construction are usually made

    A. at floor level
    B. two feet above floor level
    C. two feet below floor level
    D. midway between floors

30. In plumbing, a lead bend is usually used in the line from a

    A. slop sink   B. shower
    C. water closet   D. kitchen sink

31. The location of leaks in gas piping may be BEST detected by use of a

    A. match   B. heated filament
    C. soapy water solution   D. guinea pig

32. The one of the following items that would be MOST useful in eliminating water hammer from a water system is a

    A. magnesium anode   B. surge tank
    C. clean out   D. quick-closing valve

33. The MAIN purpose of a fixture trap is to

    A. catch small articles that may have accidentally dropped in the fixture
    B. prevent back syphonage
    C. make it easier to repair the fixture
    D. block the passage of foul air

34. In a certain district, the area of a building may be no longer than 55% of the area of the lot on which it stands. On a rectangular lot 75 ft. by 125 ft., the maximum permissible area of building is, in square feet, *most nearly*

    A. 5148   B. 5152   C. 5156   D. 5160

35. The allowable tensile stress in steel is 18,000 pounds per square inch. The maximum permissible tensile load in a 1-inch diameter steel bar is, in pounds, *most nearly*

    A. 13,500   B. 13,800   C. 14,100   D. 14,400

KEY (CORRECT ANSWERS)

1.	B	16.	C
2.	C	17.	B
3.	B	18.	D
4.	D	19.	D
5.	D	20.	B
6.	D	21.	A
7.	D	22.	C
8.	D	23.	B
9.	A	24.	C
10.	C	25.	A
11.	B	26.	D
12.	D	27.	B
13.	B	28.	D
14.	C	29.	B
15.	A	30.	C

31. C
32. B
33. D
34. C
35. C

———

TEST 3

DIRECTIONS: Each question or incomplete statement is followed by several suggested answers or completions. Select the one that BEST answers the question or completes the statement. *PRINT THE LETTER OF THE CORRECT ANSWER IN THE SPACE AT THE RIGHT.*

1. The ends of a joist in a brick building are cut to a bevel. This is done PRINCIPALLY to prevent damage to

   A. joist   B. floor   C. sill   D. wall

2. Of the following, the wood that is MOST commonly used today for floor joists is

   A. long leaf yellow pine   B. douglas fir
   C. oak   D. birch

3. Quarter sawed lumber is preferred for the best finished flooring PRINCIPALLY because it

   A. has the greatest strength
   B. shrinks the least
   C. is the easiest to nail
   D. is the easiest to handle

4. Of the following, the MAXIMUM height that would be considered acceptable for a stair riser is

   A. 6 1/2"   B. 7 1/2"   C. 8 1/2"   D. 9 1/2"

5. The part of a tree that will produce the DENSEST wood is the _____ wood.

   A. spring   B. summer   C. sap   D. heart

6. Lumber in quantity is ordered by

   A. cubic feet   B. foot board measure
   C. lineal feet   D. weight and length

7. A *chase* in a brick wall is a

   A. pilaster   B. waterstop   C. recess   D. corbel

8. *Parging* refers to

   A. increasing the thickness of a brick wall
   B. plastering the back of face brickwork
   C. bonding face brick to backing blocks
   D. leveling each course of brick

9. In brickwork, muriatic acid is commonly used to

   A. increase the strength of the mortar
   B. etch the brick
   C. waterproof the wall
   D. clean the wall

10. Cement mortar can be made easier to work by the addition of a small quantity of

    A. lime   B. soda   C. litharge   D. plaster

11. Joints in brick walls are tooled

    A. immediately after each brick is laid
    B. after the mortar has had its initial set
    C. after the entire wall is completed
    D. 28 days after the wall has been built

12. If cement mortar has begun to set before it can be used in a wall, the BEST thing to do is to

    A. use the mortar immediately as is
    B. add a small quantity of lime
    C. add some water and mix thoroughly
    D. discard the mortar

13. The BEST flux to use when soldering galvanized iron is

    A. killed acid   B. sal-ammoniac
    C. muriatic acid   D. resin

14. The type of solder that would be used in *hard soldering* is _____ solder.

    A. bismuth   B. wiping   C. 50-50   D. silver

15. Roll roofing material is usually felt which has been impregnated with

    A. cement   B. mastic   C. tar   D. latex

16. The purpose of flashing on roofs is to

    A. secure roofing materials to the roof
    B. make it easier to lay the roofing
    C. prevent leaks through the roof
    D. insulate the roof from excessive heat

17. The type of chain used with sash weights is _____ link.

    A. flat   B. round
    C. figure-eight   D. basketweave

18. The material that would be used to seal around a window frame is

    A. oakum   B. litharge   C. grout   D. calking

19. The function of a window sill is *most nearly* the same as that of a

    A. jamb   B. coping   C. lintel   D. buck

20. Lightweight plaster would be made with

    A. sand   B. cinders   C. potash   D. vermiculite

21. The FIRST coat of plaster to be applied on a three-coat plaster job is the _____ coat.

    A. brown   B. scratch   C. white   D. keene

22. The FIRST coat of plaster over rock lath should be a _____ plaster.

    A. gypsum
    B. lime
    C. Portland cement
    D. pozzolan cement

23. The PRINCIPAL reason for covering a concrete sidewalk with straw or paper after the concrete has been poured is to

    A. prevent people from walking on the concrete while it is still wet
    B. impart a rough, non-slip surface to the concrete
    C. prevent excessive evaporation of water in the concrete
    D. shorten the length of time it would take for the concrete to harden

24. Concrete is *rubbed* with a(n)

    A. emery wheel
    B. carborundum brick
    C. sandstone
    D. alundum stick

25. To prevent concrete from sticking to forms, the forms should be painted with

    A. oil   B. kerosene   C. water   D. lime

26. One method of measuring the consistency of a concrete mix is by means of a _____ test.

    A. penetration
    B. flow
    C. slump
    D. weight

27. A chemical that is sometimes used to prevent the freezing of concrete in cold weather is

    A. alum
    B. glycerine
    C. calcium chloride
    D. sodium nitrate

28. The one of the following that is LEAST commonly used for columns is

    A. wide flange beams
    B. angles
    C. concrete-filled pipe
    D. "I" beams

29. Fire protection of steel floor beams is MOST frequently accomplished by the use of

    A. gypsum block
    B. brick
    C. rock wool fill
    D. vermiculite gypsum plaster

30. A *Pittsburgh lock* is a(n)

    A. emergency door lock
    B. sheet metal joint
    C. elevator safety
    D. boiler valve

31. Of the following items, the one which is NOT used in making fastenings to masonry or plaster walls is a(n)

    A. lead shield
    B. expansion bolt
    C. rawl plug
    D. steel bushing

32. The term *bell and spigot* USUALLY refers to

    A. refrigerator motors
    B. cast iron pipes
    C. steam radiator outlets
    D. electrical receptacles

33. In plumbing work, a valve which allows water to flow in one direction only is commonly known as a _____ valve.

   A. check B. globe C. gate D. stop

34. A pipe coupling is BEST used to connect two pieces of pipe of

   A. the same diameter in a straight line
   B. the same diameter at right angles to each other
   C. different diameters at a 45° angle
   D. different diameters in a 1/8th bend

35. One method of testing fuses is to connect a pair of test lamps in the circuit in such a manner that the test lamp will light up if the fuse is good and will remain dark if the fuse is bad. In the illustration, 1 and 2 are fuses. In order to test if fuse 1 is bad, test lamps should be connected between

   A. A and B B. B and D C. A and D D. C and B

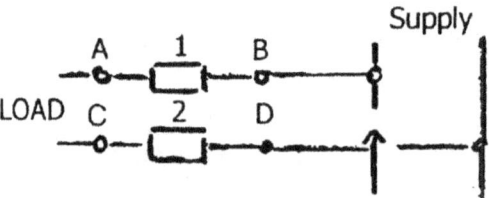

36. Operating an incandescent electric light bulb at less than its rated voltage will result in

   A. shorter life and brighter light
   B. longer life and dimmer light
   C. brighter light and longer life
   D. dimmer light and shorter life

37. In order to control a lamp from two different positions, it is necessary to use

   A. two single pole switches
   B. one single pole switch and one four-way switch
   C. two three-way switches
   D. one single pole switch and one four-way switch

38. The PRINCIPAL reason for the grounding of electrical equipment and circuits is to

   A. prevent short circuits   B. insure safety from shock
   C. save power   D. increase voltage

39. The ordinary single-pole flush wall type switch must be connected

   A. across the line
   B. in the "hot" conductor
   C. in the grounded conductor
   D. in the white conductor

40. A strike plate is MOST closely associated with a

   A. lock B. sash C. butt D. tie rod

41. A room is 7'6" wide by 9'0" long, with a ceiling height of 8'0". One gallon of flat paint will cover approximately 400 square feet of wall.
The number of gallons of this paint required to paint the walls of this room, making no deductions for windows or doors, is *most nearly* _____ gallon.

    A. 1/4 B. 1/3 C. 3/4 D. 1

42. The cost of a certain job is broken down as follows:
    Materials $375
    Rental of equipment   120
    Labor   315
    The percentage of the total cost of the job that can be charged to materials is *most nearly*

    A. 40% B. 42% C. 44% D. 46%

43. By trial, it is found that by using two cubic feet of sand, a 5 cubic foot batch of concrete is produced. Using the same proportions, the amount of sand required to produce 2 cubic yards of concrete is *most nearly* _____ cubic feet.

    A. 20 B. 22 C. 24 D. 26

44. It takes four men six days to do a certain job. Working at the same speed, the number of days it will take three men to do this job is

    A. 7 B. 8 C. 9 D. 10

45. The cost of rawl plugs is $2.75 per gross. The cost of 2,448 rawl plugs is

    A. $46.75 B. $47.25 C. $47.75 D. $48.25

KEY (CORRECT ANSWERS)

1. D	11. B	21. B	31. D	41. C
2. B	12. D	22. A	32. B	42. D
3. B	13. C	23. C	33. A	43. B
4. B	14. D	24. B	34. A	44. B
5. D	15. C	25. A	35. C	45. A
6. B	16. C	26. C	36. B	
7. C	17. A	27. C	37. C	
8. B	18. D	28. B	38. B	
9. D	19. B	29. D	39. B	
10. A	20. D	30. B	40. A	

EXAMINATION SECTION
TEST 1

DIRECTIONS: Each question or incomplete statement is followed by several suggested answers or completions. Select the one that BEST answers the question or completes the statement. *PRINT THE LETTER OF THE CORRECT ANSWER IN THE SPACE AT THE RIGHT.*

1. Of the following materials, the one which has the HIGHEST tendency to spontaneous heating is

    A. lanolin
    B. linseed oil
    C. coconut oil
    D. turpentine

    1._____

2. The one of the following fabrics used in the manufacture of clothing that is MOST flammable is

    A. wool   B. acetate   C. cotton   D. linen

    2._____

3. Which of the following substances has the LOWEST boiling point?

    A. Turpentine
    B. Benzene
    C. Mineral spirits
    D. Cellosolve

    3._____

4. Which of the following non-solid fuels has the HIGHEST ignition temperature?

    A. Acetone
    B. Carbon monoxide
    C. Ethylene
    D. Methyl alcohol

    4._____

5. Assume that the cellar of a building is 100 feet long, 100 feet wide, and 10 feet high. If natural gas were distributed evenly throughout the cellar, and all openings from the cellar are closed, which one of the following volumes of natural gas would create an explosive atmosphere if suddenly released into this cellar?
    _____ cubic feet.

    A. 2,500   B. 7,500   C. 17,500   D. 25,000

    5._____

6. A lighted cigarette is LEAST likely to start a fire if dropped and left

    A. on a kapok pillow
    B. on cotton bed clothes
    C. in an explosive vapor-air mixture
    D. on dry grass

    6._____

7. A fire marshal inspecting a number of buildings where explosions are suspected as having been caused by dynamite would find that the scene of the dynamite explosion is MOST likely the one where

    A. a large section of wall has toppled, with its mortar remaining intact
    B. there are fragments of shattered cast iron
    C. a window frame has been pushed out from the wall surface, with some or all of the windows remaining intact
    D. the light bulbs in the building have remained unbroken

    7._____

8. During apparatus field inspection of a restaurant located in a building erected in 1972, a fireman finds that the filters for the cooking equipment exhaust system are cleaned every three months and the entire system is cleaned once a year.
   This maintenance procedure is

   A. *correct*
   B. *incorrect,* because the filters should be discarded at least every three months and the system cleaned at least once a year
   C. *incorrect,* because the filters should be discarded at least once a year and the system cleaned at least once a year
   D. *incorrect,* because both the filters and the entire system should be cleaned at least every three months

9. A group home is a facility for the care and maintenance of not less than three nor more than twelve children and is classified by the building code in the same occupancy group as a one-family dwelling.
   This much of the definition of a group home GENERALLY is

   A. *correct*
   B. *incorrect,* because a group home may not have less than seven children
   C. *incorrect,* because a group home is for adults, not children
   D. *incorrect,* because a group home is classified in the same occupancy group as a rooming house

10. A fifty-foot high, five-story multiple dwelling built in 1974 has a floor area of 7,000 square feet on each floor. It is equipped with a non-automatic dry standpipe system. During apparatus field inspection duty, a member discovers that a control valve on the standpipe is in closed position with no placard indicating that this was the normal position of the valve. Further investigation reveals that there is no one in the building who has a certificate of fitness to maintain the standpipe system. Of the following statements concerning the above situation, the one that is CORRECT is that the situation as described is

    A. *legal*
    B. *illegal,* because an individual with a certificate of fitness must be on the premises
    C. *illegal,* because an automatic system is required
    D. *illegal,* because the control valve must be in the open position

11. A tank truck with a capacity of 4,400 gallons is delivering #4 fuel oil to a multiple dwelling. According to the specifications for tank trucks, the person in control of the truck and supervising this delivery

    A. *does not* require a certificate of fitness because the capacity of the tank is less than 5,000 gallons
    B. *does not* require a certificate of fitness because the tank has light oil
    C. *does not* require a certificate of fitness because the delivery is being made to a non-commercial occupancy
    D. *requires* a certificate of fitness because a fire department permit is needed for all tank trucks delivering #4 fuel oil

12. The multiple dwelling law states that sprinkler systems in lodging houses shall have a supervisory and maintenance service satisfactory to the fire department. The fire department requires a valid inspection of the sprinkler control valve AT LEAST once

A. daily
B. semi-weekly
C. weekly
D. monthly

13. Anhydrous ammonia is being used in a duplicating machine located in a school office. There is no one in the school with a certificate of fitness for the storage and use of ammonia or for the servicing of the duplicating machine. In this situation, a certificate of fitness is GENERALLY

    A. *not* required because the machine is considered office equipment
    B. *not* required unless the quantity of anhydrous ammonia being stored on the premises is more than two 150-lb. cylinders
    C. *not* required because schools, with regular supervised fire drills, are exempt from certain requirements of the fire prevention code
    D. *required* whether or not a permit is needed under the fire prevention code

13._____

14. According to the labor law, fire drills are required to be conducted in certain factory buildings.
    Which of the following statements is CORRECT with respect to such fire drills?

    A. Fire drills are required to be conducted in every factory building in which there are more than 75 persons above or below the street floor.
    B. Fire drills are not required to be conducted in factory buildings less than 100 feet in height.
    C. Fire drills are required to be conducted in every factory building over two stories in height in which more than twenty-five persons are employed above the ground floor unless the sprinkler system and number of occupants of the building are in accordance with the other provisions of the labor law.
    D. The sprinklering of a factory building is not a factor in determining whether or not a building is required to conduct fire drills.

14._____

15. An officer tells members during a drill that a red light and a placard should serve to locate the Siamese hose connection of a temporary standpipe system in a building under construction.
    The officer's instructions are

    A. *correct,* because both the red light and a placard are required
    B. *incorrect,* because only the red light is required
    C. *incorrect,* because only a placard is required
    D. *incorrect,* because neither the red light nor a placard is required

15._____

16. During apparatus field inspection duty, a fireman inspecting a 40-story office building occupied by 1,000 people is unable to find a fire safety director or deputy fire safety director in the building. The manager of the building states that the fire safety director is out to lunch, that there is no deputy fire safety director, and that he, the manager, is acting as the fire safety director pending the return of the fire safety director. Because the manager does not have a fire safety director certificate of fitness, the fireman issues a violation to him.
    The fireman's action in this situation is

16._____

A. *correct,* because local law requires a fire safety director with a certificate of fitness in a building this high to be on duty whenever the building is occupied by more than 500 people
B. *incorrect,* because local law permits the fire safety director to be temporarily relieved, for short intervals, by responsible individuals who do not have the required certificate of fitness
C. *correct,* because local law requires a fire safety director with a certificate of fitness to be on duty in a building this high, regardless of the occupancy of the building
D. *incorrect,* because whenever local law is not complied with, a referral report should be forwarded, and no violation issued

17. A commercial vehicle without a fire department permit is transporting 500 pounds of dynamite from a neighboring outside county through the city to another out-of-town county without stopping to make any deliveries enroute. There is no department pumping engine escort. The situation as described is

    A. *legal,* because the shipment contains less than 1,000 pounds of dynamite
    B. *illegal,* because a pumping engine escort is required whenever explosives are transported without a fire department permit through the city
    C. *legal,* even though a fire department permit has not been issued, because the shipment does not contain any blasting caps
    D. *illegal,* because dynamite may not be transported through the city from one out-of-town location to another

18. Of the following exit doors in buildings erected in 1976, the one that does NOT have to swing outward is a(n)

    A. corridor door from a room used for office purposes with an occupancy of 80 persons
    B. corridor door from a lecture room in a school building where the room has an occupancy of 80 persons
    C. exterior street-floor exit door from a space 2,000 square feet in area in a business building, where the space is occupied by fewer than 50 persons and the maximum travel distance to the door is 50 feet
    D. exterior street-floor exit door from a lobby in a hotel, where the lobby will not be occupied by more than 50 persons and the maximum travel distance to the door is 50 feet

19. During apparatus field inspection duty, a fireman inspecting a 90-foot high apartment house erected in 1972 finds that the standpipe hose is missing from every hose rack in the building. Of the following statements concerning this situation, the one that is CORRECT is that

    A. the situation as described may be legal but the fire-man needs additional information to make a final decision
    B. all such buildings, regardless of when erected, must have the standpipe hose racks equipped with hose
    C. all such buildings, if erected under the new building code, must have their standpipe hose racks equipped with hose
    D. the situation as described would be acceptable for an office building but not for an apartment house

20. A permit is required to store empty combustible packing boxes in a building whenever the   20.____

    A. boxes occupy more than two thousand cubic feet
    B. storage space is less than 50 feet from the nearest wall of a building occupied as a hospital, school, or theater
    C. boxes are of cardboard or similarly combustible material
    D. building is of non-fireproof construction

21. An inspector, taking some clothing to a dry cleaner in his neighborhood, noticed that   21.____
    inflammable cleaning fluid was stored in a way which created a fire hazard. The fireman called this to the attention of the proprietor, explaining the danger involved.
    This method of handling the situation was

    A. *bad;* the fireman should not have interfered in a matter which was not his responsibility
    B. *good;* the proprietor would probably remove the hazard and be more careful in the future
    C. *bad;* the fireman should have reported the situation to the fire inspector's office without saying anything to the proprietor
    D. *good;* since the fireman was a customer, he should treat the proprietor more leniently than he would treat other violators

22. According to the Building Code, a vertical iron ladder to an escape manhole opening in   22.____
    the sidewalk is required from a cellar room when the room is being used as a

    A. coal storage room   B. restaurant kitchen
    C. boiler room   D. factory

23. In a building of public assembly, the provisions of the Fire Prevention Code prohibit the   23.____
    use of decorations, drapes, or scenery made of combustible material which have not been rendered fireproof.
    Of the following types of occupancies, the one that is exempt from the provisions of this section is a

    A. school   B. hospital   C. church   D. museum

24. As used in the Building Code, a *4-hour fire rating* of a wall means that in a standard fire   24.____
    test of four hours duration, the

    A. wall will not collapse
    B. unexposed side of the wall will not char or smolder
    C. temperature on the unexposed side of the wall will not rise
    D. temperature on the unexposed side of the wall will not rise more than a predetermined amount

25. The prohibition against smoking in retail stores applies   25.____

    A. to all stores
    B. only to stores employing more than 25 persons
    C. only to stores accommodating more than 300 persons
    D. only to stores employing more than 25 persons or accommodating more than 300 persons

KEY (CORRECT ANSWERS)

1.	C	11.	D
2.	D	12.	C
3.	B	13.	D
4.	D	14.	C
5.	C	15.	A
6.	C	16.	D
7.	A	17.	B
8.	D	18.	C
9.	B	19.	A
10.	D	20.	A

21. B
22. C
23. C
24. D
25. A

TEST 2

DIRECTIONS: Each question or incomplete statement is followed by several suggested answers or completions. Select the one that BEST answers the question or completes the statement. *PRINT THE LETTER OF THE CORRECT ANSWER IN THE SPACE AT THE RIGHT.*

1. The one of the following which is NOT required by the Code for the protection of openings into public halls in old-law tenements less than four stories high is that every 1.____

   A. door opening into the public hall shall be fireproof, having a fire-resisting rating of at least one hour
   B. door opening into the public hall shall be self-closing
   C. glazed panel in a door opening into a public hall shall be glazed with wire glass
   D. transom opening upon any public hall shall be glazed with wire glass and firmly secured in a closed position

2. Firestopping of the space above a hung ceiling into areas not exceeding 3,000 square feet is REQUIRED when the 2.____

   A. structural members within the concealed space are individually protected with materials having the required fire resistance
   B. concealed space is sprinklered
   C. ceiling contributes to the required fire resistance of the floor or roof assembly
   D. ceiling is not an essential part of the fire-resistive assembly

3. When a deluge sprinkler system is provided around the perimeter of a theater stage, manual operating devices as well as automatic controls are required by the Building Code. 3.____
   The MOST complete and accurate statement concerning these manual operating devices is that they should be located

   A. at the emergency control station
   B. adjacent to one exit from the stage
   C. at the emergency control station and adjacent to one exit from the stage
   D. at the emergency control station, adjacent to one exit from the stage, and at the deluge valve

4. Yellow painted Siamese caps on office buildings will indicate that the Siamese serves ONLY 4.____

   A. the standpipe in pressurized stairs
   B. the sprinklers in sub-basement locations
   C. a combination standpipe and sprinkler system
   D. as a supply line to the fire pump for the upper level standpipe outlets

5. Of the following buildings, the one that MUST have emergency smoke-venting equipment is a 5.____

   A. new office building, 275 feet high, equipped throughout with automatic sprinklers
   B. new office building, 175 feet high, without an air conditioning system

C. new office building, 75 feet high, without sprinklers and with a central air conditioning system serving more than the floor on which the equipment is located
D. one-story building, classified in occupancy group B-1, greater in depth than 100 feet from a frontage space

6. A factory building was erected in 1912 and was occupied continuously as such until 1950 when it became completely vacant. After many years, it was reoccupied with factory occupancies.
This structure

   A. must comply with the State Labor Law affecting factory buildings erected after October 1, 1913
   B. may be reoccupied as a factory building without changing its classification as one erected before October 1, 1913
   C. may be reoccupied as a factory building erected before October 1, 1913 provided an automatic sprinkler system is installed
   D. cannot be reoccupied as a factory unless it is of fireproof construction

7. A five-story fireproof factory building erected in 1909 has the following occupancies:
   First floor - dress manufacturing
   Second floor - tannery
   Third floor - artificial flower manufacturing
   Fourth floor - machine shop
   Fifth floor - vacant
Under the State Labor Law, an automatic extinguishing system is

   A. *not required* because the building is classed as fireproof
   B. *required* for the artificial flower factory and all floors above
   C. *not required* if the tannery is moved to the fifth floor
   D. *required* throughout

8. Which one of the following statements does NOT correctly describe the protection requirements for vertical separation of openings?
In buildings classified in occupancy group

   A. E exceeding three stories or 40 feet in height, openings located vertically above one another in exterior walls except in stairway enclosures required to have a fire resistance rating of one hour or more shall be separated by a spandrel wall at least three feet high between the top of one opening and the bottom of the opening immediately above
   B. D exceeding three stories or 40 feet in height, openings located vertically above one another in exterior walls except in stairway enclosures shall have each such opening above the lower one protected against fire by an opening protective
   C. C exceeding three stories or 40 feet in height, openings located vertically above one another in exterior walls except in stairway enclosures shall be protected by a fire canopy of non-combustible materials extending out at least two feet horizontally from the wall and at least as long as the width of the lower opening
   D. B, spandrels and fire canopies shall be constructed to provide at least the fire-resistance rating required for the exterior wall, but in no event less than one hour

9. It is MOST complete and accurate to state that, according to the Manual of Fire Communications, in the event the officer in command of a fire or emergency operation requires additional manpower, in lieu of transmitting additional alarms or special calls, he may

   A. telephone the Office of the Chief of Department, specifying the kind of aid required and when it should be sent
   B. notify the dispatcher by radio of the assistance required, specifying the number of officers and fire-men, and the location to which they shall report
   C. telephone the dispatcher specifying the assistance required, including the number of officers and fire-men needed, location to which they shall report, and the expected time additional manpower will be released
   D. notify the Office of the Chief of Department, specifying the assistance required, the location to which they shall report, the reason for calling additional manpower, and the amount of time they can be expected to be detained

10. While inspecting a sprinklered building, a fire officer is asked by the building manager for his opinion about painting the wooden water tank on the roof. The manager explains it is his understanding that painting the tank will extend its useful life.
    Of the following, it would probably be MOST appropriate for the fire officer to indicate that

    A. painting the interior of the tank below water level will prolong the life of the tank, but painting the exterior may tend to hide structural defects
    B. painting a wooden tank may be desirable from the standpoint of appearance, but it is of questionable value in increasing the life of the tank
    C. the use of paint is undesirable for any purpose on either the exterior or interior of the tank
    D. the manager should consult a painting contractor to find out what his experience and recommendations are

11. In a large warehouse facility, the GREATEST fire hazard potential will result if rubber automotive tires are stored on the

    A. side in stacked piles   B. tread in racks
    C. side on pallets   D. tread in stacked piles

12. During a fire prevention inspection, a firefighter may find a condition which could be the immediate cause of death in the event of a fire.
    Which one of the following conditions in a restaurant is the MOST dangerous?

    A. Blocked exit doors
    B. A crack in the front door
    C. A window that does not open
    D. A broken air conditioning system

13. Firefighters must regularly inspect office buildings to determine whether fire prevention laws have been obeyed. Some of these fire prevention laws are as follows: DOORS: Doors should be locked as follows:
    I. Doors on the ground floor may be locked on the street side to prevent entry into the stairway.
    II. Doors in office buildings that are less than 100 feet in height may be locked on the stairway side on each floor above the ground floor.
    III. Doors in office buildings that are 100 feet or more in height may be locked on the stairway side except for every fourth floor.

    The doors in an office building which is less than 100 feet in height may be locked on the stairway side

    A. on all floors including the ground floor
    B. on all floors above the ground floor
    C. except for every fourth floor
    D. on all floors above the fourth floor

14. SIGNS: Signs concerning stairways should be posted in the following manner:
    I. A sign shall be posted near the elevator on each floor, stating, *IN CASE OF FIRE, USE STAIRS UNLESS OTHERWISE INSTRUCTED.* The sign shall contain a diagram showing the location of the stairs and the letter identification of the stairs.
    II. Each stairway shall be identified by an alphabetical letter on a sign posted on the hallway side of the stair door.
    III. Signs indicating the floor number shall be attached to the stairway side of each door.
    IV. Signs indicating whether re-entry can be made into the building, and the floors where re-entry can be made, shall be posted on the stairway side of each door.

    Which one of the following CORRECTLY lists the information which should be posted on the stairway side of a door?

    A sign will indicate the
    A. floor number, whether re-entry can be made into the building, and the floors where re-entry can be made
    B. alphabetical letter of the stairway, whether re-entry can be made into the building, and the floors where re-entry can be made
    C. alphabetical letter of the stairway and the floor number
    D. alphabetical letter of the stairway, the floor number, whether re-entry can be made into the building, and the floors where re-entry can be made

15. The Fire Department now uses companies on fire duty, with their apparatus, for fire prevention inspection in commercial buildings.
    The one of the following changes which was MOST important in making this inspection procedure practicable was the

    A. reduction of hours of work of firemen
    B. use of two-way radio equipment
    C. use of enclosed cabs on fire apparatus
    D. increase in property values during the post-war period

16. The MAXIMUM length of unlined linen hose which shall be permitted at any standpipe hose outlet valve is

    A. 50' B. 75' C. 100' D. 125'

17. The State Labor Law requires that fire drills be conducted monthly in factory buildings over two stories in height in which more than 25 persons are employed above the ground floor.
    The one of the following statements that is MOST complete and accurate is that the law provides for automatic exemption from this requirement to factory buildings which are

    A. completely sprinklered
    B. completely sprinklered by a system having two adequate sources of water supply
    C. completely sprinklered by a system having two adequate sources of water supply and a maximum number of occupants of any one floor not more than 50 percent above the capacity of the exits required for the same building if unsprinklered
    D. completely sprinklered by a system having two adequate sources of water supply, a maximum number of occupants of any one floor not more than 50 percent above the capacity of the exits required for the same building if unsprinklered and an interior fire alarm system

18. Automatic sprinkler systems installed in the public halls of converted multiple dwellings with a required Siamese are subjected to a hydrostatic pressure test before acceptance. The test pressure for such systems is to be NOT less than

    A. 30 pounds per square inch
    B. 30 pounds per square inch in excess of the normal pressure required for such systems when in service
    C. 200 pounds per square inch
    D. 200 pounds per square inch in excess of the normal pressure required for such systems when in service

19. According to the rules of the Board of Standards and Appeals, when flameproofed materials are subjected to prescribed tests, they shall meet established standards for each of the following properties EXCEPT

    A. flashing   B. duration of flame
    C. duration of glow   D. temperature of flame

20. Each year many children die in fires which they have started while playing with matches. Of the following measures, the one that would be MOST effective in preventing such tragedies is to

    A. warn the children of the dangers involved
    B. punish parents who are found guilty of neglecting their children
    C. keep matches out of the reach of children
    D. use only safety matches

21. Sparks given off by welding torches are a serious fire hazard.
The BEST of the following methods of dealing with this hazard is to conduct welding operations

   A. only in fireproof buildings protected by sprinkler systems
   B. only out-of-doors on a day with little wind blowing
   C. only on materials certified to be non-combustible by recognized testing laboratories
   D. only after loose combustible materials have been cleared from the area and with a man standing by with a hose line

22. A two-story, Class 3, non-fireproof building was originally occupied as a store on the first floor and one apartment on the second floor. Upon inspection, you find that the second floor is now being used for offices. The building is 20' x 50'. There is one stairway made of wood, enclosed with fire-retarded stud partitions, leading directly to the street from the second floor.
The one of the following statements that is MOST complete and accurate is that the situation as described

   A. complies with applicable laws
   B. is illegal because the stair should be of incombustible material
   C. is illegal because there should be two means of egress
   D. is illegal because there should be two means of egress and the stair should be of incombustible material

Questions 23-25.

DIRECTIONS: Questions 23 through 25 are to be answered SOLELY on the basis of the following passage.

Automatic sprinkler systems are installed in many buildings. They extinguish or keep from spreading 96% of all fires in areas they protect. Sprinkler systems are made up of pipes which hang below the ceiling of each protected area and sprinkler heads which are placed along the pipes. The pipes are usually filled with water, and each sprinkler head has a heat sensitive part. When the heat from the fire reaches the sensitive part of the sprinkler head, the head opens and showers water upon the fire in the form of spray. The heads are spaced so that the fire is covered by overlapping showers of water from the open heads.

23. Automatic sprinkler systems are installed in buildings to

   A. prevent the build-up of dangerous gases
   B. eliminate the need for fire insurance
   C. extinguish fires or keep them from spreading
   D. protect 96% of the floor space

24. If more than one sprinkler head opens, the area sprayed will be

   A. flooded with hot water
   B. overlapped by showers of water
   C. subject to less water damage
   D. about 1 foot per sprinkler head

25. A sprinkler head will open and shower water when 25.____
    A. it is reached by heat from a fire
    B. water pressure in the pipes gets too high
    C. it is reached by sounds from a fire alarm
    D. water temperature in the pipes gets too low

KEY (CORRECT ANSWERS)

1.	A		11.	B
2.	C		12.	A
3.	C		13.	B
4.	C		14.	A
5.	D		15.	B
6.	B		16.	D
7.	D		17.	C
8.	A		18.	C
9.	B		19.	D
10.	B		20.	C

21. D
22. A
23. C
24. B
25. A

TEST 3

DIRECTIONS: Each question or incomplete statement is followed by several suggested answers or completions. Select the one that BEST answers the question or completes the statement. *PRINT THE LETTER OF THE CORRECT ANSWER IN THE SPACE AT THE RIGHT.*

1. The one of the following which is the MOST valid statement in the Fire Prevention Code regarding height restrictions on combustible fiber storage is that

    A. a clearance of at least 18 inches shall be maintained below the sprinkler head
    B. storage shall be no higher than 20 feet above the floor
    C. storage shall be no higher than 2/3 of the distance from floor to ceiling
    D. storage shall be piled to a height not greater than 6 inches below the top of the enclosing wall

2. The one of the following which is NOT among the Fire Prevention Code protection requirements for the storage of television special effects is that

    A. partitions in the storage room shall have at least a one-hour fire resistive rating
    B. the roof of the storage room shall have at least a 1 1/2 hour fire resistive rating
    C. there shall be one sprinkler head for each 80 square feet of floor space in the storage room
    D. there shall be mechanical ventilation providing at least four air changes per hour

3. According to the Fire Prevention Code, of the following containers, the ones which are NOT legal for the transportation of gasoline are

    A. 5-gallon cans with metal seals
    B. glass bottles not exceeding 4 ounces each
    C. 55-gallon steel barrels or drums
    D. 10-gallon safety cans

4. The following conditions have been found during an inspection:
    I. 10,000 small arms cartridges in a store authorized to sell gunpowder
    II. 500 small arms cartridges in a pawn shop
    III. 200 small arms cartridges in a liquor store
    IV. 100 small arms cartridges in a drug store

    Which of the following choices lists ONLY those of the above conditions that comply with the Fire Prevention Code either because a permit may be issued or because a pernit is not required?

    A. I, II, III   B. I, II, IV
    C. I, III, IV   D. II, III, IV

5. While inspecting a building, an officer notices that a standard enclosure having a three-hour fire resistance rating has been constructed above ground on the lowest floor of the building.
    According to the Building Code, the MAXIMUM size fuel oil storage tank that can be placed in this enclosure is one with a capacity of _____ gallons.

    A. 1,100   B. 2,500   C. 10,000   D. 20,000

6. The one of the following which is NOT a Class B multiple dwelling is a   6._____

   A. hotel
   B. boarding school
   C. clubhouse
   D. hospital

7. When inspecting an industrial plant, an officer discovers a conveyor passing through a   7._____
   fire wall with no fire shutter for the opening.
   The MOST valid of the following statements concerning alternate forms of protection is
   that

   A. no alternate is acceptable; a shutter having fire resistance equal to the wall fire
      resistance is required
   B. a sprinkler head located in the opening to provide at least 3 gallons per square foot
      per minute is acceptable
   C. two sprinkler heads to provide a water curtain for the entire opening is acceptable
   D. four water spray nozzles on each side of the opening controlled by an automatic
      valve actuated by a heat detector is acceptable

8. A new restaurant in a multiple-story building of Class I construction has a false front on   8._____
   the outside of the building representing an English castle.
   The one of the following which meets the Building Code requirement for this condition
   to be legal is that the false front is of

   A. fire retardant treated wood not over 40 feet high
   B. fire retardant treated wood covering less than 2,000 square feet of surface
   C. slow burning plastic, not over 25 feet high, covering not over 1,000 square feet of
      surface
   D. slow burning plastic, not over 40 feet high, covering less than 5% of the building
      surface

9. At a recent fire on the third floor of a building, firemen could not open the locked windows   9._____
   nor could they break the plastic glazing.
   For such conditions, the Building Code requires that

   A. keys to the windows be available in the lobby
   B. one window for each 50 feet of street front be openable from the inside or outside
   C. all plastic glazing be replaced by glass
   D. all locks be removed and replaced with spring latches

10. Showroom spaces located in office buildings over 100 feet high are required to be sprin-   10._____
    klered when the

    A. building air conditioning system serves more than the floor in which the equipment
       is located, and the showroom space exceeds 7,500 square feet in area and is
       located more than 40 feet above curb level
    B. showroom space is over 1,000 square feet in area and is located more than 40 feet
       above curb level
    C. showroom space is over 7,500 square feet in area, is not equipped with an
       approved smoke detection alarm system, and is served by a one-floor mechanical
       ventilation system
    D. showroom space exceeds 2,500 square feet in area and is located more than 75
       feet above curb level

3 (#3)

11. In a building classified as occupancy group E, occupied or arranged to be occupied for an occupant load of more than one hundred persons above or below the street level or more than a total of five hundred persons in the entire building, a building evacuation supervisor performs his training activities under the direction of

    A. the battalion chief on duty
    B. the building fire safety director
    C. the building fire brigade supervisor
    D. someone other than any of the above

11.___

12. The one of the following which BEST identifies where a Class E fire alarm signal system will sound continuously upon operation of a manual station is only on the floor where

    A. actuated
    B. actuated and the floor above
    C. actuated and the next two floors above
    D. actuated, the floor above, and the floor below

12.___

13. The ONLY one of the following occupancies in which portable kerosene space heaters approved by the Board of Standards and Appeals may be used in the event of failure of the central heating unit is in

    A. private dwellings
    B. multiple dwellings
    C. places of public assembly
    D. schools

13.___

14. The one of the following which is NOT a requirement relating to oxygen and acetylene torch operations in a building under demolition is that there be

    A. one fire guard in the area of torch operation equipped with a 2 1/2" hose line
    B. one fire guard for each torch operator and an addi-tional fire guard on the floor or level below
    C. fire guards to make an inspection of the exposed area one half hour after completion of torch operations
    D. fire guards to make an inspection of the exposed area one hour after completion of torch operations

14.___

15. Upon responding to an alarm of fire in a building, an officer notes that the Siamese connections are painted yellow.
    This color coding indicates that

    A. the sprinkler system protects only showrooms located not over 40 feet above the curb line
    B. the standpipe riser is only four inches in size
    C. a floor control valve is provided for the sprinkler system on each floor
    D. the Siamese connection supplies a high-expansion foam system

15.___

16. The one of the following which does NOT correctly describe what can happen during manual operation of an elevator with the keyed switch in the *Fireman Service* position is that the

    A. doors will open on all floors but the fire floor
    B. direction of travel can be changed after a floor selection has been made

16.___

78

4 (#3)

C. doors will open only in response to the *Door Open* button in the car
D. doors can be automatically reclosed while in the process of opening

17. The Building Code places restrictions on the suspension of new ceilings below existing suspended ceilings in construction group II in order to restrict the travel of fire in hidden spaces.
The one of the following requirements which BEST describes the nature of this restriction is that the

17.____

A. concealed space shall be provided with firestops to divide the space into sections not exceeding 3,000 square feet each
B. new ceiling shall be supported directly from the ceiling carrying channels and shall have no openings from the concealed space to the area below
C. new ceiling shall be of non-combustible construction or have a flame spread rating of 25 or less, and a smoke developed rating of 50 or less
D. existing ceiling shall be completely removed before the new ceiling is suspended

18. While inspecting a 125-foot-high factory building constructed in 1912 within 20 feet of an adjacent one-story fireproof garage 12 feet in height, an officer notices that the fire windows in the factory wall facing the garage are glazed with wireglass only to the fourth floor or 65-foot level. Windows above that level are 60 feet higher vertically than the roof of the garage and are glazed with inch plate glass lights 400 square inches in area.
The one of the following which is the PROPER conclusion for the officer to draw is that

18.____

A. such windows comply with the State Labor Law
B. a violation exists since all fire windows in the wall of a factory building facing any building within 30 feet must be glazed with wireglass
C. a violation exists since the fire windows in all factory buildings erected before 1913 must have wireglass
D. none of the fire windows in the factory wall need be wireglass if there are no openings in the garage wall facing it

19. An officer submits for review a referral report containing statements about the exterior screened stairway of a factory building he has recently inspected which he considers to be in violation of the State Labor Law.
Of the officer's observations listed below, the one that is NOT a violation of the State Labor Law is:

19.____

A. No balcony connecting with the stairs at the fourth floor
B. Door connecting with the balcony at the third floor opens inward
C. Stair terminates in rear yard not communicating to a street
D. Access to balcony at second floor via sliding door

20. A five story non-fireproof factory building erected in 1908 has an area on all floors of 900 square feet with two exits remote from each other on all floors, except for the fourth floor which is used entirely as a raw material storeroom. No one is regularly employed on that floor. For security reasons, the fourth floor has only one exit.
It would be CORRECT to say that, according to the State Labor Law,

20.____

A. this arrangement is expressly forbidden, as every floor must have two exits
B. one exit from the fourth floor would be acceptable provided it is protected by an automatic sprinkler system

C. the one exit from the fourth floor is acceptable provided it conforms to the criteria for a factory exit
D. one exit from the fourth floor is acceptable provided the longest distance to the exit from any point on the floor does not exceed 75 feet

21. Buildings which have been vacated by order of the fire department are kept under surveillance.
When such buildings have been boarded up, surveillance may, with approval, be reduced to once each

    A. week   B. month
    C. quarter-year D. half-year

22. Overly detailed fire prevention inspections are to be avoided CHIEFLY because they

    A. unduly interfere with the normal activities of the occupancy, causing public resentment
    B. require excessive time which could be used to better advantage inspecting other occupancies
    C. tend to result in oversight of some fundamental hazards
    D. are beyond the capabilities of many firemen who are not specifically trained in inspectional techniques

23. Requests for sprinkler re-evaluation are accepted by the fire department, and a re-inspection made, if the petitioner states that substantial changes have been made in the sprinkler system.
The one of the following statements that is MOST accurate and complete is that such re-inspections are made by the division commander

    A. in all instances
    B. except when he has endorsed the original sprinkler order
    C. except when he has endorsed the original sprinkler order or when his workload is excessive
    D. except when he has endorsed the original sprinkler order, his workload is excessive, or the re-evaluation is extremely complex

24. Department regulations require the forwarding of reports to the Fire Commissioner relating to demolition work adjacent to or adjoining company quarters.
The one of the following statements that is MOST accurate and complete is that such reports should be forwarded when notice of the proposed demolition is

    A. received
    B. received and when the work is completed
    C. received, when the work actually starts, and when the work is completed
    D. received, when the work actually starts, when any interruption of work occurs, and when the work is completed

25. The one of the following statements that is MOST complete and accurate is that when a building inspector issues a Violation Order, the time allowed for compliance

    A. must be the specific number of days indicated on the Standard Form of Orders
    B. may be less than the specific number of days indicated on the Standard Form of Orders

C. may be more than the specific number of days indicated on the Standard Form of Orders
D. may be more or less than the specific number of days indicated on the Standard Form of Orders, depending upon the circumstances

---

KEY (CORRECT ANSWERS)

1.	C	11.	B
2.	D	12.	B
3.	D	13.	D
4.	C	14.	A
5.	D	15.	C
6.	D	16.	A
7.	D	17.	D
8.	C	18.	A
9.	B	19.	D
10.	A	20.	C

21.	C
22.	B
23.	D
24.	A
25.	B

TEST 4

DIRECTIONS: Each question or incomplete statement is followed by several suggested answers or completions. Select the one that BEST answers the question or completes the statement. *PRINT THE LETTER OF THE CORRECT ANSWER IN THE SPACE AT THE RIGHT.*

1. Of the following substances, the one that would MOST appropriately be protected with a sprinkler installation is   1.___

    A. cellulose acetate
    B. quicklime
    C. magnesium powder
    D. calcium carbide

2. Providing clearance around unprotected steel columns in storage occupancies is a practice which is GENERALLY   2.___

    A. *desirable,* chiefly because the quantity of combustibles stored is reduced
    B. *undesirable,* chiefly because flue-like conditions will prevail
    C. *desirable,* chiefly because it will allow water from sprinklers to keep the column wet
    D. *undesirable,* chiefly because stock can topple if not supported

3. National fire records indicate that over the years restaurant fires have increased in number and in total dollar loss despite technological improvements.   3.___
   The large increase in the number of restaurant fires is PRIMARILY attributable to

    A. fires of incendiary origin
    B. duct fires
    C. the use of open flames for cooking
    D. careless handling of smoking materials

4. When serving a summons for a violation of the Building Code, it is most important that proper procedure be followed.   4.___
   Of the following statements, the one that is MOST acceptable is that a summons may be

    A. mailed to the residence of the building's owner if he is not on the premises
    B. given to a superintendent to be forwarded to the owner if he is not on the premises
    C. placed on the desk or in the immediate vicinity of the owner if he refuses to accept it
    D. made out with the initials of the owner if the full name is not known

5. A dry-pipe sprinkler system is generally not considered acceptable protection for an occupancy utilizing flammable liquids MAINLY because   5.___

    A. corrosion tends to weaken these systems
    B. water is a poor extinguishing agent for flammable liquids
    C. the systems are too expensive for the purpose
    D. a fast spreading fire may be out of control by the time water arrives

6. In order to enforce the fire safety laws, firefighters must inspect buildings and stores.   6.___
   It is NOT a good idea for firefighters to let owners of buildings and stores know when they are coming because

A. firefighters will waste valuable time if the owner breaks the appointment
B. owners might try to hide fire hazards from the fire-fighters
C. firefighters can make the inspection faster without an appointment
D. owners would be angry if the firefighters were unable to keep the appointment

7. Many older buildings are modernized to give a blank wall appearance by being *wrapped*. It is INACCURATE to state, with reference to *wrapped* buildings, that

    A. the use of expanded metal panels reduces the hazard from exposure fires
    B. they are essentially windowless buildings
    C. solid metal panels may be blown loose and scale a considerable distance
    D. expanded metal panels may be hung or mounted a foot or more from the original exterior wall

8. According to the Administrative Code, it is unlawful to manufacture within the city all of the following EXCEPT

    A. blank cartridges
    B. railroad track torpedoes
    C. flashlight compositions
    D. ship signal rockets

9. A newly appointed firefighter is assigned to go with an experienced firefighter to inspect a paint store. The paint store owner refuses to allow the inspection, saying that he is closing the store early that day and going on vacation. The new firefighter demands rudely that the inspection be allowed, even though it would be permissible to delay it.
Of the following, it would be BEST for the experienced firefighter to

    A. repeat the demand that the inspection be allowed and quote the law to the store owner
    B. tell the new firefighter that it would be best to schedule the inspection after the store owner's vacation
    C. tell the store owner to step aside, and instruct the new firefighter to enter the store and begin the inspection
    D. tell the new firefighter to forget about the inspection because the store owner is uncooperative

10. One person shall be permitted to supervise more than one interior fire alarm system. The one of the following that is NOT in accord with the restrictions placed on this permission is that

    A. the buildings in which the interior fire alarm systems are located must be within an area whose diameter does not exceed six hundred feet
    B. the interior fire alarms in all buildings in the group can be tested within thirty minutes of commencing work daily
    C. the addresses of all buildings shall be listed on the one certificate of fitness
    D. records and logbooks must be kept on each premises

11. The one of the following which is NOT in accord with the Regulations for Use of Halon 1301, Extinguishing Agent, is that

    A. maximum concentration shall not exceed 10 percent where human habitation is present in the volume to be flooded
    B. minimum concentration of FE 1301 used shall not be less than 10 percent

C. a discharge rate which results in attaining the design concentration in 8 seconds is acceptable
D. a central office connection must be provided for fire detection or systems operation where human habitation is present in the volume to be flooded

12. According to the Fire Prevention Code, a person who holds a permit for the manufacture of inflammable mixtures and who wishes to manufacture combustible mixtures is

    A. *required* to obtain another permit
    B. *not required* to obtain another permit
    C. *not required* to obtain another permit unless the mixtures include stove polishes or insecticides
    D. *not required* to obtain another permit unless the mixtures include medicinal and toilet preparations

13. The one of the following statements which is MOST accurate and complete is that the Fire Prevention Code permits the hanging of fresh-cut decorative greens in places of public assembly only if they do not contain

    A. pitch
    B. pitch and are hung by means of non-combustible material
    C. pitch, are hung by means of non-combustible material, and do not remain for a period in excess of 24 hours
    D. pitch, are hung by means of non-combustible material, have been treated with an approved evaporation-retarding product, and do not remain for a period in excess of 48 hours

14. In any automatic wet-pipe sprinkler system which has standard one-half inch sprinkler heads exposed to cold and subject to freezing, shut-off valves may be provided and the water supply discontinued

    A. under no circumstances
    B. from November 15 to March 15 when there are five or less such exposed heads
    C. from November 1 to April 1 when there are ten or less such exposed heads
    D. from November 15 to April 15 when there are fifteen or less such exposed heads

15. At an inspection of a building, one floor of which is used for combustible fiber storage, the following facts are revealed:
    I. The safe bearing capacity of the floor, as certified by the Department of Buildings, is 250 lbs./sq.ft. The weight of the combustible fiber is 75 lbs./sq.ft.
    II. The floor is 10,000 sq.ft. in area, of which 6,000 sq.ft. is occupied by the fiber bales.
    III. The height from floor to ceiling is 16', and the stacked bales stand 10' high.
    In this situation, _____ of the Fire Prevention Code.

    A. Item I is in   B. Item II is in
    C. Item III is in   D. there is no

16. Carelessness in smoking is a very common cause of fire.
    A lighted cigarette placed on top of most upholstery will GENERALLY

    A. cause no damage
    B. burn to the end without starting a fire

C. cause a gradually increasing fire
D. start a fire rapidly

17. The one of the following that is the type of automatic sprinkler system MOST commonly found in museums, art galleries, and storage places for records or valuable merchandise is the _____ system.

    A. deluge
    B. pre-action
    C. dry pipe
    D. sypho-chemical

18. The Fire Prevention Code requires that a permit be obtained for the storage of more than the equivalent of five barrels of oils and fats.
    The one of the following which is excluded from this requirement is

    A. lubricating oils
    B. grease
    C. edible oils
    D. soap stock

19. The Fire Prevention Code requires that rooms in dry cleaning establishments in which washing tanks are located be equipped with

    A. asbestos cloths or blankets
    B. carbon dioxide or dry chemical extinguishers
    C. buckets of sand
    D. automatic fire alarm device

20. The one of the following occupancies which is required to have a two-source water supply for its sprinkler system is one containing

    A. combustible fiber storage
    B. a motion picture film studio
    C. oils and fats storage
    D. a theater

21. The one of the following statements that is MOST accurate is that the Fire Prevention Code prohibits the storage of distilled liquors and alcohols in

    A. quantities aggregating more than 50 gallons, without a permit
    B. any building of wooden construction
    C. excess of one barrel for each five square feet of floor space
    D. barrels stacked more than one high

22. A special permit issued by the Fire Commissioner is required for the operation of certain businesses. Concerning parking lots, technical establishments, retail drug stores, and dry cleaning establishments, it is MOST accurate to say that special permits are required for all

    A. four of them
    B. of the above except parking lots
    C. of the above except technical establishments
    D. of the above except retail drug stores

23. The one of the following chemicals which may NOT be manufactured or stored in a drug and chemical supply house in any quantity is

    A. acetone
    B. benzole
    C. chloride of nitrogen
    D. metallic magnesium

24. A permit is required for the storage of empty wooden packing boxes in buildings if the quantity stored exceeds

    A. one ton
    B. 2,000 square feet of area
    C. 2,000 cubic feet of space
    D. one ton or 2,000 square feet of area, whichever is the smaller amount

25. The MAXIMUM number of excess liquefied petroleum gas cylinders that may be stored in a single structure protected by an approved dry sprinkler system is

    A. 25 B. 50 C. 75 D. 100

KEY (CORRECT ANSWERS)

1. A		11. B	
2. C		12. B	
3. A		13. C	
4. C		14. C	
5. D		15. D	
6. B		16. B	
7. A		17. B	
8. D		18. C	
9. B		19. A	
10. C		20. B	

21. B
22. A
23. C
24. C
25. B

READING COMPREHENSION
UNDERSTANDING AND INTERPRETING WRITTEN MATERIAL
EXAMINATION SECTION
TEST 1

DIRECTIONS: Each question or incomplete statement is followed by several suggested answers or completions. Select the one that BEST answers the question or completes the statement. *PRINT THE LETTER OF THE CORRECT ANSWER IN THE SPACE AT THE RIGHT.*

Questions 1-3.

DIRECTIONS: Questions 1 through 3 are to be answered SOLELY on the basis of the following paragraph.

The aging housing inventory presents a broad spectrum of conditions, from good upkeep to unbelievable deterioration. Buildings, even relatively good buildings, are likely to have numerous minor violations rather than the gross and evident sanitary violations of an earlier age. Except for the serious violations in a relatively small number of slum buildings, the task is to deal with masses of minor violations that, though insignificant in themselves, amount in the aggregate to major deprivations of health and comfort to tenants. Caused by wear and tear, by the abrasions of time, and aggravated by neglect, these conditions do not readily yield to the dramatic *vacate and restore* measures of earlier times. Moreover, the lines between *good* and *bad* housing have become blurred in many parts of our cities; we find a range of *shades of gray* blending into each other. Different kinds of code enforcement efforts may be required to deal with different degrees of deterioration.

1. The above passage suggests that code enforcement efforts may have to be   1.____

    A. developed to cope with varying levels of housing dilapidation
    B. aimed primarily at the serious violations in slum buildings
    C. modeled on the *vacate and restore* measures of earlier times
    D. modified to reduce unrealistic penalties for petty violations

2. According to the above passage, during former times some buildings had sanitary violations which were   2.____

    A. irreparable and minor
    B. blurred and gray
    C. flagrant and obvious
    D. insignificant and numerous

3. According to the above passage, the aging housing stock presents a   3.____

    A. great number of rent-controlled buildings
    B. serious problem of tenant-caused deterioration
    C. significant increase in buildings without intentional violations
    D. wide range of physical conditions

Questions 4-5.

DIRECTIONS: Questions 4 and 5 are to be answered SOLELY on the basis of the following passage.

In general, housing code provisions relating to the safe and sanitary maintenance of dwelling units prescribe the maintenance required for foundations, walls, ceilings, floors, windows, doors, stairways, and also the facilities and equipment required in other sections. The more recent codes have, in addition, extensive provisions designed to ensure that the unit be maintained in a rat-free and rat-proof condition. Also, as an example of new approaches in code provisions, one proposed Federal model housing code prohibits the landlord from terminating vital services and utilities except during temporary emergencies or when actual repairs or maintenance are in process. This provision may be used to prevent a landlord from turning off utility services as a technique of self-help eviction or as a weapon against rent strikes.

4. According to the above passage, the more recent housing codes have extensive provisions designed to

   A. maintain a reasonably fire-proof living unit
   B. prohibit tenants from participating in rent strikes
   C. maintain the unit free from rats
   D. prohibit tenants from using lead-based paints

5. According to the above passage, one housing code would permit landlords to terminate vital services during

   A. a rent strike
   B. an actual eviction
   C. a temporary emergency
   D. the planning of repairs and maintenance

Questions 6-8.

DIRECTIONS: Questions 6 through 8 are to be answered SOLELY on the basis of the following passage.

City governments have long had building codes which set minimum standards for building and for human occupancy. The code (or series of codes) makes provisions for standards of lighting and ventilation, sanitation, fire prevention, and protection. As a result of demands from manufacturers, builders, real estate people, tenement owners, and building-trades unions, these codes often have established minimum standards well below those that the contemporary society would accept as a rock-bottom minimum. Codes often become outdated so that meager standards in one era become seriously inadequate a few decades later as society"s concept of a minimum standard of living changes. Out-of-date codes, when still in use, have sometimes prevented the introduction of new devices and modern building techniques. Thus, it is extremely important that building codes keep pace with changes in the accepted concept of a minimum standard of living.

6. According to the above passage, all of the following considerations in building planning would probably be covered in a building code EXCEPT

   A. closet space as a percentage of total floor area
   B. size and number of windows required for rooms of differing sizes
   C. placement of fire escapes in each line of apartments
   D. type of garbage disposal units to be installed

7. According to the above passage, if an ideal building code were to be created, how would the established minimum standards in it compare to the ones that are presently set by city governments?
   They would

   A. be lower than they are at present
   B. be higher than they are at present
   C. be comparable to the present minimum standards
   D. vary according to the economic group that sets them

8. On the basis of the above passage, what is the reason for difficulties in introducing new building techniques?

   A. Builders prefer techniques which represent the rock-bottom minimum desired by society.
   B. Certain manufacturers have obtained patents on various building methods to the exclusion of new techniques.
   C. The government does not want to invest money in techniques that will soon be outdated.
   D. New techniques are not provided for in building codes which are not up-to-date.

Questions 9-11.

DIRECTIONS: Questions 9 through 11 are to be answered SOLELY on the basis of the following paragraph.

When constructed within a multiple dwelling, such storage space shall be equipped with a sprinkler system and also with a system of mechanical ventilation in no way connected with any other ventilating system. Such storage space shall have no opening into any other part of the dwelling except through a fireproof vestibule. Any such vestibule shall have a minimum superficial floor area of fifty square feet, and its maximum area shall not exceed seventy-five square feet. It shall be enclosed with incombustible partitions having a fire-resistive rating of three hours. The floor and ceiling of such vestibule shall also be of incombustible material having a fire-resistive rating of at least three hours. There shall be two doors to provide access from the dwelling, to the car storage space. Each such door shall have a fire-resistive rating of one and one-half hours and shall be provided with a device to prevent the opening of one door until the other door is entirely closed.

9. According to the above paragraph, the one of the following that is REQUIRED in order for cars to be permitted to be stored in a multiple dwelling is a(n)

   A. fireproof vestibule   B. elevator from the garage
   C. approved heating system   D. sprinkler system

10. According to the above paragraph, the one of the following materials that would NOT be acceptable for the walls of a vestibule connecting a garage to the dwelling portion of a building is

    A. 3" solid gypsum blocks
    B. 4" brick
    C. 4" hollow gypsum blocks, plastered both sides
    D. 6" solid cinder concrete blocks

10.____

11. According to the above paragraph, the one of the following that would be ACCEPTABLE for the width and length of a vestibule connecting a garage that is within a multiple dwelling to the dwelling portion of the building is

    A. 3'8" x 13'0"   B. 4'6" x 18'6"
    C. 4'9" x 14'6"   D. 4'3" x 19'3"

11.____

Questions 12-13.

DIRECTIONS: Questions 12 and 13 are to be answered SOLELY on the basis of the following paragraph.

It shall be unlawful to place, use, or maintain in a condition intended, arranged, or designed for use, any gas-fired cooking appliance, laundry stove, heating stove, range or water heater or combination of such appliances in any room or space used for living or sleeping in any new or existing multiple dwelling unless such room or space has a window opening to the outer air or such gas appliance is vented to the outer air. All automatically operated gas appliances shall be equipped with a device which shall shut off automatically the gas supply to the main burners when the pilot light in such appliance is extinguished. A gas range or the cooking portion of a gas appliance incorporating a room heater shall not be deemed an automatically operated gas appliance. However, burners in gas ovens and broilers which can be turned on and off or ignited by non-manual means shall be equipped with a device which shall shut off automatically the gas supply to those burners when the operation of such non-manual means fails.

12. According to the above paragraph, an automatic shut-off device is NOT required on a gas

    A. hot water heater   B. laundry dryer
    C. space heater   D. range

12.____

13. According to the above paragraph, a gas-fired water heater is permitted

    A. only in kitchens   B. only in bathrooms
    C. only in living rooms   D. in any type of room

13.____

Questions 14-18.

DIRECTIONS: Questions 14 through 18 are to be answered SOLELY on the basis of the information contained in the statement below.

No multiple dwelling shall be erected to a height in excess of one and one-half times the width of the widest street on which it faces, except that above the level of such height, for each one foot that the front wall of such dwelling sets back from the street line, three feet shall be added to the height limit of such dwelling, but such dwelling shall not exceed in maximum height three feet plus one and three-quarter times the width of the widest street on which it faces.

Any such dwelling facing a street more than one hundred feet in width shall be subject to the same height limitations as though such dwelling faced a street one hundred feet in width.

14. The MAXIMUM height of a multiple dwelling set back five feet from the street line and facing a 60 foot wide street is ____ feet.

    A. 60   B. 90   C. 105   D. 165

15. The MAXIMUM height of a multiple dwelling set back six feet from the street line and facing a 120 foot wide street is _____ feet.

    A. 198   B. 168   C. 120   D. 105

16. The MAXIMUM height of a multiple dwelling is

    A. 100 ft.   B. 150 ft.   C. 178 ft.   D. unlimited

17. The MAXIMUM height of a multiple dwelling set back 10 feet from the street line and facing a 110 foot wide street is ____ feet.

    A. 178   B. 180   C. 195   D. 205

18. The MAXIMUM height of a multiple dwelling set back eight feet from the street line and facing a 90 foot wide street is ____ feet.

    A. 135   B. 147   C. 178   D. 159

Questions 19-23.

DIRECTIONS: Questions 19 through 23 are to be answered SOLELY on the basis of the following statement.

The number of persons accommodated on any story in a lodging house shall not be greater than the sum of the following components,

   a. 22 persons for each full multiple of 22 inches in the smallest clear width for each means of egress approved by the department, other than fire escapes
   b. 20 persons for each lawful fire escape accessible from such story.

19. The MAXIMUM number of persons that may be accommodated on a story in a lodging house depends on the

    A. number of lawful fire escapes *only*
    B. number of approved means of egress *only*
    C. smallest clear width in each approved means of egress *only*
    D. number of lawful fire escapes and sum total of smallest clear widths in each approved means of egress

20. The MAXIMUM number of persons that may be accommodated on a story of a lodging house having one lawful fire escape and a sum total of 44 inches in the smallest clear widths of the two approved means of egress is

    A. 20   B. 22   C. 42   D. 64

21. The MAXIMUM number of persons that may be accommodated on a story of a lodging house having two lawful fire escapes and a sum total of 60 inches in the smallest clear width of the approved means of egress is

    A. 64   B. 84   C. 100   D. 106

22. The MAXIMUM number of persons that may be accommodated on a story of a lodging house having one lawful fire escape and a sum total of 33 inches in the smallest clear width of the approved means of egress is

    A. 42   B. 53   C. 64   D. 73

23. The MAXIMUM number of persons that may be accommodated on a story of a lodging house having two lawful fire escapes and two approved means of egress, with 40 inches and 44 inches in the smallest clear widths, respectively, is

    A. 84   B. 104   C. 106   D. 108

Questions 24-25.

DIRECTIONS: Questions 24 and 25 are to be answered SOLELY on the basis of the following paragraph.

Though the recent trend toward apartment construction may appear to be the Region's response to large-lot zoning and centralized industry, it really is not. It is mainly a function of the age of the population. Most of the apartments are occupied by one- and two-person families young people out of school but without a family of their own and older people whose children have grown. Both groups have been increasing in number; and, in this Region, they characteristically live in apartments. It is this increased demand for apartments and the simultaneous decrease in demand for one-family houses that dramatically raised the percentage of building permits issued for multi-family housing units from 36 percent in 1977 to 67 percent in 1981. The fact that three-fourths of the apartments were built in the Core between 1977 and 1981 at the same time as the Core was losing population underscores the failure of the apartment boom to slow the outward spread of the population.

24. According to the above paragraph, one of the reasons for the increase in the number of building permits issued for multi-family construction in the City Metropolitan Region is

    A. that workers in industry want to live close to their jobs
    B. an increase in the number of elderly people living in the Region
    C. the inability of many families to afford the large lots necessary to build private homes
    D. the new zoning ordinance made it easier to build apartments

25. According to the above paragraph, the apartment construction boom

    A. increased the population density in the Core
    B. spurred a population shift to the suburbs
    C. did not halt the outward flow of the population from the Core
    D. was most significant in the outer areas of the Region

KEY (CORRECT ANSWERS)

1. A
2. C
3. D
4. C
5. C

6. A
7. B
8. D
9. D
10. B

11. C
12. D
13. D
14. C
15. B

16. C
17. A
18. D
19. D
20. D

21. B
22. A
23. C
24. B
25. C

TEST 2

DIRECTIONS: Each question or incomplete statement is followed by several suggested answers or completions. Select the one that BEST answers the question or completes the statement. *PRINT THE LETTER OF THE CORRECT ANSWER IN THE SPACE AT THE RIGHT.*

Questions 1-4.

DIRECTIONS: Questions 1 through 4 are to be answered SOLELY on the basis of the following paragraph.

Although the suburbs have provided housing and employment for millions of additional families since 1950, many suburban communities have maintained controls over the kinds of families who can live in them. Suburban attitudes have been formed by reaction against a perception of crowded, harassed city life and threatening alien city people. As population, taxable income, and jobs have left the cities for the suburbs, the *urban crisis* of substandard housing, declining levels of education and public services, and decreasing employment opportunities has been created. The crisis, however, is not urban at all, but national, and in part a result of the suburban policy that discourages outward movement by the urban poor.

1. According to the above paragraph, the quality of urban life   1.____

    A. is determined by public opinion in the cities
    B. has worsened in recent years
    C. is similar to rural life
    D. can be changed by political means

2. According to the above paragraph, suburban communities have   2.____

    A. tried to show that the urban crisis is really a national crisis
    B. avoided taking a position on the urban crisis
    C. been involved in causing the urban crisis
    D. been the innocent victims of the urban crisis

3. According to the above paragraph, the poor have   3.____

    A. become increasingly sophisticated in their attempts to move to the suburbs
    B. generally been excluded from the suburbs
    C. lost incentive for betterment of their living conditions
    D. sought improvement of the central cities

4. As used in the above paragraph, the word perception means MOST NEARLY   4.____

    A. development   B. impression
    C. opposition   D. uncertainty

Questions 5-8.

DIRECTIONS: Questions 5 through 8 are to be answered SOLELY on the basis of the following paragraph.
The concentration of publicly assisted housing in central cities -- because the suburbs do not want them and effectively bar them -- is usually rationalized by a solicitous regard for

keeping intact the city neighborhoods cherished by low-income groups. If one accepted this as valid, the devotion of minorities to blighted city neighborhoods in preference to suburban employment and housing would be an historic first. Certainly no such devotion was visible among the millions who have deserted their city neighborhoods in the last 25 years even if it meant an arduous daily trip from the suburbs to their jobs in the cities.

5. The writer implies that MOST poor people

   A. prefer isolation
   B. fear change
   C. are angry
   D. seek betterment

6. The general tone of the paragraph is BEST characterized as

   A. uncertain   B. skeptical   C. evasive   D. indifferent

7. As used in the above paragraph, the word rationalize means MOST NEARLY

   A. dispute   B. justify   C. deny   D. locate

8. According to the above paragraph, publicly assisted housing is concentrated in the central cities PRIMARILY because

   A. city dwellers are unable to find satisfactory housing
   B. deterioration of older housing has increased in recent years
   C. suburbanites have opposed the movement of the poor to the suburbs
   D. employment opportunities have decreased in the suburbs

Questions 9-11.

DIRECTIONS: Questions 9 through 11 are to be answered SOLELY on the basis of the following paragraph.

In recent years, new and important emphasis has been placed upon the maximum use of conservation and rehabilitation techniques in carrying out programs of urban renewal and revitalization. In urban renewal projects where existing structures are hopelessly deteriorated or land uses are incompatible with the community's overall plans, the entire area may be acquired, cleared, and sold for redevelopment. However, where existing structures are basically sound but have deteriorated to the point where they are a blighting influence on the neighborhood, they may be salvaged through a program of rehabilitation and reconditioning.

9. According to the above paragraph, the one of the following which is MOST likely to cause area-wide razing of the buildings in urban renewal programs is

   A. a program of rehabilitation and reconditioning
   B. concerted insistence by landlords and tenants that certain buildings be bulldozed
   C. an inability of community groups to agree on priorities for staged clearance
   D. land use contrary to the community's general plan

10. According to the above paragraph, rehabilitation of structures may take place if

    A. new conservation and rehabilitation techniques are used
    B. salvaging all the buildings in the entire area is hopeless
    C. the community wishes to preserve historic structures
    D. the existing buildings are structurally sound

11. As used in the above paragraph, the word <u>blighting</u> means MOST NEARLY   11.____

    A. ruining   B. infrequent   C. recurrent   D. traditional

Questions 12-13.

DIRECTIONS: Questions 12 and 13 are to be answered SOLELY on the basis of the following paragraphs.

We must also find better ways to handle the relocation of people uprooted by projects. In the past, many renewal plans have foundered on this problem, and it is still the most difficult part of the community development. Large-scale replacement of low-income residents -- many ineligible for public housing -- has contributed to deterioration of surrounding communities. However, thanks to changes in housing authority procedures, relocation has been accomplished in a far more satisfactory fashion. The step-by-step community development projects we advocate in this plan should bring further improvement.

But additional measures will be necessary. There are going to be more people to be moved; and, with the current shortage of apartments, large ones especially, it is going to be tougher to find places to move them to. The city should have more freedom to buy or lease housing that comes on the market because of normal turnover and make it available to relocatees.

12. According to the above paragraphs, one of the reasons a neighborhood may deteriorate is that   12.____

    A. there is a scarcity of large apartments
    B. step-by-step community development projects have failed
    C. people in the given neighborhood are uprooted from their homes
    D. a nearby renewal project has an inadequate relocation plan

13. From the above paragraphs, one might conclude that the relocation phase of community renewal has been improved.   13.____

    A. by changes in housing authority procedures
    B. by development of step-by-step community development projects
    C. through expanded city powers to buy housing for relocation
    D. by the addition of huge sums of money

Questions 14-15.

DIRECTIONS: Questions 14 and 15 are to be answered SOLELY on the basis of the following paragraphs.

Provision of decent housing for the lower half of the population (by income) was thus taken on as a public responsibility. Public housing was to assist the poorest quarter of urban families while the 221(d)(3) Housing Program would assist the next quarter. But limited funds meant that the supply of subsidized housing could not stretch nearly far enough to help this half of the population. Who were to be left out in the rationing process which was accomplished by the sifting of applicants for housing on the part of public and private authorities?

Discrimination on the grounds of race or color is not allowed under Federal law. In all sections of the country, encouragingly, housing programs are found which follow this law to the letter. Yet, housing programs in some cities still suffer from the residue of racial segregation policies and attitudes that for years were condoned or even encouraged.

Some sifting in the 221(d)(3) Housing Program follows the practice of many public housing authorities, the imposition of requirements with respect to character. This is a delicate matter. To fill a project overwhelmingly with broken families, alcoholics, criminals, delinquents, and other problem tenants would hardly make it a wholesome environment. Yet the total exclusion of such families is hardly an acceptable alternative. To the extent this exclusion is practiced, the very people whose lives are described in order to persuade lawmakers and the public to instigate new programs find the door shut in their faces when such programs come into being. The proper balance is difficult to achieve, but society's neediest families surely should not be totally denied the opportunities for rejuvenation in subsidized housing.

14. From the above paragraphs, it can be assumed that the 221(d)(3) Housing Program

    A. served a population earning more than the median income
    B. served a less affluent population than is served by public housing
    C. excludes all problem families from its projects
    D. is a subsidized housing program

15. According to this text, the provision of housing for the poor

    A. has not been completely accomplished with public monies
    B. is never influenced by segregationist policies
    C. is limited to providing housing for only the neediest families
    D. is primarily the responsibility of the Federal government

16. Five hundred persons attended a public hearing at which a proposed public housing project was being considered. Less than half favored the project while the majority opposed the project.
    According to the above statement, it is REASONABLE to conclude that

    A. the proposal stimulated considerable community interest
    B. the public housing project was disapproved by the city because a majority opposed it
    C. those who opposed the project lacked sympathy for needy persons
    D. the supporters of the project were led by militants

17. A vacant lot close to a polluted creek is for sale. Two buyers compete. One owns an adjacent factory which provides 300 high paying unskilled jobs. He needs to expand or move from the city. If he expands, he will provide 300 additional jobs. The other is a community group in a changing residential area close by. They hope to stabilize the neighborhood by bringing in new housing. They would build an apartment building with 100 dwelling units on the lot.
    According to the above paragraph, it is REASONABLE to conclude that

    A. jobs are more important than housing
    B. there is conflict between the factory owners and the neighborhood group
    C. the neighborhood group will not succeed in stabilizing the area by constructing new housing
    D. the polluted creek should be cleaned up

18. The housing authority faces every problem of the private developer, and it must also assume responsibilities of which private building is free. The authority must account to the community; it must conform to federal regulations; it must provide durable buildings of good standard at low cost; it must overcome the prejudices against public operations, of contractors, bankers, and prospective tenants. These authorities are being watched by anti-housing enthusiasts for the first error of judgment or the first evidence of high costs, to be torn to bits before a Congressional committee.
On the basis of this statement, it would be MOST correct to state that

   A. private builders do not have the opposition of contractors, bankers, and prospective tenants
   B. Congressional committees impede the progress of public housing by petty investigations
   C. a housing authority must deal with all the difficulties encountered by the private builder
   D. housing authorities are no more immune from errors in judgment than private developers

19. Another factor that has considerably added to the city's housing crisis has been the great influx of low-income workers and their families seeking better employment opportunities during wartime and defense boom periods. The circumstances of these families have forced them to crowd into the worst kind of housing and have produced on a renewed scale the conditions from which slums flourish and grow.
On the basis of this statement, one would be justified in stating that

   A. the influx of low-income workers has aggravated the slum problem
   B. the city has better employment opportunities than other sections of the country
   C. the high wages paid by our defense industries have made many families ineligible for tenancy in public housing projects
   D. the families who settled in the city during wartime and the defense build-up brought with them language and social customs conducive to the growth of slums

20. Much of the city felt the effects of the general postwar increase of vandalism and street crime, and the greatly expanded public housing program was no exception. Projects built in congested slum areas with a high incidence of delinquency and crime were particularly subjected to the depredations of neighborhood gangs. The civil service watchmen who patrolled the projects, unarmed and neither trained nor expected to perform police duties, were unable to cope with the situation.
On the basis of this statement, the MOST accurate of the following statements is:

   A. Neighborhood gangs were particularly responsible for the high incidence of delinquency and crime in congested slum areas having public housing programs
   B. Civil service watchmen who patrolled housing projects failed to carry out their assigned police duties
   C. Housing projects were not spared the effects of the general postwar increase of vandalism and street crime
   D. Delinquency and crime affected housing projects in slum areas to a greater extent than other dwellings in the same area

21. Another peculiar characteristic of real estate is the absence of liquidity. Each parcel is a discrete unit as to size, location, rental, physical condition, and financing arrangements. Each property requires investigation, comparison of rents with other properties, and individualized haggling on price and terms.
On the basis of this statement, the LEAST accurate of the following statements is:

    A. Although the size, location, and rent of parcels vary, comparison with rents of other properties affords an indication of the value of a particular parcel
    B. Bargaining skill is the essential factor in determining the value of a parcel of real estate
    C. Each parcel of real estate has individual peculiarities distinguishing it from any other parcel
    D. Real estate is not easily converted to other types of assets

21.____

22. In part, at least, the charges of sameness, monotony, and institutionalism directed at public housing projects result from the degree in which they differ from the city's normal housing pattern. They seem alike because their very difference from the usual makes them stand apart.
In many respects, there is considerably more variety between public housing projects than there is between different streets of apartment houses or tenements throughout the city.
On the basis of this statement, it would be LEAST accurate to state that:

    A. There is considerably more variety between public housing projects than there is between different streets of tenements throughout the city
    B. Public housing projects differ from the city's normal housing pattern to the degree that sameness, monotony, and institutionalism are characteristic of public buildings
    C. Public housing projects seem alike because their deviation from the usual dwellings draws attention to them
    D. The variety in structure between public housing projects and other public buildings is related to the period in which they were built

22.____

23. The amount of debt that can be charged against the city for public housing is limited by law. Part of the city's restricted housing means goes for cash subsidies it may be required to contribute to state-aided projects. Under the provisions of the state law, the city must match the state's contributions in subsidies; and while the value of the partial tax exemption granted by the city is counted for this purpose, it is not always sufficient.
On the basis of this statement, it would be MOST accurate to state that:

    A. The amount of money the city may spend for public housing is limited by annual tax revenues
    B. The value of tax exemptions granted by the city to educational, religious, and charitable institutions may be added to its subsidy contributions to public housing projects
    C. The subsidy contributions for state-aided public housing projects are shared equally by the state and the city under the provisions of the state law
    D. The tax revenues of the city, unless supplemented by state aid, are insufficient to finance public housing projects

23.____

24. Maintenance costs can be minimized and the useful life of houses can be extended by building with the best and most permanent materials available. The best and most permanent materials in many cases are, however, much more expensive than materials which require more maintenance. The most economical procedure in home building has been to compromise between the capital costs of high quality and enduring materials and the maintenance costs of less desirable materials.
    On the basis of this statement, one would be justified in stating that:

    A. Savings in maintenance costs make the use of less durable and less expensive building materials preferable to high quality materials that would prolong the useful life of houses constructed from them
    B. Financial advantage can be secured by the home builder if he judiciously combines costly but enduring building materials with less desirable materials which, however, require more maintenance
    C. A compromise between the capital costs of high quality materials and the maintenance costs of less desirable materials makes it easier for a home builder to estimate construction expenditures
    D. The most economical procedure in home building is to balance the capital costs of the most permanent materials against the costs of less expensive materials that are cheaper to maintain

25. Personnel selection has been a critical problem for local housing authorities. The pool of qualified workers trained in housing procedures is small, and the colleges and universities have failed to grasp the opportunity for enlarging it. While real estate experience makes a good background for management of a housing project, many real estate men are deplorably lacking in understanding of social and governmental problems. Social workers, on the other hand, are likely to be deficient in business judgment.
    On the basis of this statement, it would be MOST accurate to state that:

    A. Colleges and universities have failed to train qualified workers for proficiency in housing procedures
    B. Social workers are deficient in business judgment as related to the management of a housing project
    C. Real estate experience makes a person a good manager of a housing project
    D. Local housing authorities have been critical of present methods of personnel selection

KEY (CORRECT ANSWERS)

1. B
2. C
3. B
4. B
5. D

6. B
7. B
8. D
9. D
10. D

11. A
12. D
13. A
14. D
15. A

16. A
17. B
18. C
19. A
20. C

21. B
22. B
23. C
24. B
25. A

DOCUMENTS AND FORMS
PREPARING WRITTEN MATERIALS
EXAMINATION SECTION
TEST 1

DIRECTIONS: Each question or incomplete statement is followed by several suggested answers or completions. Select the one that BEST answers the question or completes the statement. *PRINT THE LETTER OF THE CORRECT ANSWER IN THE SPACE AT THE RIGHT.*

1. Of the following types of documents, it is MOST important to retain and file
   A. working drafts of reports that have been submitted in final form
   B. copies of letters of good will which conveyed a message that could not be handled by phone
   C. interoffice orders for materials which have been received and verified
   D. interoffice memoranda regarding the routine of standard forms

2. The MAXIMUM number of 2¾" x 4¼" size forms which may be obtained from one ream of 17" x 22" paper is
   A. 4,000   B. 8,000   C. 12,000   D. 16,000

3. On a general organization chart, staff positions NORMALLY should be pictured
   A. directly above the line positions to which they report
   B. to the sides of the main flow lines
   C. within the box of the highest level subordinate positions pictured
   D. directly below the line positions which report to them

4. When an administrator is diagramming an office layout, of the following, his PRIMARY job generally should be to indicate the
   A. lighting intensities that will be required by each operator
   B. noise level that will be produced by the various equipment employed in the office
   C. direction of the work flow and the distance involved in each transfer
   D. durability of major pieces of office equipment currently in use or to be utilized

5. One common guideline or rule-of-thumb ratio for evaluating the efficiency of files is the number of records requested divided by the number of records filed. Generally, if this ratio is very low, it would point MOST directly to the need for
   A. improving the indexing and coding systems
   B. improving the charge-out procedures
   C. exploring the need for transferring records from active storage to the archives
   D. exploring the need to encourage employees to keep more records in their private files

6. The GREATEST percentage of money spent on preparing and keeping the usual records in an office generally is expended for which one of the following?
   A. Renting space in which to place the record-keeping equipment
   B. Paying salaries of record-preparing and record-keeping personnel
   C. Depreciation of purchased record-preparation and record-keeping machines
   D. Paper and forms upon which to place the records

7. In a certain office, file folders are constantly being removed from the files for use by administrators. At the same time, new material is coming in to be filed in some of these folders.
   Of the following, the BEST way to avoid delays in filing of the new material and to keep track of the removed folders is to
   A. keep a sheet listing all folders removed from the file, who has them, and a follow-update to check on their return; attach to this list new material received for filing
   B. put an "out" slip in the place of any file folder removed, telling what folder is missing, date removed, and who has it; file new material received at front of files
   C. put a temporary "out" folder in place of the one removed, giving title or subject, date removed, and who has it; put into this temporary folder any new material received
   D. keep a list of all folders removed and who has them; forward any new material received for filing while a folder is out to the person who has it

8. Folders labeled "Miscellaneous" should be used in an alphabetic filing system MAINLY to
   A. provide quick access to recent material
   B. avoid setting up individual folders for infrequent correspondence
   C. provide temporary storage for less important documents
   D. temporarily hold papers which will not fit into already crowded individual folders

9. Out-of-date and seldom-used records should be removed periodically from the files because
   A. overall responsibility for records will be transferred to the person in charge of the central storage files
   B. duplicate copies of every record are not needed
   C. valuable filing space will be regained and the time needed to find a current record will be cut down
   D. worthwhile suggestions on improving the filing system will result whenever this is done

10. Of the following, the BEST reason for discarding certain material from office files would be that the
    A. files are crowded
    B. material in the files is old
    C. material duplicates information obtainable from other sources in the files
    D. material is referred to most often by employees in an adjoining office

11. Of the following, the MAIN factor contributing to the expense of maintaining an office procedure manual would be the
    A. infrequent use of the manual
    B. need to revise it regularly
    C. cost of loose-leaf binders
    D. high cost of printing

11._____

12. The suggestion that memos or directives which circulate among subordinates be initialed by each employee is a
    A. *poor* one, because, with modern copying machines, it would be possible to supply every subordinate with a copy of each message for his personal use
    B. *good* one, because it relieves the supervisor of blame for the action of subordinates who have read and initialed the messages
    C. *poor* one, because initialing the memo or directive is no guarantee that the subordinate has read the material
    D. *good* one, because it can be used as a record by the supervisor to show that his subordinates have received the message and were responsible for reading it

12._____

13. Of the following, the MOST important reason for microfilming office records is to
    A. save storage space needed to keep records
    B. make it easier to get records when needed
    C. speed up the classification of information
    D. shorten the time which records must be kept

13._____

14. Your office filing cabinets have become so overcrowded that it is difficult to use the files.
    Of the following, the MOST desirable step for you to take FIRST to relieve this situation would be to
    A. assign your assistant to spend some time each day reviewing the material in the files and to give you his recommendations as to what material may be discarded
    B. discard all material which has been in the files more than a given number of years
    C. submit a request for additional filing cabinets in your next budget request
    D. transfer enough material to the central storage room of your agency to give you the amount of additional filing space needed

14._____

15. In indexing names of business firms and other organizations, one of the rules to be followed is:
    A. The word "and" is considered an indexing unit
    B. When a firm name includes the full name of a person who is not well known, the person's first name is considered as the first indexing unit
    C. Usually, the units in a firm name are indexed in the order in which they are written
    D. When a firm's name is made up of single letters (such as ABC Corp.), the letters taken together are considered as more than one indexing unit

15._____

16. Assume that your unit processes confidential forms which are submitted by persons seeking financial assistance. An individual comes to your office, gives you his name, and states that he would like to look over a form which he sent in about a week ago because he believes he omitted some important information.
Of the following, the BEST thing for you to do FIRST is to
    A. locate the proper form
    B. call the individual's home telephone number to verify his identity
    C. ask the individual if he has proof of his identity
    D. call the security office

17. An employee has been assigned to open her division head's mail and place it on his desk. One day, the employee opens a letter which she then notices is marked "Personal."
Of the following, the BEST action for her to take is to
    A. write "Personal" on the letter and staple the envelope to the back of the letter
    B. ignore the matter and treat the letter the same way as the others
    C. give it to another division head to hold until her own division head comes into the office
    D. leave the letter in the envelope and write "Sorry-opened by mistake" on the envelope, and initial it

18. The MOST important reason for having a filing system is to
    A. get papers out of the way
    B. have a record of everything that has happened
    C. retain information to justify your actions
    D. enable rapid retrieval of information

19. The system of filing which is used MOST frequently is called _____ filing.
    A. alphabetic   B. alphanumeric
    C. geographic   D. numeric

20. In judging the adequacy of a standard office form, which of the following is LEAST important?
    A. Date of the form   B. Legibility of the form
    C. Size of the form   D. Design of the form

21. Assume that the letters and reports which are dictated to you fall into a few distinct subject-matter areas.
The practice of trying to familiarize yourself with the terminology in these areas is
    A. *good*, because you will have a basis for commenting on the dictated material
    B. *good*, because it will be easier to take the dictation at the rate at which it is given
    C. *poor*, because the functions and policies of an office are not of your concern
    D. *poor*, because it will take too much time away from your assigned work

22. A letter was dictated on June 9 and was ready to be typed on June 12. The
letter was typed on June 13, signed on June 14, and mailed on June 14.
The date that, ORDINARILY, should have appeared on the letter is June
   A. 9　　　　　B. 12　　　　　C. 13　　　　　D. 14

23. Of the following, the BEST reason for putting the "key point" at the beginning of a letter is that it
   A. may save time for the reader
   B. is standard practice in writing letters
   C. will more likely to be typed correctly
   D. cannot logically be placed elsewhere

24. As a supervisor, you have been asked to attend committee meetings and take the minutes.
The body of such minutes GENERALLY consists of
   A. the date and place of the meeting and the list of persons present
   B. an exact verbatim report of everything that was said by each person who spoke
   C. a clear description of each matter discussed and the action decided on
   D. the agenda of the meeting

25. When typing a rough draft from a recorded transcription, a stenographer under your supervision reaches a spot on the recording that is virtually inaudible.
Of the following, the MOST advisable action that you should recommend to her is to
   A. guess what the dictator intended to say based on what he said in the parts that are clear
   B. ask the dictator to listen to his unsatisfactory recording
   C. leave an appropriate amount of space for that portion that is inaudible
   D. stop typing the draft and send a note to the dictator identifying the item that could not be completed

KEY (CORRECT ANSWERS)

1.	D	11.	B
2.	D	12.	D
3.	B	13.	A
4.	C	14.	A
5.	C	15.	C
6.	B	16.	C
7.	C	17.	D
8.	B	18.	D
9.	C	19.	A
10.	C	20.	A

21.	B
22.	D
23.	A
24.	C
25.	C

TEST 2

DIRECTIONS: Each question or incomplete statement is followed by several suggested answers or completions. Select the one that BEST answers the question or completes the statement. *PRINT THE LETTER OF THE CORRECT ANSWER IN THE SPACE AT THE RIGHT.*

1. To tell a newly employed clerk to fill a top drawer of a four-drawer cabinet with heavy binders which will be often used and to keep lower drawers only partly filled is
   A. *good*, because a tall person would have to bend unnecessarily if he had to use a lower drawer
   B. *bad*, because the file cabinet may tip over when the top drawer is opened
   C. *good*, because it is the most easily reachable drawer for the average person
   D. *bad*, because a person bending down at another drawer may accidentally bang his head on the bottom of the drawer when he straightens up

2. If you have requisitioned a "ream" of paper in order to duplicate a single page office announcement, how many announcements can be printed from the one package of paper?
   A. 200   B. 500   C. 700   D. 1,000

3. In the operations of a government agency, a voucher is ORDINARILY used to
   A. refer someone to the agency for a position or assignment
   B. certify that an agency's records of financial transactions are accurate
   C. order payment from agency funds of a stated amount to an individual
   D. enter a statement of official opinion in the records of the agency

4. Of the following types of cards used in filing systems, the one which is generally MOST helpful in locating records which might be filed under more than one subject is the _____ card.
   A. out
   B. tickler
   C. cross-reference
   D. visible index

5. The type of filing system in which one does NOT need to refer to a card index in order to find the folder is called
   A. alphabetic   B. geographic   C. subject   D. locational

6. Of the following, records management is LEAST concerned with
   A. the development of the best method for retrieving important information
   B. deciding what records should be kept
   C. deciding the number of appointments a client will need
   D. determining the types of folders to be used

7. If records are continually removed from a set of files without "charging" them to the borrower, the filing system will soon become ineffective.
   Of the following terms, the one which is NOT applied to a form used in the charge-out system is a
   A. requisition card
   B. out-folder
   C. record retrieval form
   D. substitution card

8. A new clerk has been told to put 500 cards in alphabetical order. Another clerk suggests that she divide the cards into four groups, such as A to F, G to L, M to R, and S to Z, and then alphabetize these four smaller groups.
   The suggested method is
   A. *poor*, because the clerk will have to handle the sheets more than once and will waste time
   B. *good*, because it saves time, is more accurate, and is less tiring
   C. *good*, because she will not have to concentrate on it so much when it is in smaller groups
   D. *poor*, because this method is much more tiring than straight alphabetizing

9. In Microsoft Excel, data and records are entered into
   A. pages   B. forms   C. cells   D. contracts

10. Suppose a clerk has been given pads of pre-printed forms to use when taking phone messages for others in her office. The clerk is then observed using scraps of paper and not the forms for writing her messages.
    It should be explained that the BEST reason for using the forms is that
    A. they act as a checklist to make sure that the important information is taken
    B. she is expected to do her work in the same way as others in the office
    C. they make sure that unassigned paper is not wasted on phone messages
    D. learning to use these forms will help train her to use more difficult forms

11. The high-speed printing process used for producing large quantities of superior quality copy and cost efficiency is called
    A. photocopying
    B. laser printing
    C. inkjet printing
    D. word processing

12. Of the following, the MAIN reason a stock clerk keeps a perpetual inventory of supplies in the storeroom is that such an inventory will
    A. eliminate the need for a physical inventory
    B. provide a continuous record of supplies on hand
    C. indicate whether a shipment of supplies is satisfactory
    D. dictate the terms of the purchase order

13. As a supervisor, you may be required to handle different types of correspondence.
    Of the following types of letters, it would be MOST important to promptly seal which kind of letter?
    A. One marked "confidential"
    B. Those containing enclosures
    C. Any letter to be sent airmail
    D. Those in which copies will be sent along with the original

14. While opening incoming mail, you notice that one letter indicates that an enclosure was to be included but, even after careful inspection, you are not able to find the information to which this refers.
    Of the following, the thing that you should do FIRST is
    A. replace the letter in its envelope and return it to the sender
    B. file the letter until the sender's office mails the missing information
    C. type out a letter to the sender informing him of his error
    D. make a notation in the margin of the letter that the enclosure was omitted

15. You have been given a checklist and assigned the responsibility of inspecting certain equipment in the various offices of your agency.
    Which of the following is the GREATEST advantage of the checklist?
    A. It indicates which equipment is in greatest demand.
    B. Each piece of equipment on the checklist will be checked only once.
    C. It helps to insure that the equipment listed will not be overlooked.
    D. The equipment listed suggests other equipment you should look for.

16. The BEST way to evaluate the overall state of completion of a construction project is to check the progress estimate against the
    A. inspection worksheet   B. construction schedule
    C. inspector's checklist   D. equipment maintenance schedule

17. The usual contract for agency work includes a section entitled "Instructions to Bidders," which states that the
    A. contractor agrees that he has made his own examination and will make no claim for damages on account of errors or omissions
    B. contractor shall not make claims for damages of any discrepancy, error, or omission in any plans
    C. estimates of quantities and calculations are guaranteed by the agency to be correct and are deemed to be a representation of the conditions affecting the work
    D. plans, measurements, dimensions, and conditions under which the work is to be performed are guaranteed by the agency

18. In order to avoid disputes over payments for extra work in a contract for construction, the BEST procedure to follow would be to
    A. have contractor submit work progress reports daily
    B. insert a special clause in the contract specifications
    C. have a representative on the job at all times to verify conditions
    D. allocate a certain percentage of the cost of the job to cover such expenses

19. Prior to the installation of equipment called for in the specifications, the contractor is USUALLY required to submit for approval
    A. sets of shop drawings
    B. a set of revised specifications
    C. a detailed description of the methods of work to be used
    D. a complete list of skilled and unskilled tradesmen he proposes to use

20. During the actual construction work, the CHIEF value of a construction schedule is to
    A. insure that the work will be done on time
    B. reveal whether production is falling behind
    C. show how much equipment and material is required for the project
    D. furnish data as to the methods and techniques of construction operations

KEY (CORRECT ANSWERS)

1.	B	11.	B
2.	B	12.	B
3.	C	13.	A
4.	C	14.	D
5.	A	15.	C
6.	C	16.	B
7.	C	17.	A
8.	B	18.	C
9.	C	19.	A
10.	A	20.	B

ZONING ORDINANCES IN RELATION TO THE HOUSING INSPECTION

	Page
I. Background of Zoning	1
II. Definitions	2
III. Zoning Objectives	3
IV. What Zoning Cannot Do	4
V. Content of the Ordinance	4
VI. Bulk and Height requirements	5
VII. Yard Requirements	5
VIII. Off street Parking	6
IX. Nonconforming Uses	6
X. Variances	6
XI. Exceptions	7
XII. Administration	7
XIII. How Zoning Can Benefit the Housing Inspector	7
XIV. Example of Zoning and Housing Relationships	8

ZONING ORDINANCES IN RELATION TO THE HOUSING INSPECTION

Zoning is essentially a means of ensuring that a community's hind uses are compatibly located for the health, safety, and general welfare of the community. Experience has shown that some types of controls are needed in order to provide orderly growth in relation to the community plan for development. Just as a capital improvement program governs public improvements such as streets, parks, and other recreational facilities, schools, and public buildings, so zoning governs the planning program with respect to the use of public and private property.

When a person buys or builds a house or other structure in a municipality that has a zoning ordinance in effect, he is presumed to know and obliged by law to comply with the zoning regulations governing the use of buildings and land in the section of the community in which his property is located. If he either erects a structure or converts a house or building that is within that particular district by the local zoning ordinance into another type of use he still has acquired no property right to continue the forbidden use. An example would be the conversion of a single family residence into multifamily units. Even if the owner has obtained a building permit for this work already completed, the building permit would be voided, because the work was started in violation of the zoning code and because a building permit can be valid' only when issued for a lawful purpose. The building inspector is therefore obliged to refuse issuance of a building permit if the proposed work is in violation of the zoning ordinance.

It is very important that the housing inspector know the general nature of zoning regulations, since properties in violation of both the housing code and the zoning ordinance must be brought into full compliance with the zoning ordinance before the housing code can be enforced. In many cases the housing inspector may be able to eliminate some of the properties in violation of the housing code through enforcement of the zoning ordinance.

I. Background of Zoning

Zoning regulations have been used for several centuries. In the early settlement of our country, gunpowder mills and storehouses were prohibited from being located within the heavily populated portions of town, owing to the frequent fires and explosions. Later, zoning took the form of fire districts, and under implied legislative powers, wooden buildings were prohibited from certain sections of the municipality.

Massachusetts passed one of the first zoning laws in 1692. This law authorized Boston, Salem, Charlestown, and certain other market towns in the province to assign certain locations in each town for the establishment of slaughterhouses and still houses for currying of leather.

Act and Resolves of the Province of Massachusetts Bay 1692-93 C. 23

"Be it ordained and enacted by the Governor, Council and Representatives convened in General Court or Assembly, and by the authority of the same,

Sect. 1 That the selectmen of the towns of Boston, Salem, and Charlestown respectively, or other market towns in the province, with two or more justices of the peace dwelling in the town, or two of the next justices of the country, shall at or before the last day of March, one thousand six hundred ninety-three, assign some certain places of the said towns (where it may be least offensive) for the erecting or setting up of slaughterhouses for the killing of all meat, still houses, and houses for trying of tallow and currying of leather (which houses may be erected of timber, the law referring to building with brick or stone not withstanding) and shall cause an entry to be made in the town book of what places shall be by them so assigned, and make known the same by posting it up in some public places of the town; by which houses and places respectively, and no other, all butchers, slaughter men, distillers, chandlers, and curriers shall exercise and practice their respective trades and mysteries; on pain that any butcher or slaughter man transgressing of this act by killing of meat in any other place, for every conviction thereof before one or more justices of the peace, shall forfeit and pay the sum of twenty shillings (shilling worth about 12-16¢); and any distiller, chandler or currier offending against this act, for every conviction thereof before their majesties justices at the general sessions of the peace for the county, shall forfeit and pay the sum of five pounds (a pound equals 20 shillings and was worth somewhere between $2.40 and $3.20); one-third part of said forfeitures to be the use of the majesties for the support of the government of the province and incident charges thereof, one-third to the poor of the town when such offense shall be committed, and the other third to him or them that shall inform and sue for the same ....

II. Definitions

A. Accessory Structure - A detached building or structure in a secondary or subordinate capacity from the main or principal building or structure on the same premises. Example: garage behind a single-family dwelling.

B. Accessory Use - A use incidental and subordinate to the principal use of a structure. Example: a home-located physician's office.

C. Alteration - A change or rearrangement of the structural parts of a building, or an expansion or enlargement of the building.

D. Building Area - That portion of the lot remaining available for construction after all required open space and yard requirements are met.

E. Dwelling - Any enclosed space that is wholly or partially used or intended to be used for living or sleeping by human occupants provided that temporary housing shall not be regarded as a dwelling. Temporary housing is defined as any tent, trailer, mobile home, or any other shelter designed to be transportable and not attached to the ground, to another structure, or to any utility system on the same premises for more than 30 consecutive days.

F. Dwelling, Two Family - A structure containing two dwelling units and designed for occupancy by no more than two families.

G. Dwelling, Multifamily - A residential structure equipped with more than two dwelling units.

H. Dwelling Unit - Any room or group of rooms located within a dwelling and forming a single habitable unit with facilities that are used or intended to be used by a single family for living, sleeping, cooking, and eating.

I. Exception - Sometimes called "special use." An exception is a land use that can be made compatible with a district upon the imposition by the board of adjustment of special provisions covering its development, even though it would not otherwise be permitted in the district. Example: Fire substation being permitted to locate in a residential area.

J. Family - One or more individuals living together and sharing common living, sleeping, cooking, and eating facilities.

K. Home Occupation - An occupation conducted in a dwelling unit subject to the restrictions of the zoning ordinance. Limitations of interest to housing inspectors are the following: (a) Only the occupant or members of his family residing on the premises shall be engaged in the occupation, (b) the home occupation use shall be subordinate to its use for residential purposes and shall not occupy more than 25 per cent of the floor area of the dwelling unit, (c) the home occupation shall not be conducted in an accessory structure, (d) no offensive noise, glare, vibration, heat, smoke, dust, or odor shall be produced.

L. Lot- Parcel of land considered as a unit devoted to either a particular use or to occupancy by a building and its accessory structures.

M. Lot Depth - The average horizontal distance between the front and rear lot line measured at right angles to the structure.

N. Lot Width - The average horizontal distance between the sides of a lot measured at right angles to the lot depth.

O. Nonconforming Use - (a) Use of a building or use of land that does not conform to the regulations of the district in which located. (b) Nonconforming use also means a building or land use that does not conform to the regulations of the district in which the building or land is but that is nevertheless legal since it existed before enactment of the ordinance.

P. Open Space - Unoccupied space that is open to the sky and on the same lot with the building.

Q. Variance - Easing or lessening of the terms of the zoning ordinance by a public body so that relief for hardships will be provided but with the public interest still protected.

Inspectors should refer to the definitions in the zoning ordinance of their municipality for additions and changes.

III. Zoning Objectives

As stated earlier, the purpose of a zoning ordinance is to ensure that the land uses within the community are regulated not only for the health, safety, and welfare of the community but also in keeping with the comprehensive plan for community development. The objectives contained in the zoning ordinance that help to achieve a development providing for the health, safety, and welfare are the following:

A. Regulate Height, Bulk, and Area of Structure. In order to provide established standards of healthful housing within the community, regulations dealing with building heights, lot coverage, and floor areas must be established. These regulations then ensure that adequate natural lighting, ventilation, privacy, and recreational area for children will be realized. These are all fundamental physiological needs that have been determined to be necessary for a healthful environment.

Safety from fires is enhanced because of building separations needed to meet yard and open-space requirements.

Through prescribing minimum lot area per dwelling unit, population density controls are established.

B. Avoid Undue Levels of Noise, Vibration, Glare, Air Pollution, and Odor. By providing land use category districts, these environmental stresses upon the individual can be reduced. As in the first item, the absence of these stresses has been determined to be a fundamental physiological individual need.

C. Lessen Street Congestion Through Off-Street Parking and Off-Street Loading Requirement.

D. Facilitate Adequate Provisions of Water, Sewerage, Schools, Parks, and Playgrounds.

E. Secure Safety From Flooding.

F. Conserve Property Values. Through careful enforcement of the provisions property values will be stabilized and conserved.

IV. What Zoning Cannot Do

In order to understand more fully the difference between zoning and the other devices such as subdivision regulations, building codes, and housing ordinances, the housing inspector must know the things that cannot be accomplished by a zoning ordinance.

Items that cannot be accomplished in a zoning ordinance include:

A. Correcting Existence of Overcrowding or Substandard Housing. Zoning is not retroactive and cannot correct conditions such as those cited. These are corrected through enforcement of a minimum standards housing code.

B. Materials and Methods of Construction. Materials and methods of construction are enforced through the building codes rather than through zoning.

C. Cost of Construction. Quality of construction and hence construction costs are often regulated through deed restrictions or covenants. Zoning does, however, stabilize property values in an area by prohibiting incompatible development such as the location of a heavy industry in the midst of a well-established subdivision.

D. Subdivision Design and Layout. Design and layout of subdivisions as well as provisions for parks and streets are controlled through subdivision regulations.

V. Content of the Ordinance

Zoning ordinances establish districts of whatever size, shape, and number the municipality deems best for carrying out the purposes of the zoning ordinance. Most cities use three major districts: residential, commercial, and industrial. These three may then be subdivided into many sub districts, depending on local conditions. These districts specify the principal and accessory uses, exceptions, and prohibitions.

In general these permitted land uses are based on intensity of land use, a less intense land use being permitted in a more intense district but not vice versa. For example, a single-family residence is a less intense land use than a multifamily dwelling. A multifamily dwelling would not, however, be permitted in a single-family district.

In recent years, some ordinances are being partially based on performance standards rather than solely on land use intensity. For example, some types of industrial developments may be permitted in a less intense use district provided that the proposed land use creates no noise, glare, smoke, dust, vibration, or other environmental stress exceeding acceptable standards and provided further that adequate off street parking, screening, landscaping, and other similar measures are taken.

VI. Bulk and Height Requirements

To further achieve the earlier stated objectives of the zoning ordinance, other regulations within a particular zoning district are imposed to gain control of population densities and to provide adequate light, air, privacy, and other elements needed for a safe and healthy environment.

Most early zoning ordinances stated that within a particular district the height and bulk of any structure could not exceed certain dimensions and specified that dimensions for front, side, and rear yards must be provided. Today some zoning ordinances use floor area ratios for regulation. Floor area ratio is the relationship between the floor space of the structure and the size of the lot on which it is located. For example, a floor area ratio of 1 would permit either a two-story building covering 50 per cent of the lot, or a one-story building covering 100 per cent of the lot. This is illustrated in Figure 1. Other zoning ordinances specify the maximum amount of the lot that can be covered or else merely require that a certain amount of open space must be provided for each structure and leave the flexibility of the location to the builder. Still other ordinances, rather than specify a particular height for the structure, specify an angle of light obstruction within a particular district that will assure air and light to the surrounding structures. An example of this is shown in Figure 2.

VII. Yard Requirements

Zoning ordinances also contain yard requirements that are divided into front, rear, and side yard requirements. These requirements, in addition to stating the lot dimensions, usually designate the amount of setback

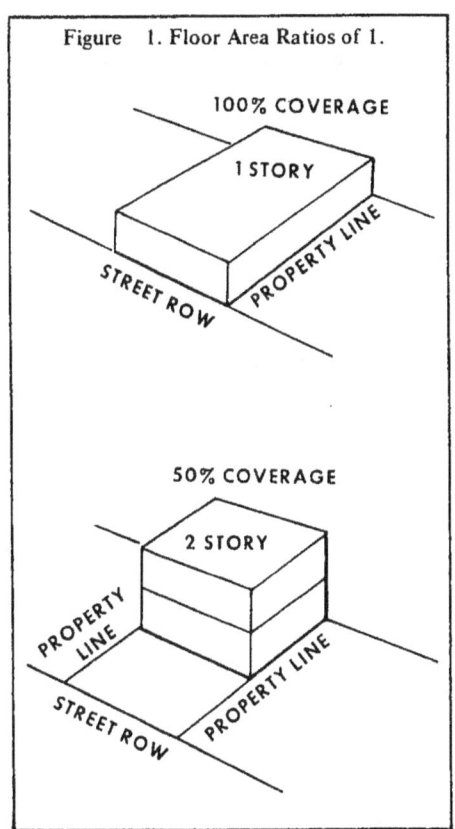

Figure 1. Floor Area Ratios of 1.

required. Most ordinances permit the erection of auxiliary buildings in rear yards provided they are located at stated distances from all lot lines and provided sufficient stated open space is maintained. If the property is a corner lot, additional requirements are set to allow visibility for motorists.

VIII. Off street Parking

Space for off street parking and off street loading is also contained in the ordinance. These requirements are based on standards relating floor space or seating capacity to land use. For example, a furniture store would require fewer off street parking spaces in relation to the floor area than a movie theater would.

IX. Nonconforming Uses

Since zoning is not retroactive, all zoning ordinances must contain a provision for nonconforming uses. If a use has already been established within a particular district before adoption of the ordinance, it must be permitted to continue. Provisions are, however, put into

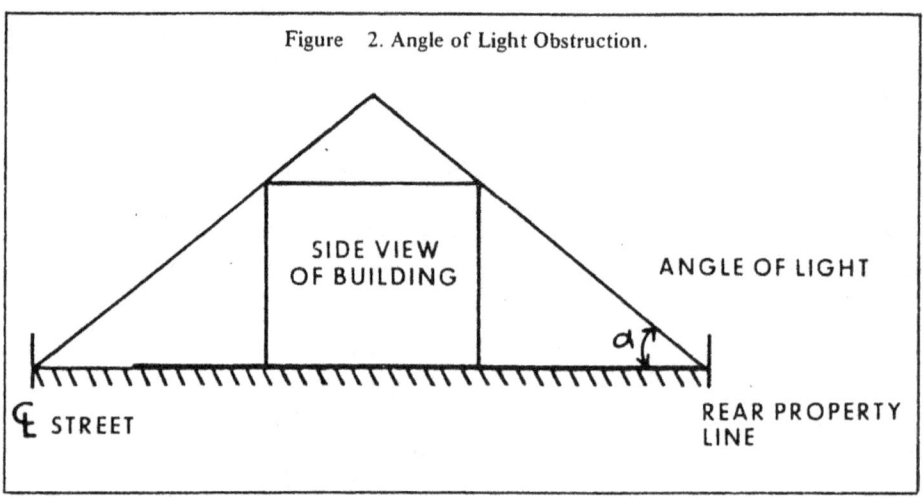
Figure 2. Angle of Light Obstruction.

The ordinance to aid in eliminating nonconforming use. These provisions generally prohibit the following: (1) An enlargement or expansion of the nonconforming uses, (2) reconstruction of the nonconforming use if more than a certain portion is destroyed, (3) resumption of the use after it has been abandoned for a period of specified time, and (4) changing the use to a higher classification or to another nonconforming use. Some zoning ordinances further provide a period of amortization during which the nonconforming land use must be phased out.

X. Variances

Zoning ordinances contain provisions for permitting variances and providing a method of granting these variances subject to certain specified conditions. A variance may be granted when, owing to a particular lot shape, topography, or other lot characteristics, an undue hardship would be imposed on the owner if the exact content of the ordinance is adhered to. For example, assume we have a piece of irregularly shaped property located in a district having the side yard requirements of 20 feet on a side and total lot size requirement of 10,000 square feet. Suppose that our property contains 10,200 feet and thus meets the area requirements; however, let us further assume that, owing to the irregular shape of the property, we can provide side yards of only 15 feet on a side. Since a hardship would be imposed if the exact letter of the law is held to, the zoning board of adjustment could be asked for a variance. Since there is sufficient total open area and since a lessening of the ordinance is not detrimental to the surrounding property, a variance would probably be granted.

Before a variance can be granted, it must be shown that (1) there is a practical hardship, (2) that the variance is needed for the owner to realize a reasonable return on the property, (3) that the original intent of the ordinance will be adhered to, (4) that the character of the neighborhood will not be changed, and (5) that the public's safety and welfare will be preserved.

XI. Exceptions

An exception is often confused with a variance. In every city there are some necessary uses that do not correspond to the permitted land uses within the district. The zoning code recognizes, however, that if proper safeguards were to be provided, these uses would not have a detrimental effect on the district. An example would be a fire substation, which could be permitted in a residential area provided the station house is designed to resemble a residential dwelling and further provided the property is properly landscaped.

XII. Administration

The key man in the zoning process is the zoning inspector, since he must come in contact with each case. In many cases the zoning inspector may also be the building inspector or the housing inspector. Since the building inspector or housing inspector is already in the field making inspections, it is relatively easy for him to check compliance with a zoning ordinance. This compliance can be checked by comparing the actual land use against that allowed for the area and shown on the zoning map.

Each zoning ordinance has a map as a part of the ordinance giving the permitted usage for each block. By taking a copy of this map with him, the inspector can make a preliminary check of the land use in the field. If the use does not conform, the inspector must then check with the Zoning Board to see if the property in question was a "nonconforming use" at the time of passage of the ordinance and if an exception has been granted. In cities where up-to-date records of existing nonconforming uses and exceptions granted are maintained, the inspector can check the use in the field against the records.

When violation is observed and the property owner is duly notified of the violation, he then has the right of hearing before a Zoning Board of Adjustment (sometimes also called the Zoning Board of Appeals). The Board may uphold the zoning enforcement officer or may rule in favor of the property owner. If the action of the zoning enforcement officer is upheld, the property owner may, if he so desires, seek relief through the courts; otherwise the violation will be corrected to conform to the zoning code.

XIII. How Zoning Can Benefit the Housing Inspector

It is of critical importance for the housing inspector, the building inspector, and the zoning inspector to work closely together in cities where these positions and responsibilities are separate. Experience has shown that when illegal conversions or uses of properties occur, these illegally converted properties are often among the most substandard encountered in the city and often contain especially dangerous housing code violations.

In communities where the zoning code is enforced effectively, the resulting zoning compliance in new and existing housing helps advance, as well as sustain, many of the minimum standards of the housing code such as occupancy, ventilation, light, and unimpeded egress. By the same token, building or housing inspectors can often aid the zoning inspector by helping eliminate some nonconforming uses through code enforcement.

XIV. Example of Zoning and Housing Relationships

The following cases will illustrate these relationships:

A Case 1

Two and one-half-story, 13-room house. Originally it had these features:

a Five-room dwelling unit on first floor including a three-piece bathroom.

b Eight-room dwelling unit occupying the second and third floors including one bathroom of three pieces on the second floor. The second and third floors are served by only one staircase.

c Two oil burners, one heating first floor, the other the second and third floors.

It is located in a residential zoning district where two-family housing is the maximum use permitted.

Five years later, while making a regular inspection, the zoning officer found this house in the process of being converted into a three-family use in violation of the zoning ordinance. The owner has already done these things.

a Made second floor into a separate five-room dwelling unit.

b Started converting the three rooms on the third floor into another apartment by:

1. Installing a three-piece bathroom, 35 square feet in area, against the windowless west wall of the center bedroom, the habitable area being thus reduced to 40 square feet, and setting up the remainder of the area as the living room by providing a coffee table, lamp, and two overstuffed chairs;

2. Putting in a wall kitchenette consisting of a sink with cold water and a stove, plus a table, lamp, and cupboards in the rear bedroom that is 60 square feet in area;

3. Equipping the front bedroom that is 90 square feet in size with two beds, chest of drawers, and other bedroom furnishings for two.

He admitted, however, that he had not checked on state tenement house law requirements since he did not realize multiple dwellings of three families or more are covered by this law.

Question: How many violations (either housing or zoning) can you find?

Answer: As a result of these actions by the owner, the house now has one more dwelling unit than is permitted by the zoning ordinance in this residential district and also contains these obvious housing code violations:

(a) Threatened over occupancy of the third-floor dwelling unit (only 190 square feet available, but 250 square feet habitable floor space is the minimum required for two occupants).

(b) Size of the front bedroom inadequate by 30 square feet if it is used by two occupants. The back bedroom lacks the requirements needed for occupancy by one person (70 square feet). If a third person lived in the dwelling unit the minimum required habitable floor area would then become 350 square feet.

(c) The bathroom does not meet the light and ventilation requirements.

(d) The kitchen sink does not have hot water.

(e) No refrigerator is provided.

(f) From the description it sounds as if one might have to go through a sleeping room to reach the bathroom. This would be a violation.

(g) Both the second and third floor units are in violation since they lack two means of egress.

B Case 2

Assume that a three-family dwelling unit is the largest size permitted in the zoning district where the building in question is located. The housing inspector's investigation of the three-story dwelling from cellar to roof showed that it contained:

1. Four dwelling units, two with six rooms each and two with three rooms each.

2. Five families, three in separate dwelling units and the two on the third floor in one unit.

3. A bathroom and a kitchen on the second floor shared by two families.

4. The bathroom and kitchen on the third floor also being shared by two families.

5. Inadequate means of egress from the dwelling unit in the third floor.

Question: If you were the housing inspector, what actions would you take?

Answer: In this situation there are definite housing code violations. The housing inspector also knows there is a zoning violation. Because he knows that the property must meet zoning requirements before complying with the housing code, the inspector would refer this case to the zoning department for action.

The housing inspector should never speak for the zoning department and tell the owner that he is in violation of a zoning ordinance unless he and the zoning inspector are the same individual. The housing inspector should complete his housing inspection and leave. Responsibility for informing the owner of any zoning violation lies with the zoning department.

In this particular case, some housing code violations will be corrected through enforcement of zoning. However, there are still violations of requirements for egress, a third kitchen, and a third bathroom.

After compliance with the zoning ordinance has been obtained, the zoning department should notify the housing inspector so that he can then enforce any housing violations that may still exist.

C Case 3

Mr. Jones, a zoning inspector, gets a report that at 1212 Oak Street the owner, Mr. Smith, is converting his single-family house into two apartments and has already started alterations. Investigations of the zoning map shows that in this district, apartments, up to four, are permitted if 1,500 square feet of open land area is provided for each apartment. Mr. Jones checks and finds that no building permit has been issued. A site investigation reveals that Mr. Smith has only 2,000 square feet of open area available. He then informs Mr. Smith that he is in violation of the zoning ordinance.

Mr. Smith then appeals to the Zoning Board of Adjustment for a variance to allow him to have two apartments even though he does not have the required 3,000 square feet 0 f open area. His appeal is denied by the board since no real hardship exists. As a result, Mr. Smith must rent the property as a single-family dwelling and is unable to recover the money he has already spent in starting alterations.

Discuss:

1. The actions of Mr. Jones.

Answer: Mr. Jones was justified in citing Mr. Smith for a zoning violation since the proposed open area would have been inadequate.

2 The action of the Board of Adjustment.

Answer: The Board of Adjustment was also justified in upholding the zoning regulations. If the board had not acted in this manner, the crowding on this property could well have started deterioration in surrounding properties.

3 The action of Mr. Smith.

Answer: Mr. Smith had no legitimate complaint when the Board ruled against him. If he had first sought to obtain a building permit, as required by law, he would have been told that his proposed alterations would not meet zoning regulations and hence would not have suffered a monetary loss.

D Case 4

Mr. Edwards requests a building permit to change a three-story single-family house into a two-family unit. Since two-family units are permitted in this district and he has sufficient open area, the permit is granted.

Six months later, the housing inspector, while making a systematic code enforcement inspection, finds that the converted house now has an apartment on each of the three floors. The bath on the second floor is shared by families on the second and third floors. This is a violation of the housing code.

Knowing that all the other houses on this street are only one- or two-family units, he also suspects a zoning violation. After returning to the office, he contacts the zoning department and learns that Mr. Edwards is in violation of the zoning ordinance as well as of the housing code.

Question: Which ordinance must be enforced first and why?

Answer: The zoning ordinance must be enforced first, since a zoning ordinance is a "primary" ordinance and determines the land use of a particular property. A housing code ordinance is a "secondary" ordinance and sets standards of residential usage on the property.

E Case 5

During a routine inspection, the housing inspector finds a house with three families, one of which is living in a cellar apartment.

Question: What actions should he take?

Answer: The inspector should immediately cite the owner for a violation of the ordinance and then follow through to see that the situation is corrected. If the family living in the cellar requires housing assistance as a result of corrective measures taken, the housing inspector should inform them of public agencies available for assistance.

F Case 6

During a routine inspection of a district zoned for up to three-family use, the housing inspector encounters a house that the owner says contains two dwelling units in addition to his own, and also one rooming unit. The inspector finds a cook stove in the "rooming unit."

Question: What actions should he take?

Answer: Although a rooming unit would be permitted in this district, the addition of a cook stove changes the rooming unit into a dwelling unit.

The inspector should refer this case to the zoning department for immediate action and then follow up for housing violations at a later date.

G Case 7

The housing inspector is investigating a complaint of alleged housing violations. The owner refuses to admit the inspector inside the building and becomes belligerent.

Question: What should the inspector do next?

Answer: The inspector should remain courteous and not lose his temper. If the inspector is not able to obtain permission to inspect without further arousing the owner, he should leave.

Since recent decisions of the U.S. Supreme Court have dictated the inclusion of requirements to obtain a search warrant in cases where entry to the inspector is denied, the inspector should obtain a warrant. He will then return at a later time with someone to serve the warrant.

H Case 8

During an inspection in July, the housing inspector finds a house that has been converted into two apartments. While checking the basement, he sees that the furnace appears in an unsafe condition. Further checking reveals that there is no provision for heat in the second apartment.

Question: What action should the inspector take since it is July and heat is not now needed. Besides, how does he know that the owner will not install heat before winter?

Answer: The inspector should cite the owner for a violation of the housing code anyway. In his notice of violations, because it is July, he can give the owner sufficient time to comply. He would also send a copy of the letter to the heating inspector for follow up.

I Case 9

During an inspection, the housing inspector is greeted at the door by a 10-year-old boy who is alone. The boy says it is all right to make the inspection.

Question: Should he? Why?

Answer: No. Permission to enter must be obtained from a responsible adult. Suppose that instead of the 10-year-old boy, he had found a 16-year-old girl.

Question: How would these change things? Why?

Answer: It would not change things, since the 16-year-old girl is not considered a responsible adult. For the protection of the inspector, some housing departments would not permit him to enter alone when the house is occupied by only a female, especially one under age.

J Case 10

During his inspections the housing inspector finds a house that has no bathroom but does have an outside pit privy.

Question: What action should be taken?

Answer: The inspector should issue a violation for lack of indoor toilet facilities and follow through the regular steps established. by his housing department. A copy of the violation should also be sent to the health department for any actions that they may wish to take for elimination of the privy.

K Case 11

A number of violations are found in a residence, but the family is occupying the unit under a land purchase contract agreement with the landlord. The owner holds title until enough rent is paid to equal the sale price. The repairs needed are more than the family can afford and are such that the building should be declared unfit for occupancy. The family now has $2,000 worth of equity in the property.

Questions: What actions should the inspector take? Who is responsible for repairs? Who will lose money?

Answer: The inspector would cite the owner of record for a housing violation, since the owner of record is responsible for repairs. If the owner will not bring the building into compliance with the code, the building should be posted as unfit for habitation and the family removed.

The family buying will probably lose in this situation. Before contracting to buy, they should have obtained a certificate of inspection from the housing department showing any violations existing at the time of purchase.

L   Case 12

The property at 112 East Street is owned by an out-of-state individual. The housing inspector found the property unfit for habitation and has had the family renting the property removed. The house is now vacant and the out-of-town owners will not make the repairs since the cost of the necessary

repairs would be too great in relation to the value of the property. The property is in an area that will probably be included in a future urban renewal project within the next few years.

Complaints have been made to the housing department by the neighbors that the house has its windows broken out and its doors broken open. Children play inside during the day and have almost set the building on fire several times. Moreover, vagrants occasionally sleep inside at night.

Question: What action would you take if you were the housing inspector?

Answer: After following standard department procedures, the housing inspector should recommend, that the house be demolished and this cost assessed as a lien against the property. If allowed to remain, the house will be a detriment to surrounding properties and also to the neighborhood.

M   Case 13

During a routine inspection, you find a house with very poor premises sanitation and evidence of roaches, flies, and rats. The property meets minimum housing standards otherwise.

Question: What action can you take?

Answer: The action depends on local regulations and procedures. In many communities the housing program is organizationally located within the health department. In that case, the housing inspector would probably follow through in requiring elimination of the infestation. If the housing inspection program were located within a department other than the health department, the housing inspector may refer the case to the health department for action.

N Case 14

While making a systematic code inspection, the housing inspector encounters a lady who questions the inspector regarding his findings on the house next door, which she is sure is much worse than hers.

Question: How should the inspector deal with the lady?

Answer: The inspector must be very courteous and tactful in his conversation and inform her that he is not permitted to discuss his survey findings for other properties.

BUILDING ASPECTS OF A HOUSING INSPECTION

CONTENTS

		Page
I.	Background Factors	1
II.	Housing Construction Terminology	1
III.	Structure	4
IV.	Discussion of Inspection Techniques	15
V.	Noise as an Environmental Stress	17

BUILDING ASPECTS OF A HOUSING INSPECTION

The principle function of a house is to furnish protection from the elements. In its current stage, however, our civilization requires that a home provide not only shelter but also privacy, safety, and reasonable protection of our physical and mental health. A living facility that fails to offer these essentials through adequately designed and properly maintained interiors and exteriors cannot be termed "healthful housing."

I. Background Factors

In this chapter, a building will be considered in terms of its major components: heating, plumbing, and electrical systems. Each of these items will be examined in detail in future chapters. Attention will be given in this chapter to the portions of a building not visible upon completion of the ceiling, roof, and interior and exterior walls in order to give the reader an understanding of generally accepted construction practices. Emphasis, however, will be placed upon the visible interior and exterior parts of a completed dwelling that have a bearing on the soundness, state of repair, and safety of the dwelling both during intended use and in the event of a fire. These are some of the elements that the housing inspector must examine when making a thorough housing inspection.

II. Housing Construction Terminology

(Key to Component Parts Numbered in Figure 1)

A Fireplace

1 **Chimney** - A vertical masonry shaft of reinforced concrete or other approved noncombustible, heat resisting material enclosing one or more flues. It removes the products of combustion from solid, liquid, or gaseous fuel.

2 **Flue Liner** - The flue is the hole in the chimney. The liner, usually of terra cotta, protects the brick from harmful smoke gases.

3 **Chimney Cap** - This top is generally of concrete. It protects the brick from weather.

4 **Chimney Flashing** - Sheet-metal flashing provides a tight joint between chimney and roof.

5 **Firebrick** - An ordinary brick cannot withstand the heat of direct fire, and so special firebrick is used to line the fireplace.

6 **Ash Dump** - A trap door to let the ashes drop to a pit below, from where they may be easily removed.

7 **Cleanout Door** - The door to the ash pit or the bottom of a chimney through which the chimney can be cleaned.

8 **Chimney Breast** - The inside face or front of a fireplace chimney.

9 **Hearth** - The floor of a fireplace that extends into the room for safety purposes.

B Roof

10 **Ridge** - The top intersection of two opposite adjoining roof surfaces.

11 **Ridge Board** - The board that follows along under the ridge.

12 **Roof Rafters** - The structural members that support the roof.

13 **Collar Beam** - Really not a beam at all. A tie that keeps the roof from spreading. Connects similar rafters on opposite side of roof.

14 **Roof Insulation** - An insulating material (usually rock wool or fiberglas) in a blanket form placed between the roof rafters for the purpose of keeping a house warm in the winter, cool in the summer.

15 **Roof Sheathing** - The boards that provide the base for the finished roof.

Figure 1. Housing Construction Terminology

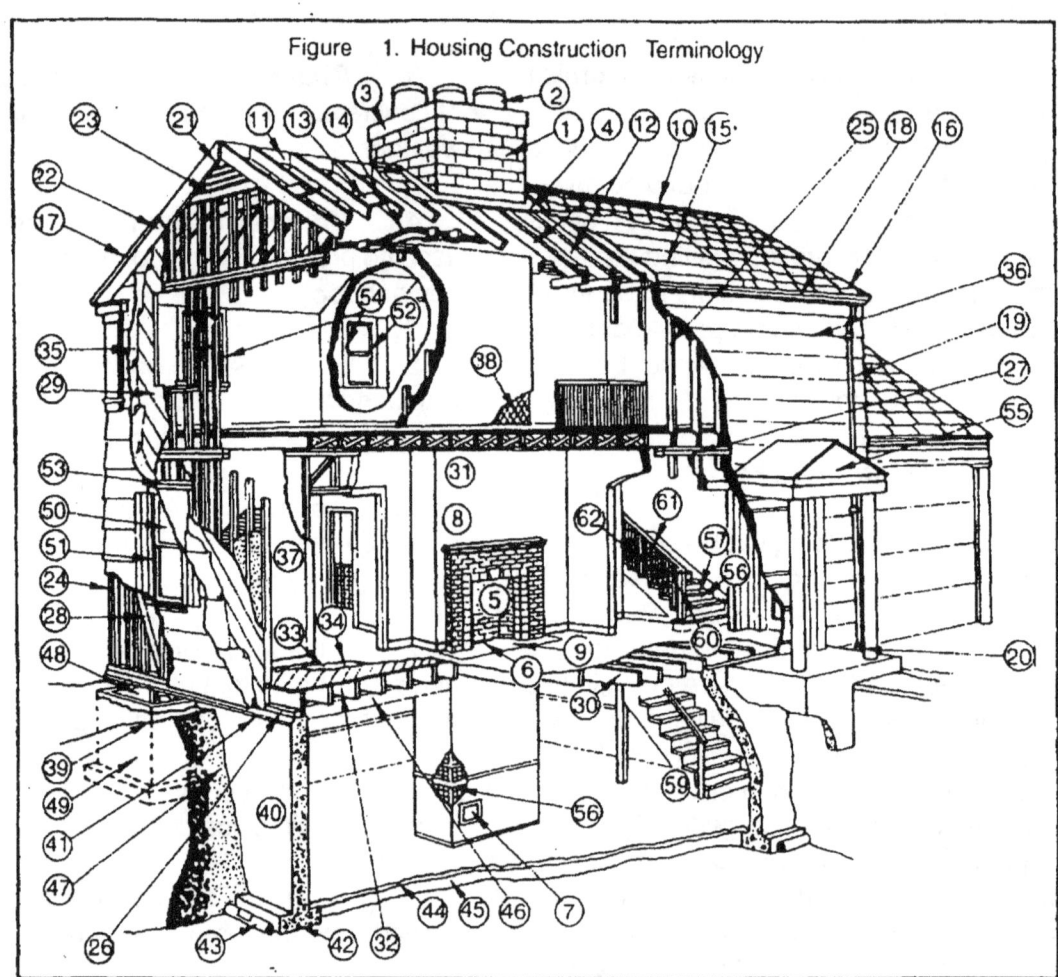

16 **Roofing** - The wood, asphalt, or asbestos shingles - or tile, slate or metal - that form the outer protection against the weather.

17 **Cornice** - A decorative element made up of molded members usually placed at or near the top of an exterior or interior wall.

18 **Gutter** - The trough that gathers rainwater from a roof.

19 **Downspouts** - The pipe that leads the water down from the gutter.

20 **Storm Sewer Tile** - The underground pipe that receives the water from the downspouts and carries it to the sewer.

21 **Gable** - The triangular end of a building with a sloping roof.

22 **Barage Board** - The fascia or board at the gable just under the edge of the roof.

23 **Louvers** - A series of slanted slots arranged to keep out rain, yet allow ventilation.

C   Walls and Floors

24 **Corner Post** - The vertical member at the corner of the frame, made up to receive inner and outer covering materials.

25 **Studs** - The vertical wood members of the house, usually 2 X 4's generally spaced every 16 inches.

26 **Sill** - The board that is laid first on the foundation, and on which the frame rests.

27 **Plate** - The board laid across the top ends of the studs to hold them even and rigid.

132

28 **Corner Bracing** - Diagonal strips to keep the frame square and plumb.

29 **Sheathing** - The first layer of outer wall covering nailed to the studs.

30 **Joist** - The structural members or beams that hold up the floor or ceiling, usually 2 X 10's or 2 X 12's spaced 16 inches apart.

31 **Bridging** - Cross bridging or solid. Members at the middle or third points of joist spans to brace one to the next and to prevent their twisting.

32 **Subflooring** - The rough boards that are laid over the joist. Usually laid diagonally.

33 **Flooring Paper** - A felt paper laid on the rough floor to stop air infiltration and, to some extent, noise.

34 **Finish Flooring** - Usually hardwood, of tongued and grooved strips.

35 **Building Paper** - Paper placed outside the sheathing, not as a vapor barrier, but to prevent water and air from leaking in. Building paper is also used as a tarred felt under shingles or siding to keep out moisture or wind.

36 **Beveled Siding** - Sometimes called clapboards, with a thick butt and a thin upper edge lapped to shed water.

37 **Wall Insulation** - A blanket of wool or reflective foil placed inside the walls.

38 **Metal Lath** - A mesh made from sheet metal onto which plaster is applied.

D   Foundation and Basement

39 **Finished Grade Line** - The top of the ground at the foundation.

40 **Foundation Wall** - The wall of poured concrete (shown) or concrete blocks that rests on the footing and supports the remainder of the house.

41 **Termite Shield** - A metal baffle to prevent termites from entering the frame.

42 **Footing** - The concrete pad that carries the entire weight of the house upon the earth.

43 **Footing Drain Tile** - A pipe with cracks at the joints to allow underground water to drain in and away before it gets into the basement.

44 **Basement Floor Slab** - The 4- or 5-inch layer of concrete that forms the basement floor.

45 **Gravel Fill** - Placed under the slab to allow drainage and to guard against a damp floor.

46 **Girder** - A main beam upon which floor joists rest. Usually of steel, but also of wood.

47 **Backfill** - Earth, once dug out, that has been replaced and tamped down around the foundation.

48 **Areaway** - An open space to allow light and air to a window. Also called a light well.

49 **Area Wall** - The wall, of metal or concrete, that forms the open area.

E   Windows and Doors

50 **Window** - An opening in a building for admitting light and air. It usually has a pane or panes of glass and is set in a frame or sash that is generally movable for opening and shutting.

51 **Window Frame** - The lining of the window opening.

52   Window Sash - The inner frame, usually movable, that holds the glass.

53   Lintel - The structural beam over a window or door opening.

54   Window Casing - The decorative strips surrounding a window opening on the inside.

F   Stairs and Entry

55   Entrance Canopy - A roof extending over the entrance door.

56   Furring - Falsework or framework necessary to bring the outer surface to where we want it.

57   Stair Tread - The horizontal strip where we put our foot when we climb up or down the stairs.

58   Stair Riser - The vertical board connecting one tread to the next.

59   Stair Stringer - The sloping board that supports the ends of the steps.

60   Newel - The post that terminates the railing.

61   Stair Rail - The bar used for a handhold when we use the stairs.

62   Balusters - Vertical rods or spindles supporting a rail.

III. Structure

A   Foundation
The word **foundation** is used to mean:
1. Construction below grade such as footings, cellar or basement walls.
2. The composition of the earth on which the building rests.
3. Special construction such as pilings and piers used to support the building.

The foundation bed may be composed of solid rock, sand, gravel, or unconsolidated sand or clay. Rock, sand, or gravel are the most reliable foundation materials. Unconsolidated sand and clay, though found in many sections of the country, are not as desirable, because they are subject to sliding and settling.

The footing (see Figure 2) distributes the weight of the building over a sufficient area of ground so as to ensure that the foundation walls will stand properly. Footings are usually constructed of a masonry-type material such as concrete; however, in the past wood and stone have been used. Some older houses have been constructed without footings.

Although it is usually difficult to determine the condition of a footing without excavating the foundation, a footing in a state of disrepair or lack of a footing will usually be indicated either by large

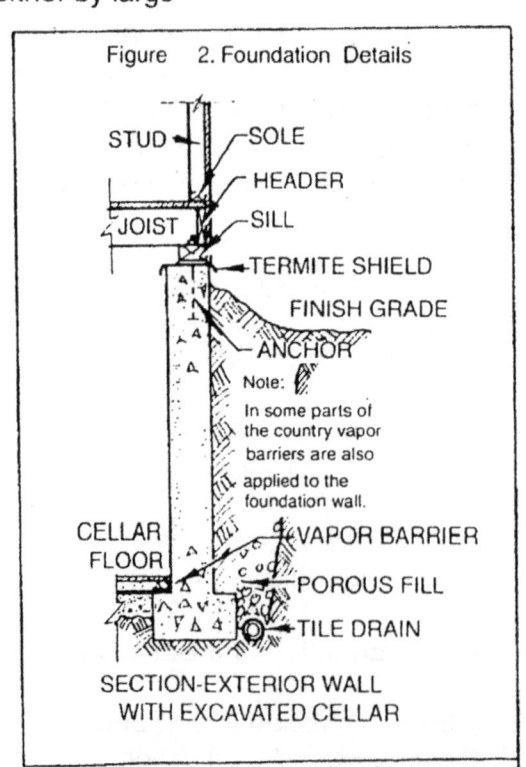

Figure 2. Foundation Details
SECTION-EXTERIOR WALL WITH EXCAVATED CELLAR

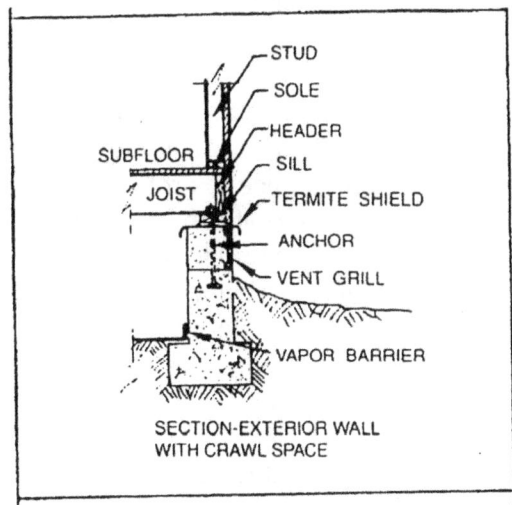

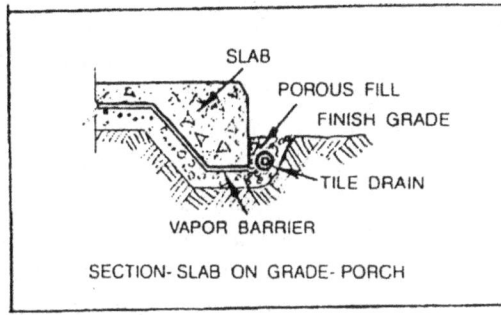

cracks or by settlement in the foundation walls (see Figure 3).

Foundation wall cracks are usually diagonal, starting from the top, the bottom; or the end of the wall. Cracks that do not extend to at least one edge of the wall may not be caused by foundation problems. Such wall cracks may be due to other structural problems and should also be reported.

The foundation walls support the weight of the structure and transfer this weight to the footings. The foundation walls may be made of stone, brick, concrete, or concrete blocks and should be moisture proofed with either a membrane of water-proof material or a coating of portland cement mortar. The membrane may consist of plastic sheeting or a sandwich of standard roofing felt joined and covered with tar or asphalt. The purpose of waterproofing the foundation walls is to prevent water from penetrating the wall material and leaving the basement or cellar walls damp.

Holes in the foundation walls are a common finding in many old houses. These holes may be caused by missing bricks or blocks. Holes and cracks in a foundation wall are undesirable because they make a convenient entry for rats and other rodents and also indicate the possibility of further structural deterioration. These holes should not be confused with adequately installed vents in the foundation wall that permit ventilation and prevent moisture entrapment.

The basement or cellar floor should be made of concrete placed on at least 6 inches of gravel. The purpose of a concrete floor is to protect the basement or cellar from invasion by rodents or from flooding. The gravel distributes ground water movements under the concrete floor, reducing the possibility of the water's penetrating the floor. A waterproof membrane, such as plastic sheeting, should be laid before the concrete is placed for additional protection against flooding.

The basement or cellar floor should be gradually but uniformly sloped towards a drain or a series of drains from all directions. These drains permit the basement or cellar floor to be drained if it becomes flooded.

Evidence of ineffective waterproofing or moisture proofing will be indicated by water or moisture marks on the floor and walls.

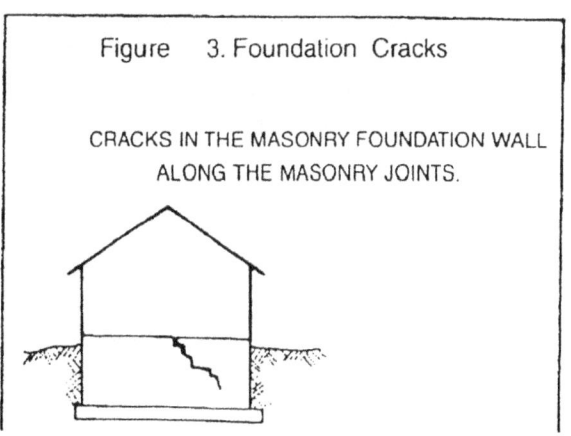

Figure 3. Foundation Cracks

CRACKS IN THE MASONRY FOUNDATION WALL ALONG THE MASONRY JOINTS.

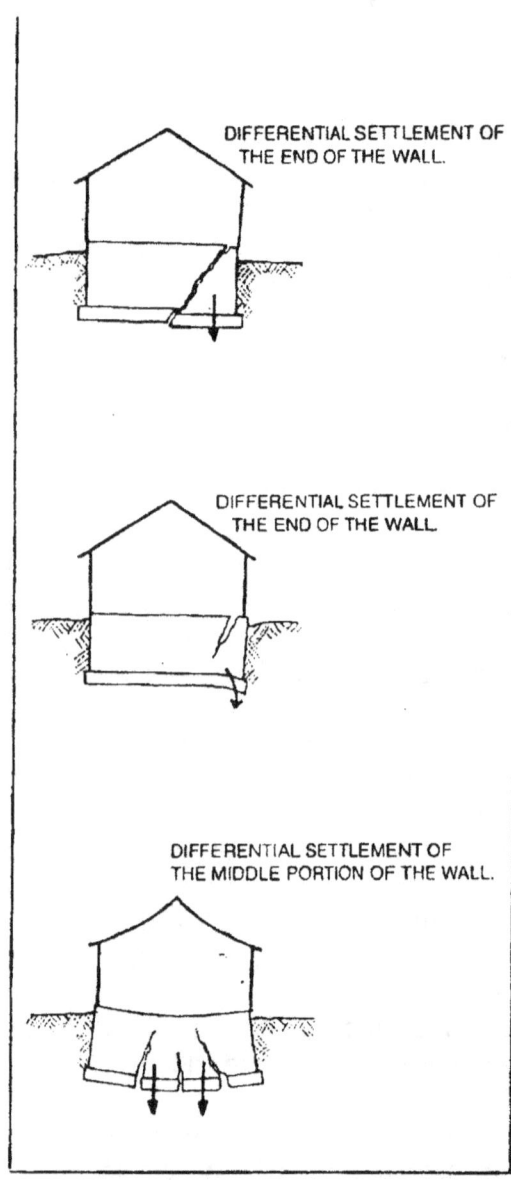

Cellar doors, hatchways, and basement windows should be weathertight and rodent proof. A hatchway can be inspected by standing at the lower portion with the doors closed; if daylight can be seen, the door probably needs repair.

B **Framing**

Many different types of house-framing systems are found in various sections of the country; however, the majority of the members in each framing system are the same. They include:

1. **Foundation Sills:** (see Figure 4 and 5). The purpose of the sill is to provide support or a bearing surface for the outside walls of the building. The sill is the first part of the frame to be placed and rests directly on the foundation wall. It is bolted to the foundation wall by sill anchors. It is good practice to protect the sill against termites by extending the foundation wall to at least 18 inches above the ground and using a non-corroding metal shield continuously around the outside top of the foundation wall.

2. **Flooring Systems:** (see Figure 5). The flooring system is composed of a combination of girders, joists, sub-flooring, and finished flooring that may be made up of concrete, steel, or wood. Joists are laid perpendicular to the girders, at about 16 inches on centers, and are the members to which the sub-flooring is attached. When the subfloor is wood, it may be nailed at either right angles or diagonally to the joists.

   As shown in Figure 5, a girder is a member that in certain framing systems supports the joists and is usually a larger section than the joists it supports. Girders are found in framing systems where there are no interior bearing walls or where the span between bearing walls is greater than the joists are capable of spanning. The most common application of a girder is to support the first floor in residences. Often a board known as a ledger is applied to the side of a wood girder or beam to form a ledge for the joists to rest upon. The girder, in turn, is supported by wood posts or steel "lally columns" which extend from the cellar or basement floor to the girder.

3. **Studs:** (see Figure 4 and 5). Wall studs are almost always 2 by 4

inches; studs 2 by 6 inches are occasionally used to provide a wall thick enough to permit the passage of waste pipes. There are two types of walls or partitions: bearing and nonbearing. A bearing wall is constructed at right angles to and supports the joists. A nonbearing wall or partition acts as a screen or enclosure; hence, the headers in it are often parallel to the joists of the floor above.

In general, studs like joists are spaced 16 inches on center. In light construction such as garages and summer cottages where plaster is omitted, or some other material is used for a wall finish, wider spacing on studs is common.

Openings for windows or doors must be framed in studs. This framing consists of horizontal members called "headers," and vertical members called "trimmers" (see Figure 1).

Since the vertical spaces between studs can act as flues to transmit flames in the event of a fire, "fire stops" are important in preventing or retarding fire from spreading through a building by way of air passages in walls, floors, and partitions. Fire stops are wood obstructions placed between studs or floor joists to prevent fire from spreading in these natural fluespaces.

4   **Interior Wall Finish:** Many types of materials are used for covering interior walls and ceilings, but the principal types are plaster and dry-wall construction. Plaster is a mixture, usually lime, sand, and water, applied in two or three coats to lath to form a hard-wall surface. Dry-wall finish is a material that requires little, if any, water for application. More specifically, dry-wall finish may be gypsum board, plywood, fiberboard, or wood in various sizes and forms.

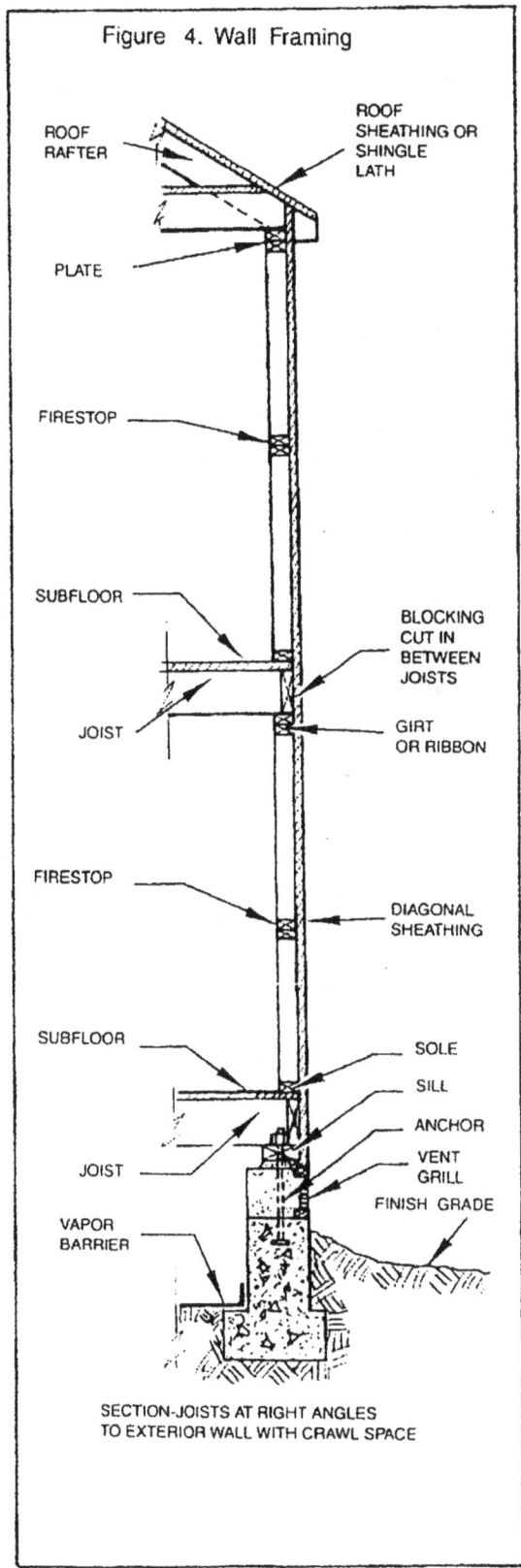

Figure 4. Wall Framing
SECTION-JOISTS AT RIGHT ANGLES TO EXTERIOR WALL WITH CRAWL SPACE

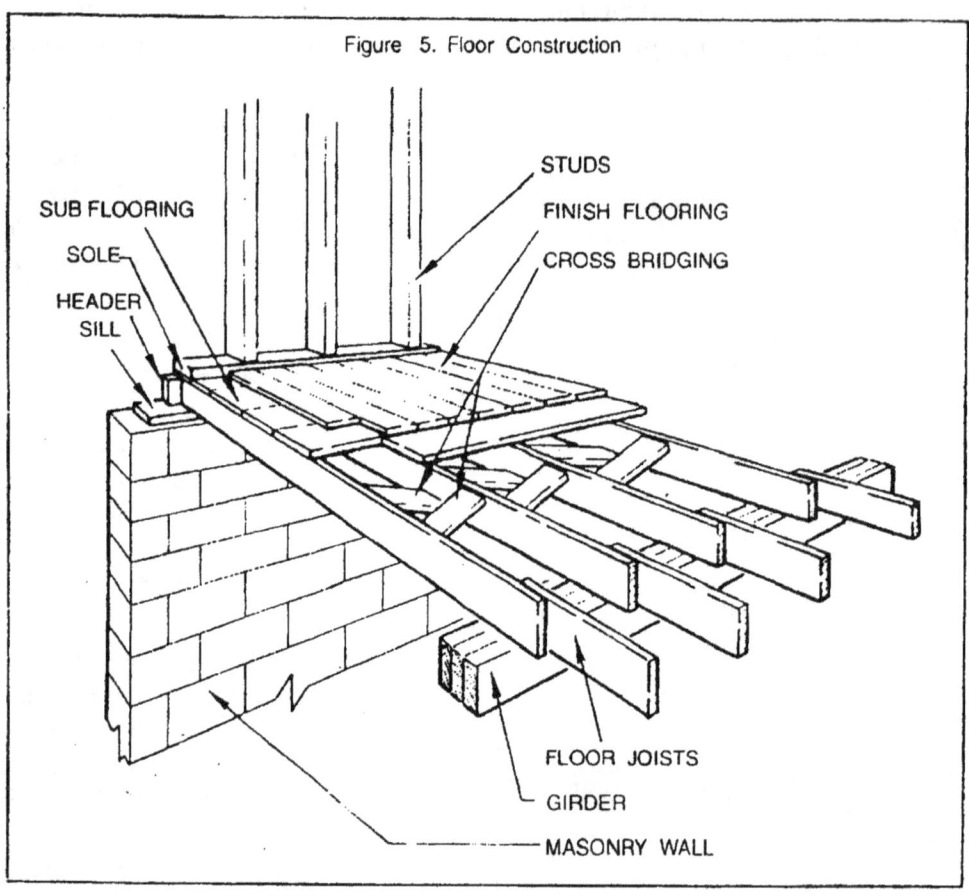

Figure 5. Floor Construction

Gypsum board is a sheet material composed of a gypsum filler faced with paper. Sheets are usually 4 feet wide and can be obtained in lengths up to 12 feet. In dry-wall construction, gypsum boards are fastened to the studs either vertically or horizontally and then painted. The edges along the length of the sheet are recessed to receive joint cement and tape.

A plaster finish requires a base upon which plaster can be spread. Wood lath at one time was the plaster base most commonly used, but today gypsum-board lath is more popular. It has paper faces with a gypsum filler. Such lath is 16 by 48 inches and 1/2 or 3/8 inches thick.

It is applied horizontally across the studs. Gypsum lath may be perforated to improve the bond and thus lengthen the time the plaster can remain intact when exposed to fire. The building codes in some cities require that gypsum lath be perforated. Expanded-metal lath may also be used as a plaster base. Expanded-metal lath consists of sheet metal slit and expanded to form openings to hold the plaster. Metal lath is usually 27 by 96 inches and is fastened to the studs.

Plaster is applied over the base to a minimum thickness of 1/2 inch. Because some drying may take place in wood-framing members after the house is completed, some shrinkage can be expected, which, in turn, may cause plaster cracks to develop around openings and in corners. Strips of lath imbedded in the plaster at these locations prevent cracks.

On the inside face of studs that form an exterior wall, vapor barriers are used to prevent condensation on the wall. The vapor barrier is an asphalted paper or metal foil through which moisture-laden air cannot travel.

5 **Stairways:** (see Figure 6). The general purpose of the standards for stairway dimensions is to ensure that there is adequate headroom, width, and uniformity in riser and tread size of every step to accommodate the expected traffic on each stairway safely.

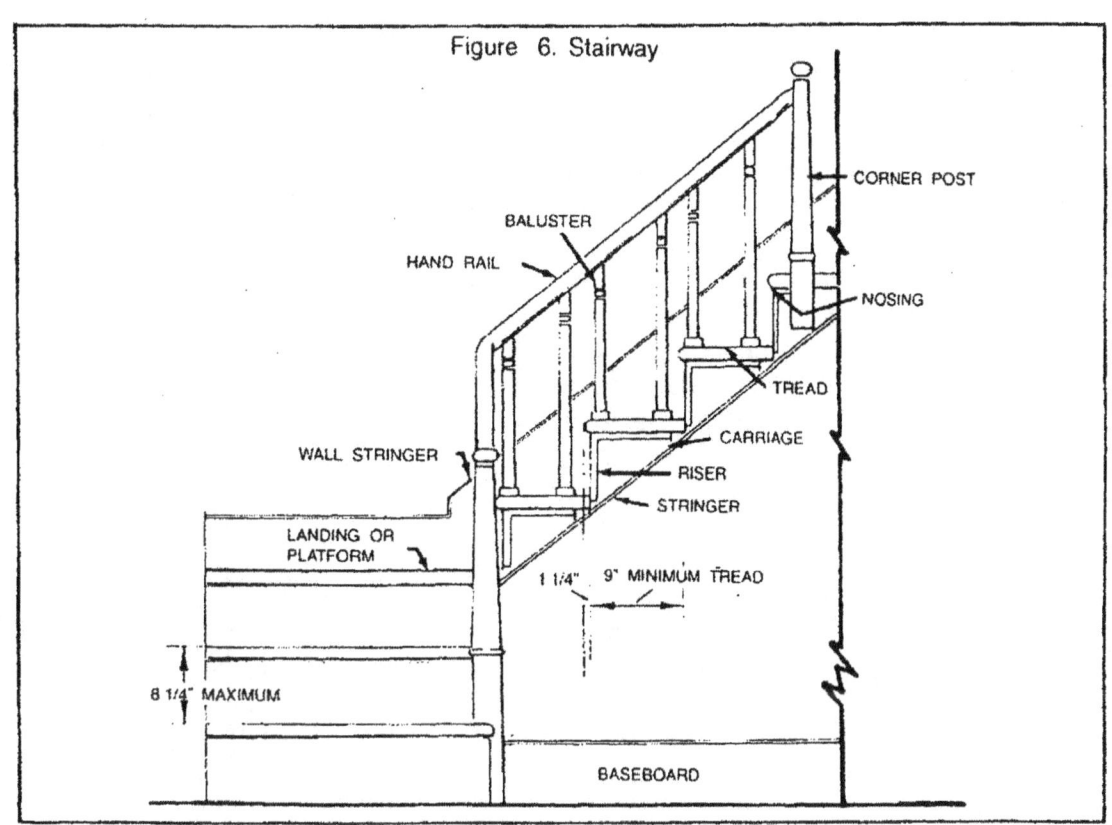

Figure 6. Stairway

Interior stairways should be not less than 44 inches in width. The width of a stairway may be reduced to 36 inches in one- and two-family dwellings. Stairs with closed risers should have maximum risers of 8 1/4 inches and a minimum tread of 9 inches plus 1 1/4-inch nosing. Basement stairs are often constructed with open risers. These stairs should have maximum risers of 8 1/4 inches and minimum treads of 9 inches plus 1/2-inch nosing. The headroom in all parts of the stair enclosure should be no less than 80 inches.

Exterior stairway dimensions should be the same as those called for in interior stairways, except that the headroom requirement does not apply.

6 **Windows:** The four general classifications of windows for residences are:

a Double-hung sash window that moves up or down, balanced by weights hung on chains or ropes, or springs on each side.

b Casement window sash is hinged at the side and can be hung so that it will swing outward or inward.

c Awning window - usually has two or more glass panes that are hinged at the top and swing about a horizontal axis.

d Sliding window - usually has two or more glass panes that slide past one another on a horizontal track.

The principal parts of a double-hung window (see Figure 4-7) are the lights, the top rail-framing members, bars or muntins that separate the lights, stiles - side-framing members, bottom rail, sash weights, and sash cords or chains. (All rails are horizontal, all stiles vertical.) The casement window's principal parts include: top and bottom rails, muntins, butt hinges, and jamb. All types of windows should open freely and close securely.

The exterior sill is the bottom projection of a window. The drip cap is a separate piece of wood projecting over the top of the window and is a component of the window casing.

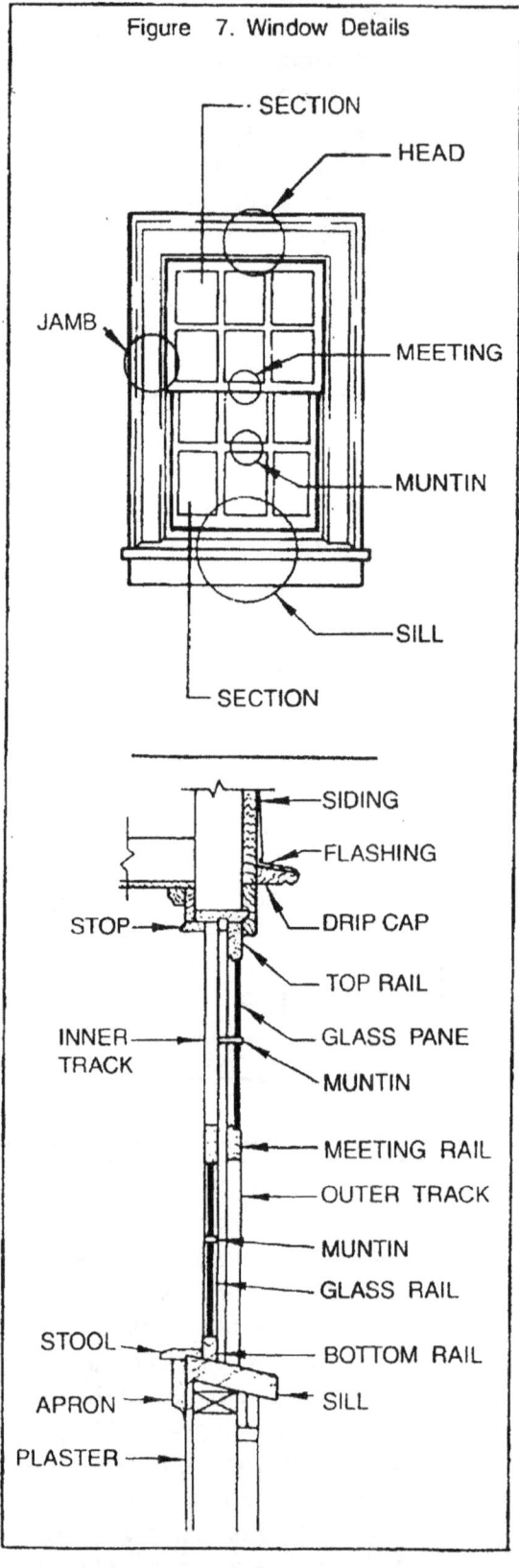

Figure 7. Window Details

7 **Doors:** There are many styles of doors both for exterior and interior use. Interior doors should offer a rea-

sonable degree of privacy. Exterior doors must, in addition to offering privacy, protect the interior of the structure from the elements. The various parts of a door have the same definitions as the corresponding parts of a window.

The most common types of doors are:

a **Batten door**: This consists of boards nailed together in various ways. The simplest is two layers nailed to each other at right angles, usually with each layer at 45 degrees to the vertical.

Another type of batten door consists of vertical boards nailed at right angles to several (two to four) cross strips called ledgers, with diagonal bracing members nailed between ledgers. If vertical members corresponding to ledgers are added at the sides, the verticals are called frames.

Batten doors are often found in cellars and other places where appearance is not a factor and economy is desired.

b **Flush doors**: Solid flush doors are perfectly flat, usually on both sides, although occasionally they are made flush on one side and paneled on the other. Flush doors sometimes are solid planking, but they are commonly veneered and possess a core of small pieces of white pine or other wood. These pieces are glued together with staggered end joints. Along the sides, top, and bottom are glued 3/4-inch edge strips of the same wood, used to create a smooth surface that can be cut or planed. The front and back faces are then covered with a 1/8-to 1/4-inch layer of veneer.

Solid flush doors may be used on both the interior and exterior.

c **Hollow-core doors**: These, like solid flush doors, are perfectly flat, but unlike solid doors, the core consists mainly of a grid of crossed wooden slats or some other type of grid construction. Faces are 3-ply plywood instead of one or two plies of veneer, and the surface veneer may be any species of wood, usually hardwood. The edges of the core are solid wood and are made wide enough at the appropriate places to accommodate locks and butts. Doors of this kind are considerably lighter than solid flush doors.

Hollow-core doors are usually used as interior doors.

d **Paneled doors**: Most doors are paneled, with most panels consisting of solid wood or plywood, either "raised" or "flat," although exterior doors frequently have one or more panels of glass, in which case they are called "lights." One or more panels may be employed although the number seldom exceeds eight. Paneled doors may be used both on the interior or exterior.

In addition to the various types of wood doors, metal is often used as a veneer or for the frame.

In general, the horizontal members are called rails and the vertical members are called stiles. Every door has a top and bottom rail, and some may have intermediate rails. There are always at least two stiles, one on each side of the door. The frame of a doorway is the portion to which the door is hinged. It consists of two side jambs and a head jamb, with an integral or attached stop against which the door closes.

Exterior door frames are ordinarily of softwood plank, with side rabbitted to receive the door in the same way as casement windows. At the foot is a sill, made of hardwood to withstand the wear of traffic, and sloped down and out to shed water.

Interior door frames are similar to exterior, except that they are often set directly on the hardwood flooring without a sill.

Building codes throughout the country call for doors in various locations within the structure to be fire resistant. These doors are often covered with metal or some other fire-resistant materials, and some are completely constructed of metal. Fire-resistant doors are usually located between a garage and a house, stairwells and hallways, all boiler rooms. The fire resistance rating required for various doors differs with local fire codes

C **Roof Framing** (see Figures 1, 4, 8, and 9)

Rafters serve the same purpose for the roof as joists do for floors, i.e., providing support for sheathing and roofing material. Rafters are usually spaced 20 inches on center.

1 **Collar Beam:** Collar beams are ties between rafters on opposite sides of the roof. If the attic is to be used for rooms, the collar beam may double as the ceiling joist.

2 **Purlin:** A purlin is the horizontal member that forms the support for the rafters at the intersection of the two slopes of a gambrel roof.

3 **Ridge Board:** A ridge board is a horizontal member against which the rafters rest at their upper ends; it forms a lateral tie to make them secure.

4 **Hip:** Like a ridge except that it slopes. The intersection of two adjacent, rather than two opposite, roof planes.

5 **Roof Boards:** The manner in which roof boards are applied depends upon the type of roofing material. Roof boards may vary from tongue-and-groove lumber to plywood panels.

6 **Dormer:** The term dormer window is applied to all windows in the roof of a building, whatever their size and shape.

D **Exterior Walls and Trim** (see Figure 4 and 9)

Exterior walls are enclosure walls whose purpose is to make the building weathertight. In most one- to three-story buildings they also serve as bearing walls. These walls may be made of many different materials.

Frequently used framed exterior walls appear to be of brick construction. In this situation, the brick is only one course thick and is called a brick veneer. It supports nothing but itself and is kept from toppling by ties connected to the frame wall.

In frame construction the base material of the exterior walls is called "sheathing." The sheathing material may be square-edge, shiplap, or tongue-and-groove boards.

In recent construction there has been a strong trend toward the use of plywood or composition panels.

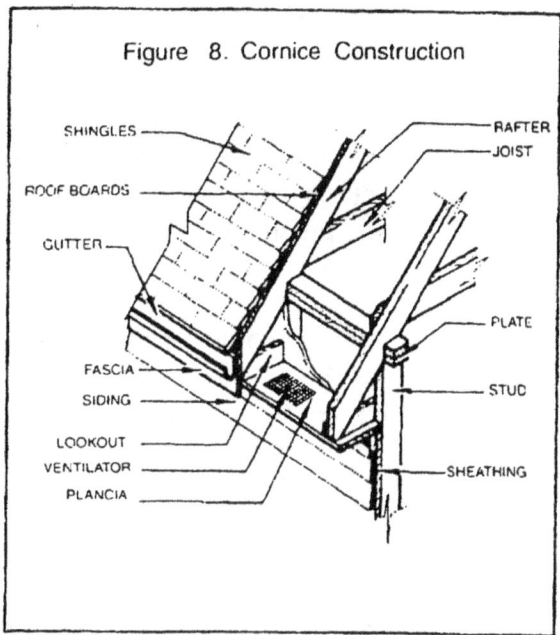

Figure 8. Cornice Construction

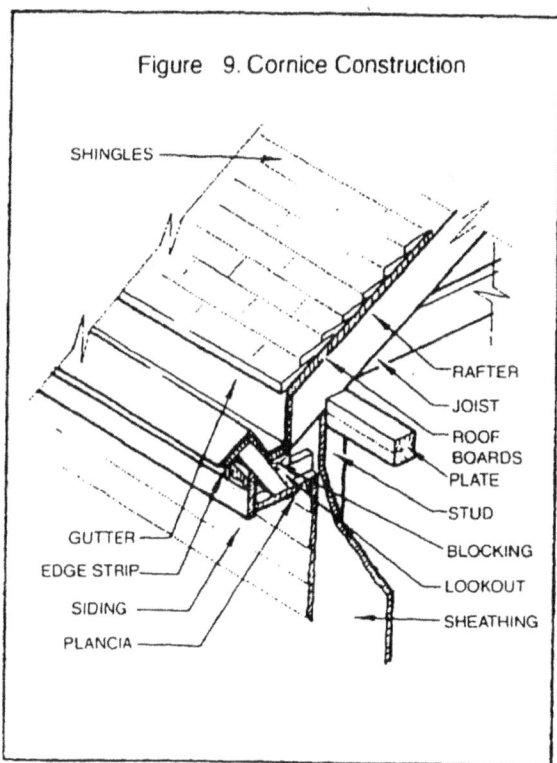

Figure 9. Cornice Construction

Sheathing, in addition to serving as a base course for the finished siding material, stiffens the frame to resist sway caused by wind. It is for this reason that sheathing has been applied diagonally on frame buildings.

The finished siding may be clapboard, shingles, aluminum, brick asphalt, wood, and so forth, or a combination thereof. Good aluminum siding has a backer board that serves as added insulation and affords rigidity to the siding. Projecting cornices are a decorative trim found at the top of the building's roofline. A parapet wall is that part of the masonry wall that extends up and beyond the roofline and is capped with a noncombustible material. It helps prevent spread of fire, provides a rest for fire department ladders, and helps prevent people on the roof from falling off.

Many types of siding, shingles, and other exterior coverings are applied over the sheathing. Wood siding, cedar, and other wood shingles or shakes, clapboard, common siding (called bevel siding), composition siding, asbestos, cement shingles, asbestos-cement siding, and the aforementioned aluminum siding are commonly used for exterior coverings. Clapboards and common siding differ only in the length of the pieces. Clapboards are 4 feet long while panel siding comes in lengths from 6 to 16 feet. Composition siding is made of felt and asphalt, which are often shaped to look like brick. Asbestos and cement shingles are rigid and produce a covering that is fire resistant. Cedar wood shingles are also manufactured with a backer board that gives insulation and fire-resistant qualities. Asbestos cement siding made of asbestos fiber and portland cement has good fire-resistant qualities and is a rigid covering.

E Roof Coverings (Flexible Material Class)

  1 **Asphalt Shingle:** The principal damage to asphalt shingle roofs is caused by the action of strong winds on shingles nailed too high. Usually the shingles affected by winds are those in the four or five courses nearest the ridge and in the area

extending about 5 feet down from the edge or rake of the roof.

2. **Asphalt Built-up Roofs:** These may be un-surfaced, the coating of bitumen being exposed directly to the weather, or they may be surfaced having slag or gravel imbedded in the bituminous coating. The use of surfacing material is desirable as a protection against wind damage and the elements. This type of roof should have enough pitch to drain water readily.

3. **Coal Tar Pitch Built-up Roofs:** This type roof must be surfaced with slag or gravel. Coal tar pitch built-up roof should always be used on deck pitched less than 1/2 inch per foot; that is, where waler may collect and stand. This type roof should be inspected on completion, 6 months later, and then at least once a year, preferably in the fall. When the top coating of bitumen shows damage or has become badly weathered, it should be renewed (rigid material class).

4. **Slate Roofs:** The most common problem with slate roofs is the replacement of broken slates. Roofs of this type normally render long service with little or no repair.

5. **Tile Roofs:** Replacement of broken shingle tiles is the main maintenance problem. This is one of the most expensive roofing materials. It requires very little maintenance and gives long service.

6. **Copper Roofs:** Usually are of 16-ounce copper sheeting and applied to permanent structures. When properly installed, they require practically no maintenance or repair. Proper installation allows for expansion and contraction with changes in temperature.

7. **Galvanized Iron Roofs:** Maintenance is done principally by removing rust and keeping roof well painted. Leaks can be corrected by re-nailing, caulking, or replacing all or part of the sheet or sheets in disrepair.

8. **Wood Shingle Roofs:** The most important factors of this type roof are its pitch and exposure, the character of wood, kind of nails used, and preservative treatment given shingles. Creosote and coal tar preservative are satisfactory for both treated and untreated shingles.

9. **Flashing:** Valleys in roofs that are formed by the junction of two downward slopes may be finished, open, or closed. In a closed valley the slates, tiles, or shingles of one side meet those of the other, and the flashing below them may be comparatively narrow. In an open valley, the flashing, which may be made of zinc, copper, or aluminum, is laid in a continuous strip, extending 12 to 18 inches on each side of the valley, while the tiles or slates do not come within 4 to 6 inches of it.

The ridges built up on a sloping roof where it runs down against a vertical projection, like a chimney or a skylight, should be weather-proofed with flashing.

Metal flashings are generally used with slate, tile, metal, and wood shingles. Failure of roof flashing is usually due to exposed nails that have come loose. The loose nails allow the flashing to lift with leakage resulting.

10. **Gutters and Leaders:** Gutters and leaders should be of noncombustible materials. They should be securely fastened to the structure and spill into a storm sewer if the neighborhood is so provided. When there is no storm sewer, a concrete or stone block placed on the ground beneath the leader prevents water from eroding the lawn. This store

block is called a splash block. Gutters will not become plugged if protected against clogging of leaves and twigs. Gutters should be checked every spring and fall and then cleaned out when necessary.

IV. Discussion of Inspection Techniques

A serious building defect may often be observed during a housing inspector's routine examination. In many cases it is beyond the scope of the housing inspector's background to analyze the underlying causes and to recommend a course of action that will facilitate repair in an efficient and economical manner. In situations such as this, it is important that the inspector realize his limitations and refer the matter to the proper expert.

A prime example of a technically complex situation that a housing inspector might observe is a leaning, buckling, or bulging foundation or bearing wall. This problem may be the result of a number of hidden or interacting problems. For example, it may be the result of differential building settlement or failure of a structural beam or girder. It is beyond the scope of the housing inspector's responsibilities to discover the cause of the defect, but it is his responsibility to note the problem and refer it to the proper authority. In this case the proper authority would be a building inspector.

In the aforementioned situation where a bulging foundation wall was discovered, this would obviously constitute a violation of the housing ordinance and should be written up as such by the housing inspector. Since the housing inspector is generally not qualified to determine whether the house should be evacuated because it is in danger of imminent collapse, he should seek the advice of a building inspector.

A question that frequently arises is *which violations should be referred to an expert?* Needless to say, circumstances that obviously fall within the jurisdiction of another department should be referred to the department. The housing inspector should discuss with his supervisor any situation in which he feels inadequate to make a decision. In all cases the inspector should inform his supervisor before referring a problem to another agency or expert.

Another reason for referral to other departments is that when a remedial action is completed the other department will be in a better position to determine whether the job is satisfactory.

This principle of referral should be applied to every portion of the inspection, whether it deals with health, heating, plumbing, gas, or electrical as well as structural defects.

Certain structural items should be recognized as unsafe by the housing inspector. For example, a beam that has sagged or slanted may cause a portion of or an entire floor to sag or slope. Where a sagging or sloping floor is found, examine the ceiling of the room below or the basement for a broken or dropped girder or joist.

Doors and windows that are out of level will not close completely. It may be possible to see outside light through openings around window rails and door jambs. If an inspector detects such a situation, the condition of the supporting girders, girts, posts, and studs should be questioned, since this condition is evidence that some of these members may be termite infested or rotted and may be causing the outside wall to sag. Glass panes in doors and windows should be replaced if found to be broken or missing. Windows should also be checked for proper operation, and items such as broken sash cords or chains noted.

If the roof of the structure appears to be sagging, the inspector should make a special effort to examine the rafters, purlin, collar beams, and ridge boards if these members are exposed as in unfinished attics. The condition of the roof boards may be examined while he is in the attic. If light can be seen between these boards the roof is unsound. Evidence of a leaking roof will be indicated by loose plaster or peeling or stained paint and wall paper. Areas of the roof where flashing occurs, such as around the chimney, are frequent origins of roof leaks. It is essential that the leak be found and repaired, not only to prevent the entrance of moisture into the building, but also to prevent the loosening of the plaster, rotting of timbers, and extension of damage to the remainder of the house.

Gutters and rain leaders should be placed around the entire building to insure proper drainage of water. This will lessen the possibility of seepage of water through siding and window frames, and entrance of water into the cellar or basement. Lack of or leaking gutters may result in rotting of the siding or erosion of the exposed portion of the cellar or basement walls. This situation commonly exists where the mortar between bricks or concrete blocks in foundation walls is found to be heavily eroded. Gutters should be free from dirt and leaves.

The exterior siding should be in sound, weathertight condition. Peeled or worn paint on wood siding will expose the bare wood to the elements and result in splitting and warping of siding. This condition will eventually lead to the entrance of rain water with resultant rotting of the sheathing and studs as well as inside dampness and falling plaster. Sound and painted siding will prevent major repairs and expenses in the future. This condition will often be particularly prevalent on the north face of the structure.

Roof and chimneys should be inspected for tilting, missing bricks, deterioration of flashing, and pointing of chimney bricks. In addition, roof covering should be checked for broken spots and missing shingles or tiles. Roof doors should be metal clad, self-closing, tight fitting, and unlockable. The roof should also be examined for weather-tightness and broken TV antennas.

Porches should be carefully examined for weakened treads, missing or cracked boards, holes, and holes covered with tin plates, railing rigidity, missing posts, handrail rigidity, condition of the columns that support the porch roof, and the condition of the porch roof itself. The open section beneath the porch should be inspected for broken lattice-work. Check under the porch for accumulation of dirt and debris that can offer a harborage for vermin and rodents.

Loose plaster and missing or peeling wallpaper or paint should be noted. Bugs and cockroaches eat the paste from the wallpaper while leaving behind loose paper.

The basic parts of a stairway that a housing inspector should be able to identify correctly are the following:

A   Riser

B   Tread

C   Nosing

D   Handrail

E   Balustrade and Balusters, the Vertical Members that Support the Handrail, and

F   The Soffit, Underpart of the Stairway.

In the examination of a stairway (be careful to turn the light on) initially check the underside, if visible, to see if it is intact. Then proceed slowly up the stairs placing full weight on each tread and checking for loose, wobbling, or uneven treads and risers. Regardless of the size of the treads or risers they should all be of uniform size. For all stairs that rise 3 or more feet, a handrail should be present and in a sound and rigid condition.

Any fireplace should conform to the requirements of the local code. An unused fireplace that has its opening covered with wallpaper or other material should have a solid seal behind the paper. Operable fireplaces should have a workable damper and a fire screen, and should be clean.

Garages and accessory structures should be inspected in the same manner as the main building.

Sidewalks and driveways, whether constructed of flagstone, concrete, or asphalt, should be checked for creaking, buckling, and other conditions dangerous to pedestrian travel.

Stone, brick, or concrete steps should be inspected for cracks, deterioration, and pointing.

Fences should be in a sound condition and painted. Fire escapes should be checked for paint condition, loose or broken treads and rails, proper operating condition, and proper connection to the house.

V. Noise as an Environmental Stress

People feel comfortable in an environment with a low-level, soothing, steady, unobstrusive level of sound, typical of the natural undisturbed environment. All of us have experienced the anguish that noise can cause, whether it be noise from a neighbor's television, the grinding of truck gears while asleep, the persistent whine of a fan motor, or the sound of children racing down the halls. These annoyances experienced in the home are producing public demands for noise control legislation.

Not only is noise disturbing, but studies also indicate that extreme noise can cause deafness and perhaps interfere with other bodily functions.

While few existing housing ordinances contain enforceable noise provisions, noise problems must be considered by the building inspector because they intimately affect and are affected by his decisions. As a housing inspector, you can help residents by suggesting corrective noise measures that can be taken; you can refer them to agencies, if needed, for corrective action; you can help them to understand that their noisy environment can place limitations on their behavior, capabilities, and satisfaction with their home.

Noise is unwanted sound. Noise can travel through air or through the building structure. The first stage of noise control is the control of sound at its source. If attempts to quiet the source are not completely successful, then other, more expensive corrective measures will be required.

Although a visual examination of a dwelling may detect some sources of noise leaks (see Figure 10) such as wide gaps or cracks at ceiling, floor, or adjoining wall edges, it is usually inadequate since it fails to detect sources of noise leaks hidden from the eye. A far more effective test is to be alert for the operation of some noisy device like a vacuum cleaner in a closed room and listen near the other side of the wall for any noise leakage. The ear is a reasonably good sensing device. If a noise leak is noticed, the partition may be surveyed at critical points with a bright flashlight while an observer looks for light leakage in a darkened room on the other side. Detection of any light leakage in the darkened room will signify a noise leak.

Noise carried as vibration by a building structure is called structure-borne noise. Detecting structure-borne noise caused by the operation of mechanical equipment is somewhat more difficult (see Figure 11). With noisy equipment in operation, the inspector can sometimes locate noise leaks or structure-borne noise paths by conducting similar hearing tests along with pressing the ear against various room surfaces or using fingertips to sense the vibration of these surfaces.

A Airborne Noise

The sources of airborne noise that cause the most frequent disturbances in the home are audio instruments such as televisions, radios, phonographs, or pianos; adults and children speaking loudly, singing, crying and shouting; household appliances such as garbage disposals, dishwashers, vacuum cleaners, clothes washers, and dryers; plumbing noises such as pipes knocking, toilets flushing, and water running.

The disturbing influences of airborne noise are generally limited to the areas near the noise source. For example, a phonograph may cause annoyance in rooms of a neighbor's apartment adjacent to the phonograph but rarely in rooms farther removed unless doors or passageways are left open. Sound absorption materials such as carpeting, acoustical tile, drapery, and upholstered furniture in the intervening rooms may often provide a significant reduction in the disturbing noise before it reaches rooms where quiet is desired.

Under no conditions should sound-absorptive materials be used on the surfaces of walls and ceilings for the sole purpose of preventing the transmission of sound as structure-borne noise. To do so would be a complete waste of effort. To illustrate, imagine the noise conducted by a wall constructed solely of drapery or acoustical tile attached to studs. The noise level in the room would be reduced, but sound produced in the room would pass through the wall to adjoining rooms with little, if any, reduction in noise level. Sound absorptive materials should be used in and near areas of high noise levels to limit airborne noise at the source of the noise and reduce the effects of noise along corridors.

The transmission of noise from one completely enclosed room to an adjoining room separated by a partition wall may be either direct transmission through the wall, indirect transmission through other walls, ceilings, and floors common to both rooms, or through corridors adjacent to such rooms.

In some older wood frame houses, the open troughs between studs and joists are efficient sound transmission paths. This noise transmission by indirect paths is known as "flanking transmission" (see Figure 10 and 11). In addition to the flanking paths, there may be noise leaks particularly along the ceiling, floor, and sidewall edges of the wall. In order to obtain the highest sound insulation performance, a partition wall must be of airtight construction. Care must be exercised to seal all openings, gaps, holes, joints, and penetrations of piping and conduits with a nonsetting caulking compound. Even hairline cracks, particularly at adjoining wall, floor, and ceiling edges, transmit a substantially greater amount of noise than would normally be expected on the basis of the size of the crack.

Figure 10. Flanking Transmission of Airborne Noise

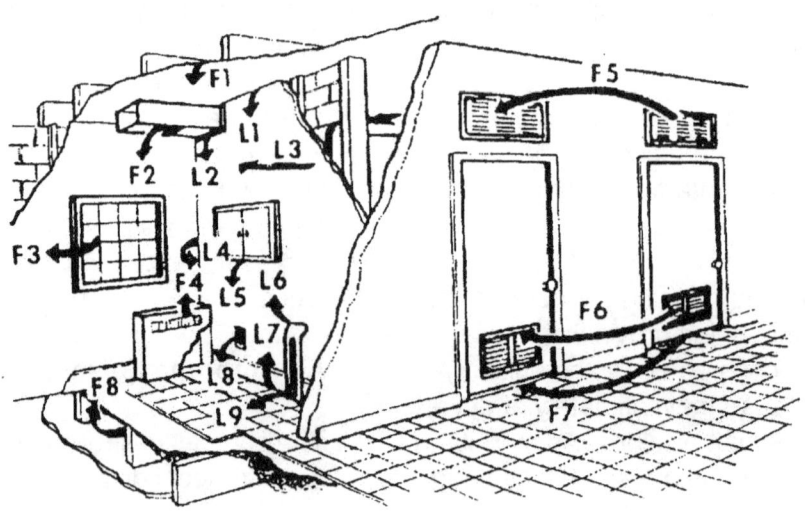

FLANKING NOISE PATHS	NOISE LEAKS
F1 Open plenums over walls, false ceilings	L1 Poor seal at ceiling edges
F2 Unbaffled duct runs	L2 Poor seal around duct penetrations
F3 Outdoor path, window to window	L3 Poor mortar joints, porous masonry block
F4 Continuous unbaffled inductor Units	L4 Poor seal at sidewall, filler panel, etc.
F5 Hall path, open vents	L5 Back-to-back cabinets, poor workmanship
F6 Hall path, louvered doors	L6 Holes, gaps at wall penetrations
F7 Hall path, openings under doors	L7 Poor seal at floor edges
F8 Open troughs in floor-ceiling structure	L8 Back-to-back electrical outlets
	L9 Holes, gaps at floor penetrations

Other points to consider are these: leaks are (a) batten strip A/O post connections of prefabricated walls, (b) under-floor pipe or service chases, (c) recessed, spanning light fixtures, (d) ceiling and floor cover plates of movable walls, (e) unsupported A/O unbacked wall-board joints (f) edges and backing of built-in cabinets and appliances, (g) prefabricated, hollow metal, exterior curtain walls.

It is often helpful to use one sound to drown out another disturbing noise; for example, music on the radio can be used to drown out the noise of traffic. The use of sound to drown out noise is particularly useful in masking noises that occur infrequently, such as accelerating or braking vehicles, periodic mechanical equipment noise, barking dogs, laughter, or shouting.

B **Structure-Borne Noise**

Structure-borne noise occurs when wall, floor, or other building elements are set into vibration by direct contact with vibrating sources such as mechanical equipment or domestic appliances. A small, vibrating pipe firmly attached to a plywood or gypsum wall panel will amplify the vibration noise. An illustration of this amplification of structure-borne noise is provided by the sound board of a piano. The major sources of structure-borne noise are the impact of walking on wood floors or of slamming doors, plumbing system noises, heating and air-conditioning system noises, noise from mechanical equipment or appliances, and vibration from sources outside the building. If the vibration is severe enough, it may have adverse effects not only on the occupants of a building but also on the building structure. Household appliances such as refrigerators, washing machines, sewing machines, clothes dryers, televisions, and pianos should be vibration isolated from the floor by means of rubber mounts placed under them if disturbing structure-borne noise is to be avoided. Residents should also be cautioned against locating these noise sources along party walls and in particular against mounting these appliances and kitchen cabinets directly on party walls so that the walls act as sounding boards in adjoining apartments. Window air-conditioners should be completely vibration isolated from the surrounding window frame by rubber gaskets and padding. The importance of isolating a vibrating source from the structure in the control of equipment noise cannot be overemphasized.

Another source of disturbing structure-borne noise is squeaking of wood floors. Some squeaks can be eliminated by lubricating the tongues of wood floor boards with mineral oil applied sparingly to the openings between adjacent boards. Loose finish flooring may be securely fastened to subflooring by surface nailing into the

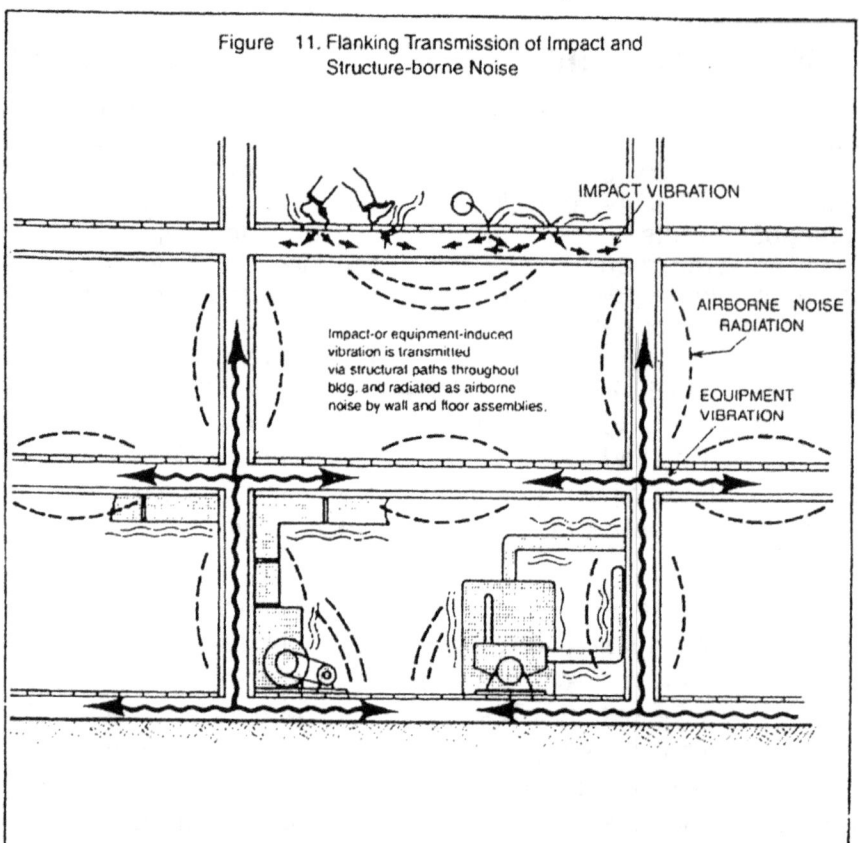

Figure 11. Flanking Transmission of Impact and Structure-borne Noise

subfloor and preferably the joists. Ring-type nails or sawtooth staples properly spaced should be used in nailing finish flooring to subflooring. In an exposed joist structure, where finish flooring is warped, driving screws up through the subfloor and into the finish floor will be effective in drawing the layers of flooring tightly together to reduce noise.

Of course, noise caused by the impact of walking or scraping can be substantially reduced by the use of carpets. In the case of door slams, the impact noise may be eliminated by the use of door closers or rubber bumpers.

The noisy hammering of a plumbing system is usually caused by the sudden interruption of water-flow, for example, by a quick closing or opening of a tap.

Air chambers can be built into the plumbing system to reduce water hammer. The air pockets, rubber inserts, or spring elements in air chambers act to reduce noise. Air chambers are explained in Chapter 6.

Defective, loose, or worn valve stems create intense chattering of the plumbing system. The defective device can frequently be found without difficulty, since immediate use of the device causes the vibration, which generally occurs at some low-flow-velocity setting and diminishes or disappears at a higher flow setting. For example, if a chattering noise occurs when a particular faucet or tap is opened partially and diminishes when fully opened, the faucet more than likely has some loose or defective parts and should be repaired.

Noise can be a very complex problem. The housing inspector is not expected to be an acoustics expert. Nor is he expected to be able to analyze and solve the noise problems that an acoustics consultant would normally handle. He can, however, help teach the public that the annoyances and stress caused by noise can be partially alleviated by a simple awareness of common noise problems found in many residences.

Although the housing inspector is not an expert in the fields of zoning, plumbing, building, and electrical systems, he should be familiar with the applicable code in each of the respective fields. Familiarization with these codes will better enable him to recognize violations.

ELECTRICAL ASPECTS OF A HOUSING INSPECTION

TABLE OF CONTENTS

		Page
I.	Definitions	1
II.	Flow of Electric Current	2
III.	Electric Service Entrance	4
IV.	Grounding	6
V.	Two- or Three-Way Electric Services	7
VI.	Residential Wiring Adequacy	8
VII.	Wire Size and Types	8
VIII.	Electric Service Panel	10
IX.	Overcurrent Devices	11
X.	Electric Circuits	13
XI.	Common Electrical Violations	16
XII.	Steps Involved in Actual Inspections	18
XIII.	Wattage Consumption of Electrical Appliances	20
XIV.	Motor Currents	20

ELECTRICAL ASPECTS OF A HOUSING INSPECTION

There are two basic codes concerned with residential wiring that are of importance to the housing inspector. The first is the local electrical code. The purpose of this code is to safeguard persons and buildings and their contents from hazards arising from the use of electricity for light, heat, and power. The electrical code contains basic minimum provisions considered necessary for safety. Compliance with this code and proper maintenance will result in an installation essentially free from hazard but not necessarily efficient, convenient, or adequate for good service or future expansion.

The majority of local electrical codes are modeled after the National Electrical Code, published by the National Fire Prevention Association.

Just because an electrical installation was safe and adequate under the provisions of the electrical code at the time of installation does not indicate that the system is safe and adequate for use today. Hazards often occur because of overloading of wiring systems by methods or usage not in conformity with the code. This occurs because initial wiring did not provide for increases in the use of electricity. For this reason it is recommended that the initial installation be adequate and that reasonable provisions for system changes be made as may be required for future increase in the use of electricity.

The other code that contains electrical provisions is the local housing code. It establishes minimum standards for artificial and natural lighting and ventilation, specifies the minimum number of electric outlets and lighting fixtures per room, and prohibits temporary wiring except under certain circumstances. In addition, the housing code usually requires that all components of the electrical system be installed and maintained in a safe condition so as to prevent fire or electric shock.

This chapter contains electrical terms and major features of a residential wiring system that should be familiar to the housing inspector. It also contains a review of the steps involved in the electrical inspection, as well as commonly found conditions.

I. Definitions

A **Electricity** - is energy that can be used to run household appliances; it can produce light and heat, shocks, and numerous other effects.

B **Current** - the flow of electricity through a circuit.

  1 **Alternating current** is an electrical current that reverses its direction of flow at regular intervals: For example, it would alternate 60 times every second in a 60-cycle system. This type of power is commonly found in homes.

  2 **Direct current** is an electric current flowing in one direction. This type of current is not commonly found in today's homes.

C **Ampere** - the unit used in measuring intensity of flow of electricity. Symbol for it is "I."

D **Volt** - the unit for measuring electrical pressure or force, which is known as electromotive force. Symbol for it is "E."

E **Watt** - is the unit of electric power. Volts X Amperes = Watts.

F **Circuit** - the flow of electricity through two or more wires from the supply source to one or more outlets and back to the source.

G **Circuit Breaker** - a safety device used to break the flow of electricity by opening the circuit automatically in the event of overloading or used to open or close it manually.

H **Short Circuit** - is a break in the flow of electricity through a circuit due to the load caused by improper connection between hot and neutral wires (have the electrical inspector check for its location).

I **Conductor** - any substance capable of conveying an electric current. In the home, copper wire is usually used.

   1 **Bare conductor** is one with no insulation or covering.

   2 **Covered conductor** is one covered with one or more layers of insulation.

J **Fuse** - a safety device that cuts off the flow of electricity when the current flowing through the fuse exceeds its rated capacity.

K **Ground** - to connect with the earth as to ground an electric wire directly to the earth or indirectly through a water pipe or some other conductor. Usually a green-colored wire is used for grounding the whole electrical system to the earth. A white wire is then usually used to ground individual electrical components of the whole system.

L **Conductor Gauge** - a numerical system used to label electric conductor sizes, given in American Wire Gauge (AWG). The larger the AWG number the smaller the wire size.

M **Hot Wires** - those that carry the electric current or power to the load; they are usually black or red.

N **Service** - the conductor and equipment for delivering energy from the electricity supply system to the wiring system of the premises.

O **Service Drop** - the overhead service connectors from the last pole or other aerial support to and including the splices, if any, connecting to the service entrance conductors at the building or other structure.

P **Insulator** - a material that will not permit the passage of electricity.

Q **Neutral Wire** - the third wire in a three-wire distribution circuit; it is usually white or light gray and is connected to the ground.

R **Service Panel** - main panel or cabinet through which electricity is brought to building and distributed. It contains the main disconnect switch and fuses or circuit breakers.

S **Voltage Drop** - a voltage loss when wires carry current. The longer the cord the greater the voltage drop.

II. Flow of Electric Current

Electricity is usually generated by a generator that converts mechanical energy into electrical energy. The electricity is then run through a transformer where voltage is increased to several hundred thousand volts and in some instances to a million or more volts. This high voltage is necessary in order to increase the efficiency of power transmission over long distances.

This high-transmission voltage is then stepped down (reduced) to normal 115/230-volt household current by a transformer located near the point of use (residence). The electricity is then transmitted to the house by a series of wires called a "service drop." In areas where the electric wiring is underground, the wires leading to the building are buried in the ground.

In order for electric current to flow, it must travel from a higher to a lower potential voltage. In an electrical system the hot wires (black or red) are at a higher potential than the neutral or ground wire (white or green). Therefore, current will flow between the hot wires and the neutral or ground wires.

The voltage is a measure of the force at which electricity is delivered. It is similar to pressure in a water supply system.

Current is measured in amperes and is the quantity of flow of electricity. It is similar to measuring water in gallons per second.

A watt is equal to volts times amperes. It is a measure of how much power is flowing. Electricity is sold in quantities of watt-hours.

The earth, by virtue of moisture contained within the soil, serves as a very effective conductor. Therefore, in power transmission, instead of having both the hot and neutral wires carried by the transmission poles, one lead of the generator is connected to the ground, which serves as a conductor (see Figure 1). Only hot wires are carried by the transmission towers. At the house, or point where the electricity is to be used, the circuit is completed by another connection to ground.

The electric power utility provides a ground somewhere in its local distribution system; therefore, there is a ground wire in addition to the hot wires within the service drop. In Figure 1 this ground can be seen at the power pole that contains the stepdown transformer.

In addition to the ground connection provided by the electric utility, every building is required to have an independent ground, called a "system ground."

The system ground provides for limiting the voltage upon the circuit, which might otherwise occur through exposure to lighting, or for limiting the maximum potential to ground due to normal voltage. Therefore, the system ground's main purpose is to protect the electric system itself and offer limited protection to the user.

The system ground serves the same purpose as the power company's ground, however, being closer to the building, it has a lower resistance.

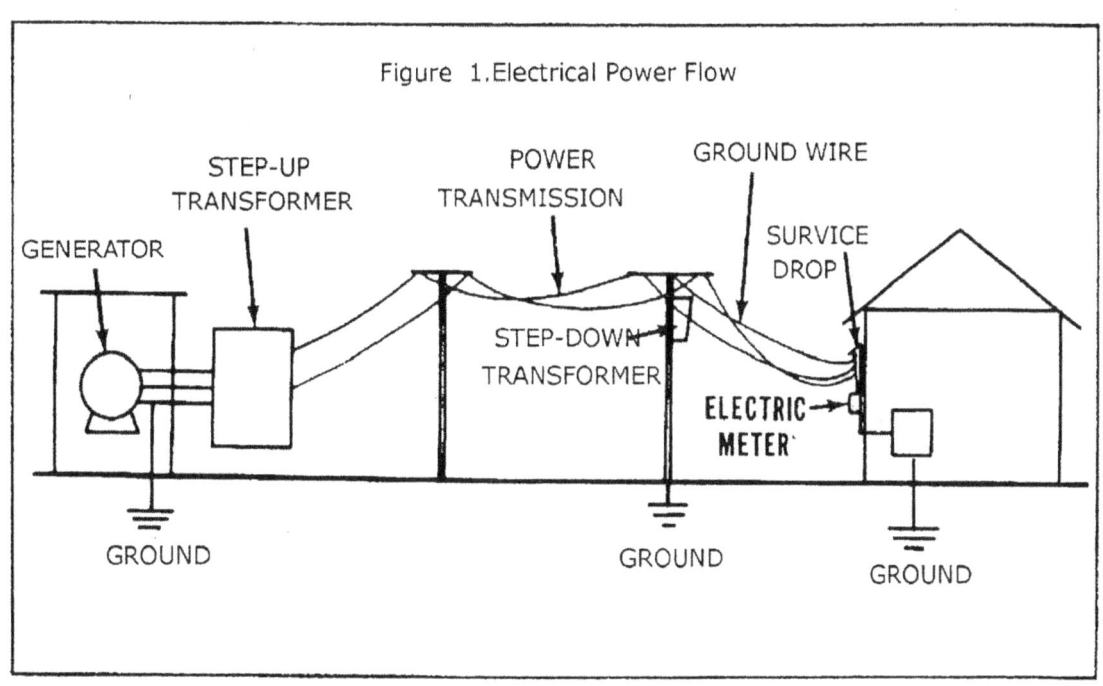

Figure 1. Electrical Power Flow

The "equipment ground," which we will discuss later in this chapter, protects man from potential harm during the use of certain electrical equipment.

The system ground should be a continuous wire of low resistance and of sufficient size to conduct current safely from lightning and overloads.

III. Electric Service Entrance

A Service Drop

The "Entrance Head" (see Figure 2) should be attached to the building at least 10 feet above ground, to prevent accidental contact by people. The conductor should clear all roofs by at least 8 feet and residential driveways by 12 feet. For public streets, alleys, roads, and driveways on other than residential property the clearance must be 18 feet.

The wires or conductor should be of sufficient size to carry the load and not smaller than No. 8 copper or equivalent.

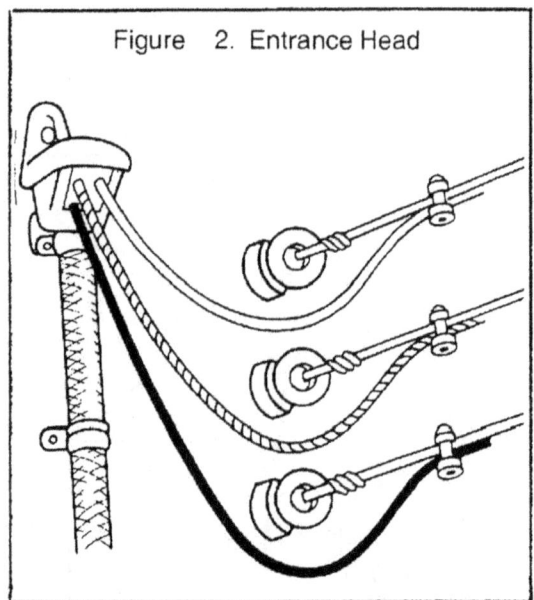

Figure 2. Entrance Head

For connecting wire from the entrance head to the service drop wires, the National Electrical Code requires that the service entrance conductors be installed either (1) below the level of the service head, or (2) below the termination of the service-entrance cable sheath. Drip loops must be formed on individual conductors. This will prevent water from entering the electric service system.

The wires that form "entrance cable" should extend 36 inches from the entrance head, to provide a sufficient length to connect service drop wires to the building with insulators (see Figure 2).

The entrance cable may be a special type of armored outdoor type of wire or it may be enclosed in a conduit. The electric power meter may be located either within or outside the building. In either instance, the meter must be located before the main power disconnect.

Figure 3 shows an armored cable service entrance. The armored cable is anchored to the building with metal straps spaced every 4 feet. The cable is run down the wall and through a hole drilled through the building. The cable is then connected to the service panel, which should be located within 1 foot of where the cable enters the building.

The ground wire need not be insulated. This ground wire may be either solid or stranded copper, or a material with an equivalent resistance.

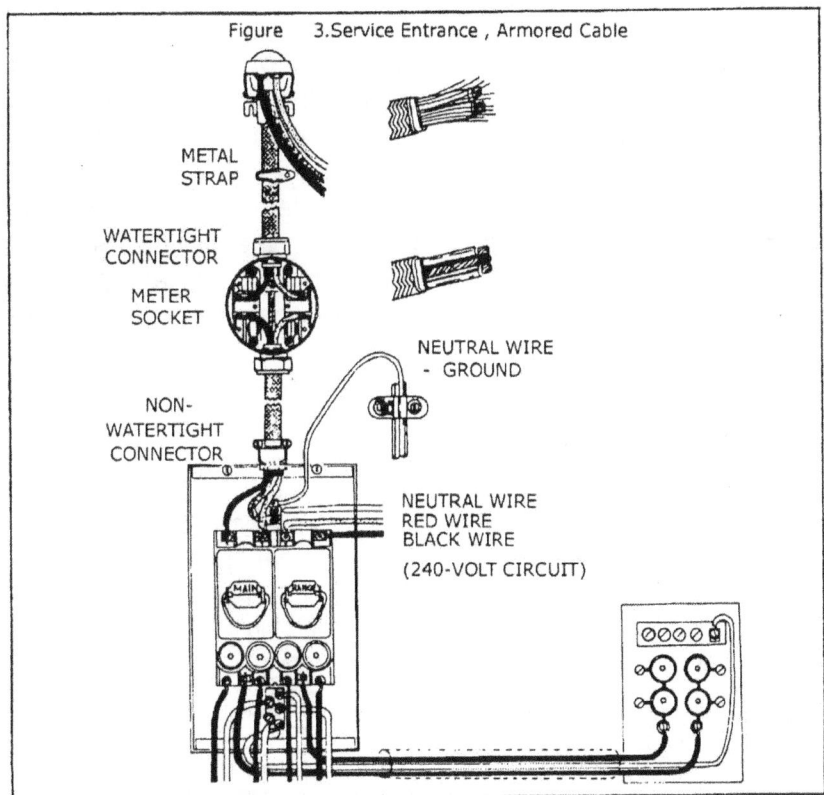

Figure 4 shows the use of thin-wall conduit in a service entrance.

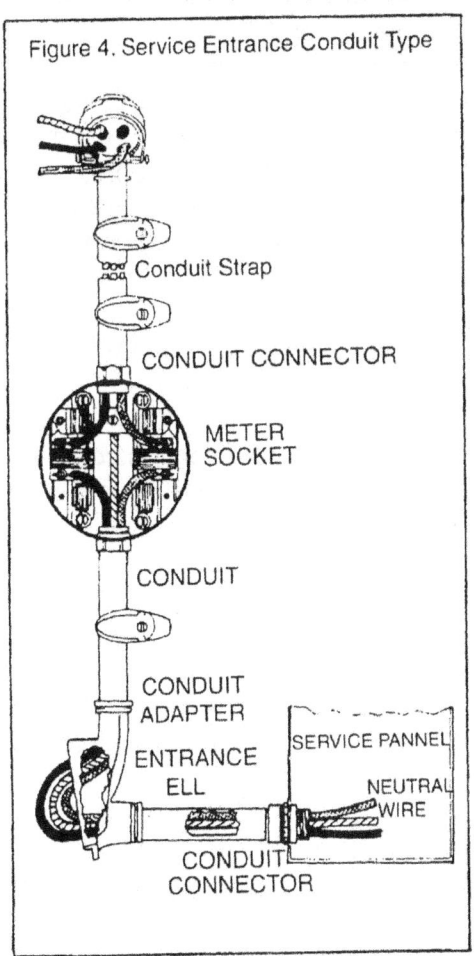

B Underground Service

When wires are run underground they must be protected from moisture and physical damage. The opening in the building foundation where the underground service enters the building must be moisture proof. Local codes should be referred to, concerning allowable materials for this type of service entrance.

C Electric Meter

The electric meter may be located inside or outside the building, as shown in Figure 3 or 4. The meter itself is weatherproof and is plugged into a weatherproof socket (see Figure 5). The electric power company furnishes the meter, the socket may or may not be furnished by the power company.

IV. Grounding

The system ground consists of grounding the neutral incoming wire as well as the neutral wire of the branch circuits. The equipment ground consists of grounding the metal parts of the service entrance, such as the service switch, as well as the service entrance conduit, armor, or cable.

The usual ground connection is to a water pipe of the city water system. The connection should be made to the street side of the cold water meter as shown in Figure 6.

If the water meter is located near the street curb, then the ground connection should be made to the cold water pipe as close as possible to where it enters the building.

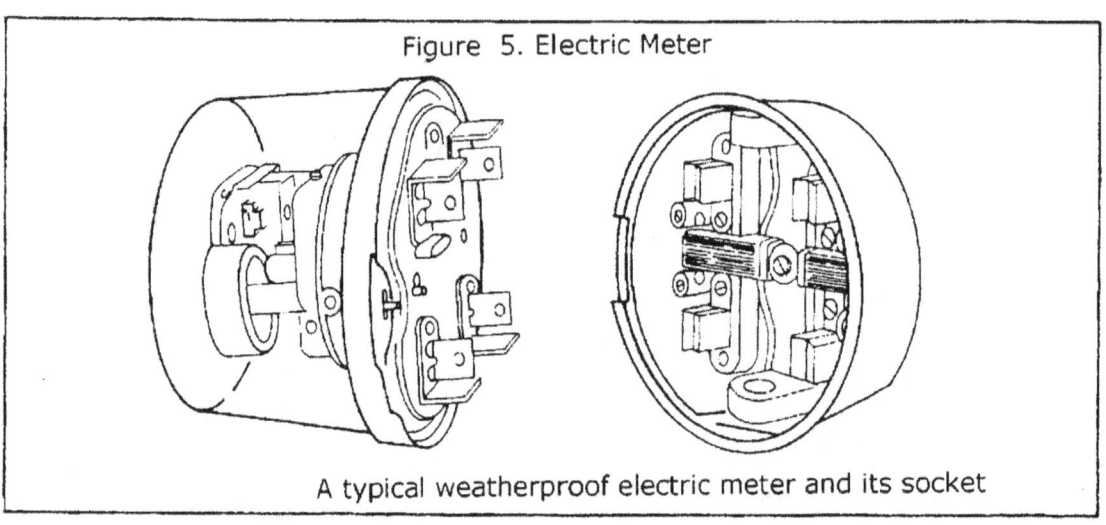

Figure 5. Electric Meter

A typical weatherproof electric meter and its socket

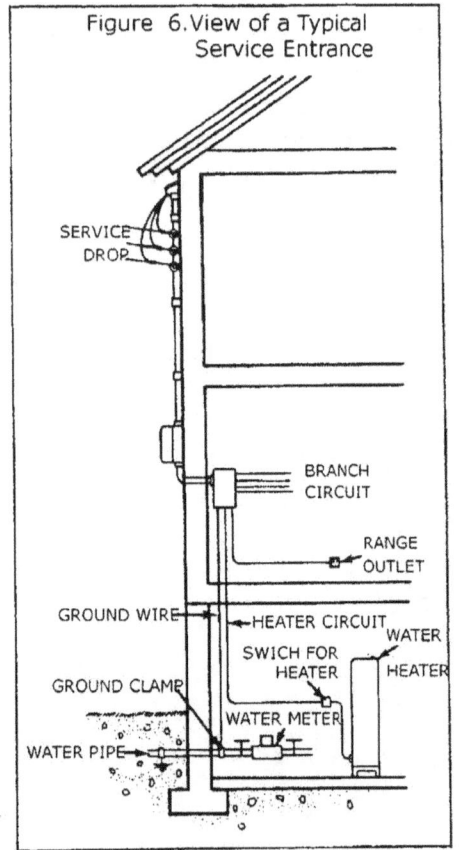

Figure 6. View of a Typical Service Entrance

It is not unusual for a water meter to be removed from a building for service. If the ground connection is made at a point in the water piping system on the building side of the water meter, the ground circuit will be broken upon removal of the meter. This broken ground circuit represents a shock hazard if both sides of the water meter connections should be touched simultaneously.

In some instances the connections between the water meter to pipes are electrically very poor. In this case, if the ground connection is made on the building side of the water meter, there may not be an effective ground.

In order to prevent the two aforementioned situations the code requires that an effective bonding shall be provided around any equipment that is likely to be disconnected for repairs or replacement. This is illustrated in Figure 7. The same jumper arrangement would be required for a water meter that is installed near the curb. In many installations the water meter mounting bracket is designed to serve as an electric jumper.

Often an amateur mechanic, in the process of doing a household repair, will disconnect the house ground. Therefore, the housing inspector should always check the house ground to see if it is properly connected.

Figure 8 shows a typical grounding scheme at the service box of a residence. In this figure, only the grounded neutral wires are shown. The neutral strap is an uninsulated metal strip that is riveted directly to the service box. The ground wires from the service entrance, branch circuits, and house ground are joined by this strip.

When a city water supply is not available for grounding, a substitute must be made. The most common ground is a pipe or rod that is driven into the ground a distance of at least 8 feet. If the pipe is made of steel or iron, it must be 3/4 inch in diameter and galvanized. A copper ground pipe of 1/2 inch diameter is sufficient.

The code requires that a ground rod be entirely independent of and kept at least 6 feet from any other ground of the type used for radio, telephone, or lightning rods.

V. Two- or Three-Wire Electric Services

One of the wires in every installation is grounded. This neutral wire is always white. The hot wires are usually black or red or some other color, but never white.

The potential difference or voltage between the hot wires and the ground or neutral of a normal residential electrical system is 115

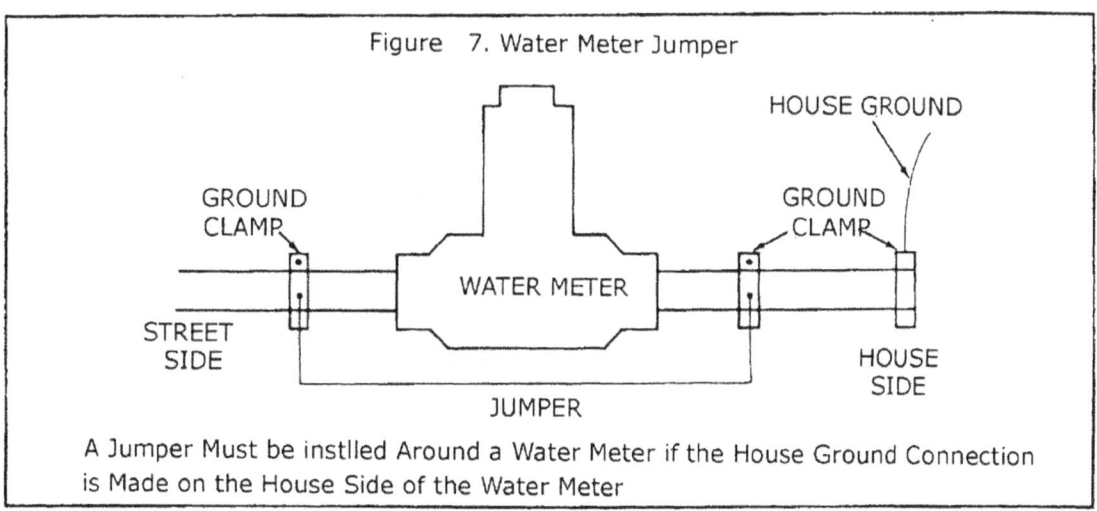

Figure 7. Water Meter Jumper

A Jumper Must be instlled Around a Water Meter if the House Ground Connection is Made on the House Side of the Water Meter

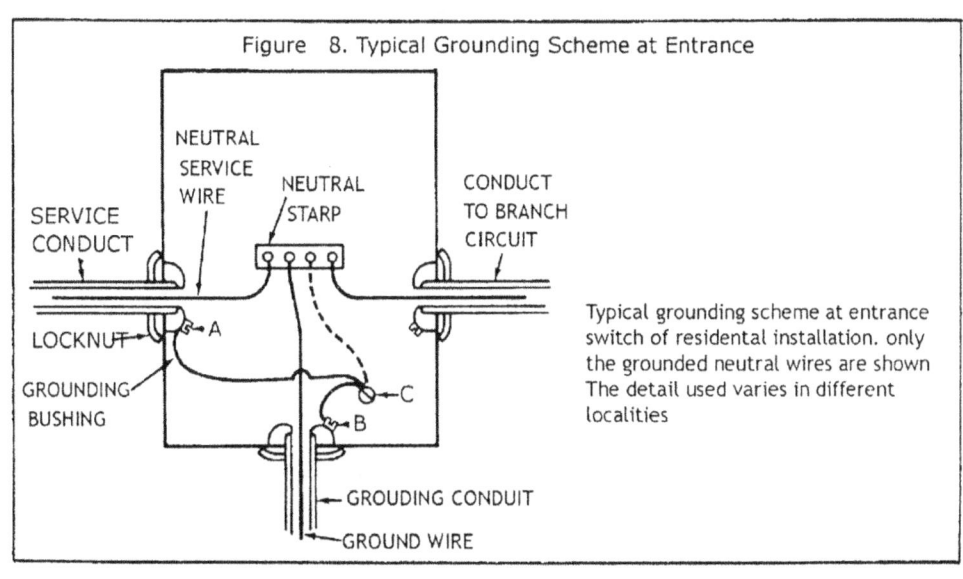

Figure 8. Typical Grounding Scheme at Entrance

Typical grounding scheme at entrance switch of residential installation. only the grounded neutral wires are shown The detail used varies in different localities

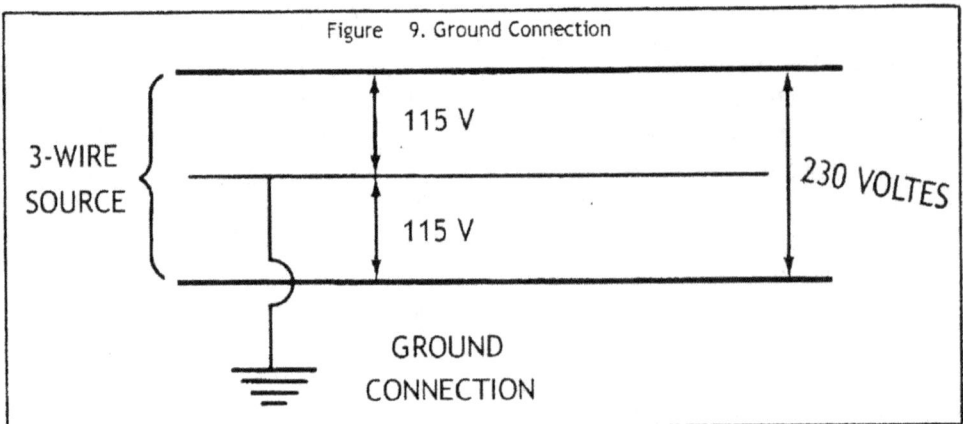

Figure 9. Ground Connection

volts. Thus, where we have a two-wire installation (one hot and one neutral) only 115-volt power is available (see Figure 9).

When three wires are installed (two hot and one neutral) either 115- or 230-volt power is available. In a three-wire system the voltage between the neutral and either of the hot wires is 115; between the two hot wires it is 230 volts.

The major advantage of a three-wire system is that it permits the operation of heavy electrical equipment such as laundry dryers, cooking ranges, and air conditioners, the majority of which require 230-volt circuits. In addition, the three-wire system is split at the service panel into two 115-volt systems to supply power for small appliances and electric lights. The result is a doubling of the number of circuits, and possibly a corresponding increase in the number of branch circuits, with a reduction of the probability of fire caused by overloading electrical circuits.

VI. Residential Wiring Adequacy

The use of electricity in the home has risen sharply since the 1930's. Many home owners have failed to repair or improve their wiring to keep it safe and up to date. The National Electrical Code recommends that individual residences be provided with a minimum of 100-ampere three-wire service. This type service is sufficient in a one-family house or dwelling unit to provide safe and adequate electric supply for the lighting, refrigerator, iron, and an 8,000-watt cooking range, plus other appliances requiring a total of up to 10,000 watts altogether.

Some homes have a 60-ampere, three-wire service. It is recommended that these homes be rewired for at least the minimum of 100 amperes recommended in the National Code since they are safely capable of supplying current only for lighting and portable appliances such as a cooking range and regular dryer (4,500 watts), or an electric hot-water heater (2,500 watts) and cannot handle additional major appliances.

Other homes today have only a 30-ampere, 115-volt, two-wire service. This system can safely handle only a limited amount of lighting, a few minor appliances, and no major appliances. Therefore, this size service is substandard in terms of modern household needs for electricity. Furthermore, it constitutes a fire hazard and a threat to the safety of the home and the occupants.

VII. Wire Size and Types

A Wire Size

Electric power flows over wire. It flows with relative ease (little resistance) in some materials such as copper and with a substantial amount of resistance in iron. If iron wire were used it would have to be 10 times as large as copper wire.

Copper wire sizes are indicated by a number. No. 14 is most commonly used in residential branch circuits. No. 14 is the smallest permitted by the Code for use in a branch circuit with a 15-ampere capacity. No. 16, 18, and 20 are progressively smaller than No. 14 and are usually used for extension wires. As the number of the wire becomes smaller the size and current capacity of the wire increases. No. 1 is the heaviest wire usually used in ordinary household wiring.

Wire of correct size must be used for two reasons: current capacity and voltage drop.

1. When current flows through a wire it creates heat. The greater the amount of flow, the greater the amount of heat generated. (Doubling the amperes without changing the wire size increases the amount of heat by four times.) The heat is electric energy that has been converted into heat energy by the resistance of the wire; the heat created by the coils in a toaster is an example. This heat developed in an electrical conductor is wasted, and thus the electric energy used to generate it is wasted. If the amount of heat generated by the flow of current through the wire becomes excessive, a fire may result. Therefore, the code sets the maximum permissible current that may flow through a certain type and size wire.
The following are examples of current capacities for copper wire of various sizes.

Size wire (AWG)	#14	#12	#10	#8
Max. capacity, amperes	15	20	30	40

2. In addition to heat generation there will be a reduction in voltage as a result of attempting to force more current through a wire than it is capable of carrying. Certain appliances, such as induction-type electric motors, may be damaged if operated at too low a voltage.

B Wire Types

1. **Wire markings** - All wires must be marked to indicate the maximum working voltage, the proper type letter or letters for the type wire specified in the code, the manufacturer's name or trademark, and the AWG size or circular-mil area.
2. **Insulations used** There are a variety of wire types which can be used for a wide range of temperature and moisture conditions. The 1975 National Electrical Code should be consulted to determine the proper wire for specific conditions.

C Types of Cable

1. **Nonmetallic Sheathed Cable** - This type of cable consists of wires wrapped in a paper layer, followed by another spiral layer of paper, and enclosed in a fabric braid, which is treated with moisture-resistant and fire-resistant compounds. Figure 10 shows this type of cable, which often is marketed under the "Romex" name. This type of cable can be used only indoors and in permanently dry locations.

2. **Armored Cable** - This type of cable is commonly known by the BX or Flex-steel trade names. Wires are wrapped in a tough paper and covered with a strong spiral flexible steel armor. This type of cable is shown in Figure 11 and may be used only in permanently dry indoor locations. Armored cable must be supported by a strap or staple every 6 feet and within 24 inches of every switch or junction box, except for concealed runs in old work where it is impossible to mount straps.

3. **Other Cable** Cables are also available with other outer coatings of metals such as copper, bronze, and aluminum for use in a variety of conditions.

D Flexible Cords

Flexible cords are used to connect lamps, appliances, and other devices to outlets. Each wire consists of many strands of fine wire for flexibility. Extension cords in AWG sizes 16 to 18 are usually fine for lamps and smaller appliances, if the cord is not too long. A commonly accepted standard limits their length to 8 feet of unspliced cord. This keeps the cords short enough to prevent the excessive voltage drops, minimizes the possibility of fire caused by overheating of the wire due to overload, and also minimizes the danger of someone's tripping over them.

E Open Wiring

Open wiring is a wiring method using knobs, nonmetallic tubes, cleats, and flexible tubing for the protection and support of insulated conductors in or on buildings and not concealed by the structure. The term "open wiring" does not mean exposed, bare wiring. In dry locations when not exposed to severe

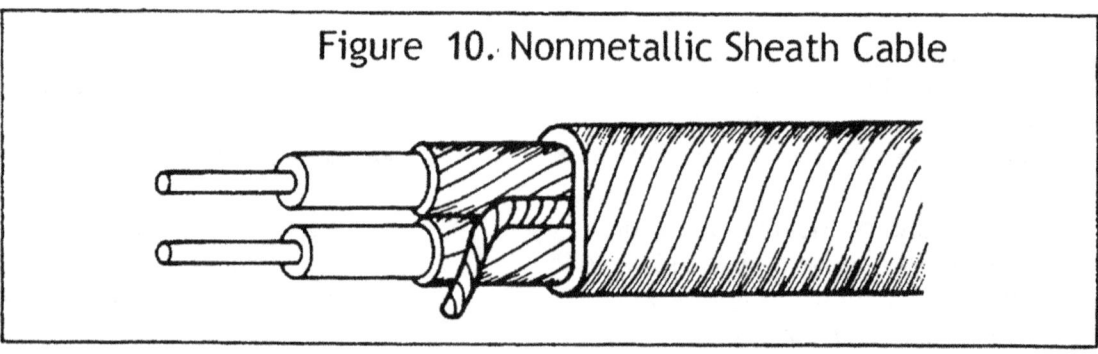

Figure 10. Nonmetallic Sheath Cable

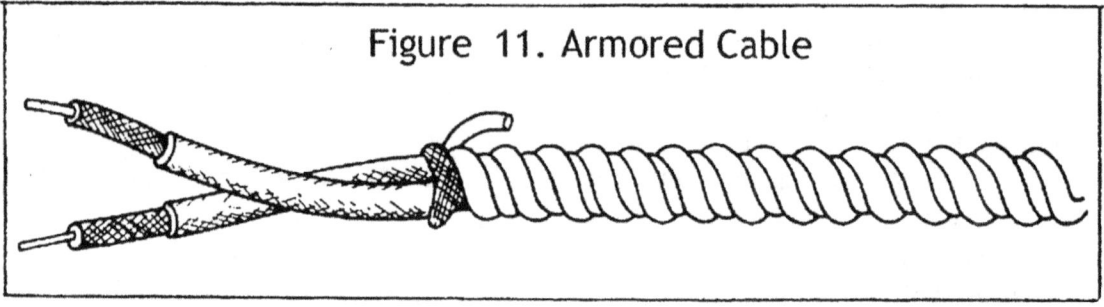

Figure 11. Armored Cable

physical damage, conductors may be separately encased in flexible tubing. Tubing should be in continuous lengths not exceeding 15 feet and secured to the surface by straps not more than 4 1/2 feet apart. They should be separated from other conductors by at least 2 1/2 inches and should have a permanently maintained airspace between them and any and all pipes they cross.

F Concealed Knob and Tube Wiring

Concealed knob and tube wiring is a wiring method using knobs, tubes, and flexible nonmetallic tubing for the protection and support of insulated wires concealed in hollow spaces of walls and ceilings of buildings. This wiring method is similar to open wiring, and like open wiring, is usually found only in older buildings.

VIII. Electric Service Panel

Service Switch

This is a main switch that will disconnect the entire electrical system at one time. The main fuses or circuit breakers are usually located within the "Service Switch" box. The branch circuit fuse or circuit breaker may also be located within this box.

According to the code, the switch must be "externally operable." This condition is fulfilled if the switch can be operated without the operator's being exposed to electrically active parts. Older switches use external handles as shown in Figure 12.

Most of today's service switches do not have hinged switch blades. Instead, the main fuse is mounted on a small insulated block that can be pulled out of the switch. When this block is removed, the circuit is broken just as if the blades had been operated with a handle.

The neutral terminal or wire of a grounded circuit must never be interrupted by a fuse or circuit breaker. In some installations the service switch is a "solid neutral" switch. This means that the neutral wire in the switch is not broken by the switch or a fuse.

When circuit breakers instead of fuses are used in homes, the use of main circuit breakers may or may not be required. If it takes not more than six movements of the hand to open all the branch-circuit breakers, no main breaker or switch or fuse will be required ahead of the branch-circuit breakers. Thus, a house with seven or more branch circuits requires a separate disconnect means or a main circuit breaker ahead of the branch-circuit breakers (see Figure 13).

IX. Overcurrent Devices

The amperage (current flow) in any wire is limited to the maximum permitted by using an overcurrent device of a

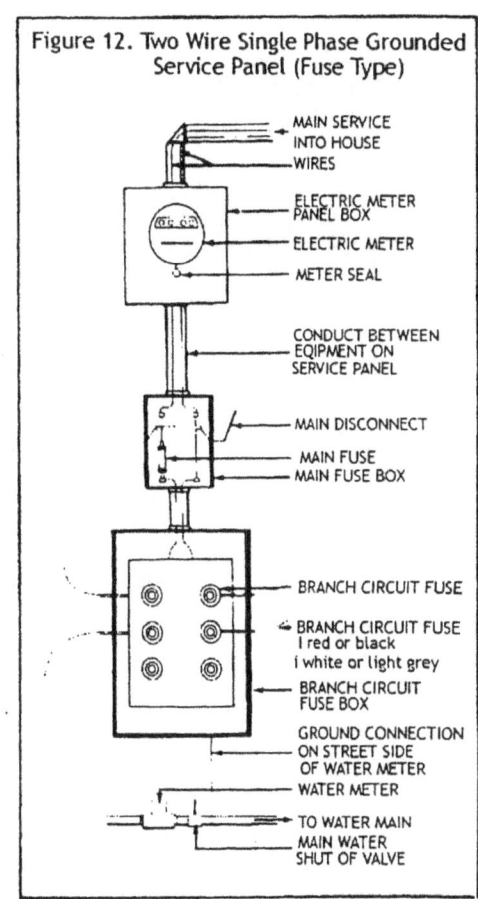

Figure 12. Two Wire Single Phase Grounded Service Panel (Fuse Type)

specific size as specified by the code. Two types of overcurrent devices are in common use: circuit breakers and fuses; both are rated in amperes. The overcurrent device must be rated at equal or lower capacity than the wire of the circuit it protects.

A Circuit Breakers (Fuseless) Service Panels

A circuit breaker (see Figure 14) looks something like an ordinary electric light switch. There is a handle that may be used to turn power on or off. Inside is a simple mechanism that, in case of a circuit overload, trips the switch and breaks the circuit. The circuit breaker may be reset by simply flipping the switch. A circuit breaker is capable of taking harmless short-period overloads (such as the heavy initial current required in the starting of a washing machine or air conditioner) without tripping but protects against prolonged overloads. After the cause of trouble

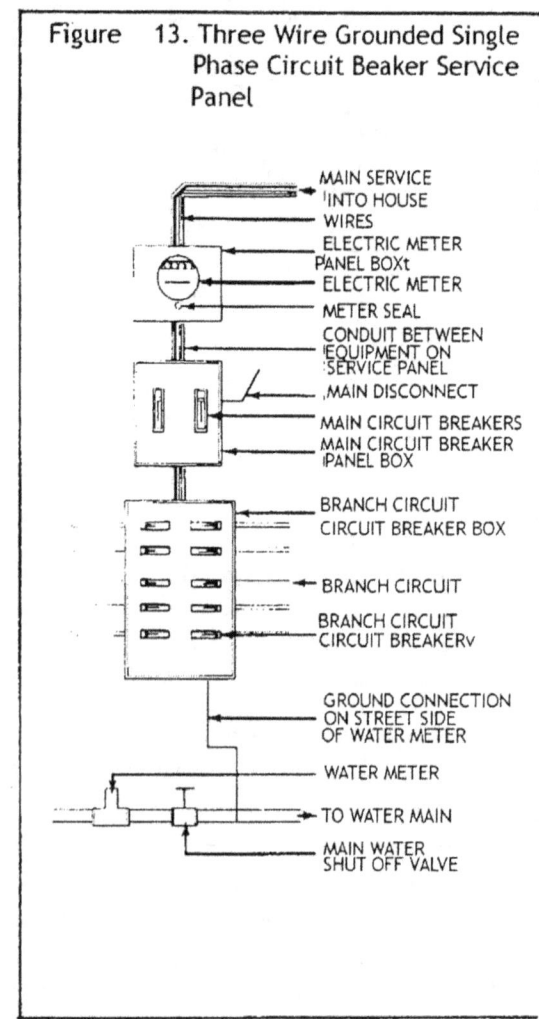

Figure 13. Three Wire Grounded Single Phase Circuit Beaker Service Panel

has been located and corrected, the power is easily restored by flipping the circuit breaker switch (circuit breakers are modern substitutes for fuses). Fuseless service panels are usually broken up into the following circuits.

1. A 100-ampere or larger main circuit breaker that shuts off all power.
2. A 40-ampere circuit for an appliance such as an electric cooking range. against the dangers of overloading
3. A 30-ampere circuit for clothes dryer, hot water heater, or central air conditioning.
4. A 20-ampere circuit for kitchen, small appliances, and power tools.
5. A 15-ampere circuit for general purpose lighting, TV, and vacuum cleaner.
6. Space for circuits to be added if needed for future use.

B Fused Ampere Service Panel or Fuse Box

Fuse-type panel boxes are generally found in older homes. They are equally as safe and adequate as a circuit breaker of equivalent capacity, provided fuses of the proper size are used.

A fuse (see Figure 15), like a circuit breaker, is designed to protect a circuit and short circuits and does this in two manners.

a. When a fuse is blown by a short circuit the metal strip is instantly heated to an extremely high temperature, and this heat causes it to vaporize. A fuse blown by a short circuit may be easily recognized because the window of the fuse usually becomes discolored.

b. In a fuse blown by overload the metal strip is melted at its weakest point, and this breaks the flow of current to the load. In this case the window of the fuse remains clear; therefore, a blown fuse caused by an overload may also be easily recognized.

Sometimes, although a fuse has not been blown, the bottom of the fuse may be severely discolored and pitted. This indicates a loose connection due to the fuse's not being screwed in properly.

Generally, all fused panel boxes are wired similarly for two- and three-wire systems. In a two-wire-circuit panel box the black or red hot wire is connected to a terminal of the main disconnect, and the white or light gray neutral wire is connected to the neutral strip, which is then grounded to the pipe on the street side of the water meter.

In a three-wire system the black and red hot wires are connected to separate terminals of the main disconnect, and the neutral wire is grounded the same as for a two-wire system (see Figure 12). Below each fuse is a terminal to which a black or red wire is connected. The white or light gray neutral wires are then connected to the neutral strip. Each fuse indicates a separate circuit.

1 **Non-tamperable Fuses** - All ordinary plug fuses, shown in Figure 15, have the same diameter and physical appearance regardless of their current capacity. Thus, if a circuit designed for a 15-ampere fuse is overloaded so that the 15-ampere fuse blows out, nothing will prevent a person from replacing the 15-ampere fuse with a 20- or 30-ampere fuse, which may not blow out. If a circuit wired with No. 14 wire (current capacity 15 amperes) is fused with a 20- or 30-ampere fuse and an overload develops, more current than the No. 14 wire is safely capable of carrying could pass through the circuit. The result would be a heating of the wire and a potential fire.

Type S fuses, shown in Figure 15, have different lengths and diameter threads for each different amperage capacity. An adapter is first inserted into the ordinary fuse holder, which adapts the fuse holder for only one capacity fuse. Once the adapter is inserted, it cannot be removed.

2 **Cartridge Fuses**

Figure 15 shows two different types of cartridge fuses. A cartridge fuse protects an electric circuit in the same manner as an ordinary plug fuse already described protects it. Cartridge fuses are often used as main fuses.

X. Electric Circuits

An electric circuit in good repair carries electricity through two or three wires from the source of supply to an outlet and back to the source.

A **Branch Circuit**

A branch circuit is an electric circuit that supplies electric current to a limited number of electric outlets and fixtures. A residence generally has many branch circuits. Each is protected against short circuits and overloads by a 15- or 20-ampere fuse or circuit breaker.

The number of outlets per branch circuit varies from building to building. The code requires enough light circuits so that 3 watts of power will be available for each square foot of floor area

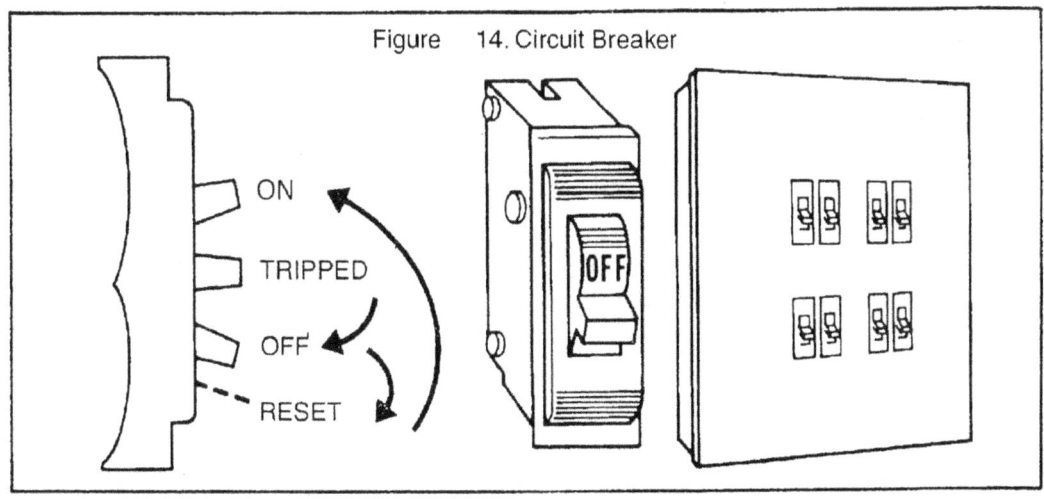

Figure 14. Circuit Breaker

Figure 15. Types of Fuses

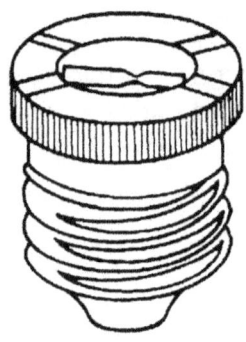

Plug fuses are not made in ratings over 30 amp.

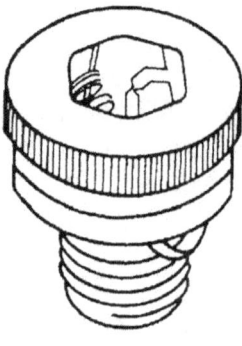

A typical Type-S non-tamperable fuse, and its adapter. Once an adapter has been screwed into a fuse-holder, it cannot be removed. This prevents use of fuses larger than originally intended.

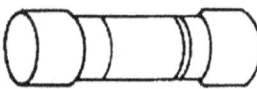

Cartridge fuses rated 60 amps, or less are of the ferrule type shown.

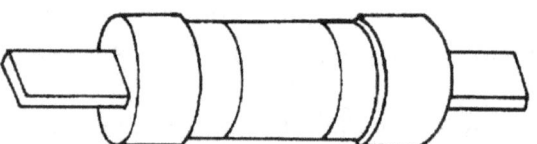

Cartridge fuses rated more than 60 amp. have knife-blade terminals shown.

in a house. A circuit wired with No. 14 wire and protected by a 15-ampere overcurrent protection device provides 15 X 115 or 1,725 watts; each circuit is obviously enough for 1,725/3 or 575 square feet.

Note that 575 is a minimum figure; if future use is considered, 500 or even 400 square feet per branch circuit should be used.

B Special Appliance Circuits

The branch circuit will provide electric power for lighting, radio, television, and small portable appliances. However, the larger electric appliances usually found in the kitchen consume more power and must have their own special circuit.

Section 220-3b of the code requires two special circuits to serve only appliance outlets in kitchen, laundry, pantry, family-room, dining room, and breakfast room. Both circuits must be extended to the kitchen; the other rooms may be served by either one or both of these circuits. No lighting outlets may be connected to these circuits, and they must be wired with No. 12 wire and protected by a 20-ampere overcurrent device. Each circuit will have a capacity of 20 X 115 or 2,300 watts, which is not too much when one considers that toasters often require over 1,600 watts.

C Individual Appliance Circuits

It is customary to provide a circuit for each of the following appliances:

1. Range
2. Water heater
3. Automatic laundry
4. Clothes dryer

5   Garbage disposer
6   Dishwasher
7   Furnace
8   Water pump

Note that these circuits may be either 115 volts or 230 volts, depending on the particular appliance or motor installed.

D   Outlet Switch and Junction Boxes

The code requires that every switch, outlet, and joint in wire or cable be housed in a box. Every fixture must be mounted on a box. Most boxes are made of metal with a galvanized finish. Figure 16 shows a typical outlet box.

When a cable of any style is used for wiring, the code requires that it be securely anchored with a connector to each box it enters.

E   Grounding Outlets

An electrical appliance may appear to be in good repair, and yet it might be a danger to the user. Consider a portable electric drill. It consists of an electric motor inside a metal casing. When the switch is depressed, the current flows to the motor, and the drill rotates. As a result of wear, however, the insulation on the wire inside the drill may deteriorate and allow the hot side of the power cord to come in contact with the metal casing. This will not affect the operation of the drill.

A person fully clothed using the drill in the living room, which has a dry floor, will not receive a shock, even though he is in contact with the electrified drill case. His body is not grounded, because of the dry floor. If, however, the operator should be standing on a wet basement floor, his body might be grounded, and when he touches the electrified drill case, current will pass through his body.

In order to protect man, the drill case is usually connected to the system ground by means of a wire called an "appliance ground." In this instance, as the drill is plugged in, current will flow between the shorted hot wire and the drill case and cause the overcurrent device to break the circuit. Thus the appliance ground has protected man. The appliance ground is the third wire found on many appliances.

The appliance ground on the appliance will be of no use unless the outlet into which the appliance is plugged is grounded. The outlet is grounded by being in physical contact with a ground outlet box. The outlet box is grounded by having a third ground wire, or a grounded conduit, as part of the circuit wiring.

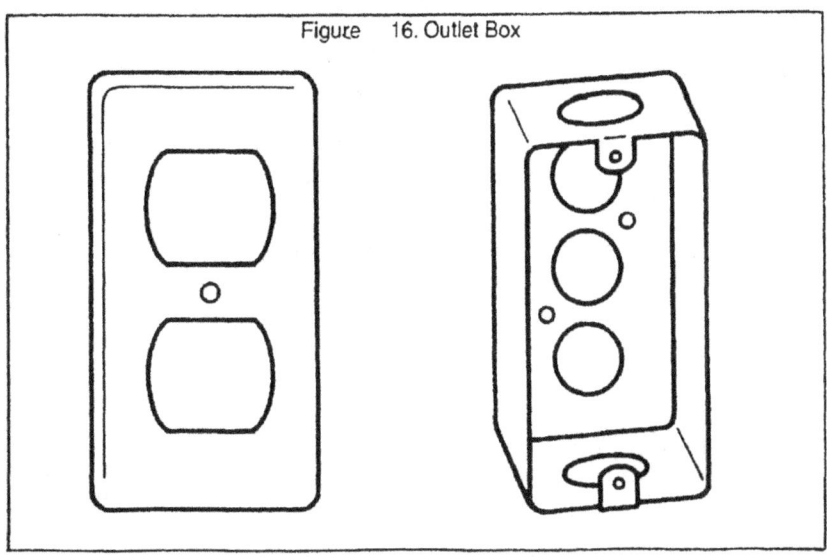

Figure 16. Outlet Box

All new buildings are required to have grounded outlets (as shown in Figure 17). The outlet may be tested by using a circuit tester. The circuit tester should light when both of its leads are plugged into the two elongated parallel openings of the outlet. In addition, the tester should light when one lead is plugged into the round third opening and the other is plugged into the hot side of the outlet.

If the conventional two-opening outlet is used, it still may be grounded. In this instance the screw that holds the outlet cover plate is the third-wire ground. The tester should light when one lead is in contact with a clean paint-free metal outlet cover plate screw and the hot side of the outlet. If the tester fails to light then the outlet is not grounded. If the outlet is not grounded then the tester will not function.

If a two-opening outlet is grounded, it may be adapted for use by a three-wire appliance by using an adapter. The loose-wire portion of the adapter should be secured behind the metal screw of the outlet plate cover.

Many appliances such as electric shavers and some new hand tools are double insulated and are safe without having a third ground wire.

XI. Common Electrical Violations

A The most apparent requirements that a housing inspector must check are the existence of the power supply; the types, locations, and conditions of the wiring in use; and the existence of the number of wall outlets or ceiling fixtures required by his local code and their condition. In making his investigations, these considerations will serve as useful guides:

1 **Power Supply** - Where is it located, is it grounded properly, and is it at least of minimum capacity required to supply current safely for lighting and the major and minor appliances in the dwelling?

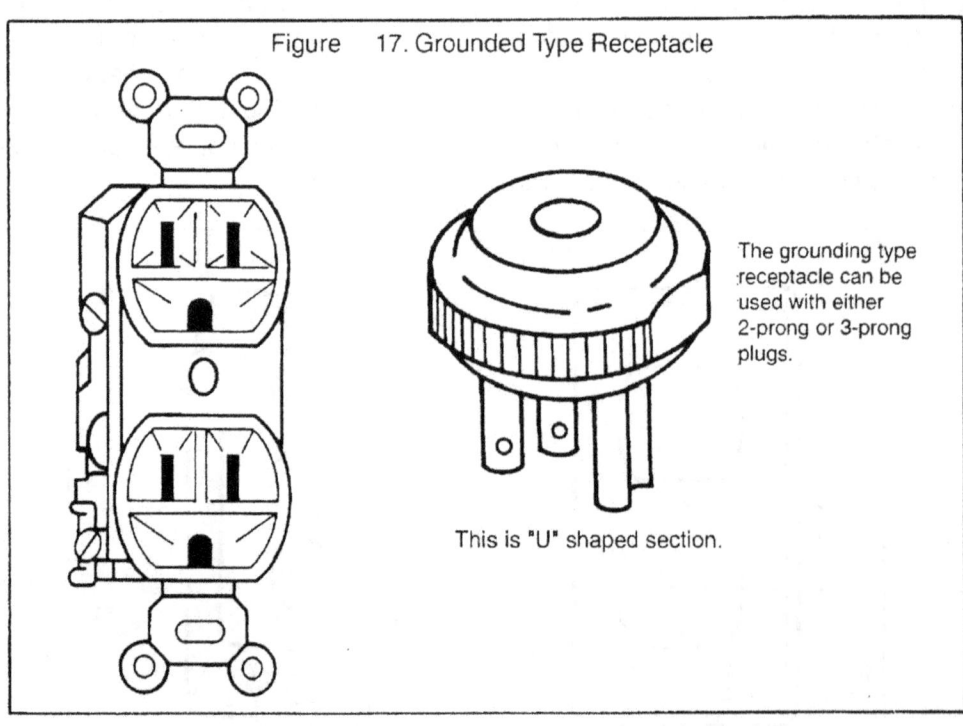

Figure 17. Grounded Type Receptacle

The grounding type receptacle can be used with either 2-prong or 3-prong plugs.

This is "U" shaped section.

2. **Panel Box Covers or Doors** - These should be accessible only from the front and should be sealed in such a way that they can be operated safely without the danger of contact with live or exposed parts of the wiring system.

3. **Switch, Outlets, and Junction Boxes** - These also must be covered to protect against danger of electric shock.

4. **Frayed or Bare Wires** - These are usually the result of long use and a drying out and cracking of the insulation, which leave the wires exposed, or else a result of constant friction and rough handling of the wire, which cause it to fray or become bare. Wiring in this condition constitutes a safety hazard, and correction of such defects should be ordered immediately.

5. **Electric Cords Under Rugs or Other Floor Coverings** - Putting electric cords in locations such as these is prohibited because of the potential fire hazard caused by continuing contact over a period of time between these heat-bearing cords and the flammable floor coverings. Direct the occupant to shift the cords to a safe location, explain why, and make sure it is done before you leave.

6. **Bathroom Lighting** - It should include at least one permanently installed ceiling or wall light fixture with a wall switch and plate so located and maintained that there is no danger of short circuiting from use of other bathroom facilities or splashing of water. Fixture or cover plates should be insulated or grounded.

7. **Lighting of Public Hallways, Stairways, Landings, and Foyers** A common standard here is sufficient lighting to provide illumination of 10 foot-candles on every part of these areas at all times. Sufficient lighting means that a person can clearly see his feet on all parts of the stairways and halls. Every public hall and stairway in a structure containing *less than three* dwelling units may be supplied with conveniently located light switches controlling an adequate lighting system that may be turned on when needed, instead of full-time lighting.

8. **Habitable Room Lighting** - The standard here may be two floor convenience outlets although floor outlets are dangerous unless protected by proper dust and water covers or one convenience outlet and one wall or ceiling electric light fixture. This number constitutes an absolute and often inadequate minimum given the contemporary widespread use of electricity in the home. The minimum should be that number required to provide adequate lighting and power to accommodate lighting and appliances normally used in each room.

9. **Octopus Outlets or Wiring** - This term is applied to outlets into which plugs have been inserted and are being used to permit more than two lights or portable appliances, such as a TV, lamp, or radio, to be connected to the electrical system. The condition occurs where the number of outlets is insufficient to accommodate the normal use of the room. This practice overloads the circuit and is a potential source of fire, which may be caused by overloading the circuit.

10. **Outlet Covers** - Every outlet and receptacle must be covered by a protective plate to prevent contact of its wiring or terminals with the body, combustible object or splashing water.

The following items are conditions that cause needless dangers and must also be corrected:

a. **Excessive or faulty fusing** - The wire's capacity must not be exceeded by the fuse or circuit breaker capacity or be left unprotected by faulty fusing or circuit breakers. Fuses and circuit breakers are safety devices designed to "blow" as a means of protection against overloadings of the electrical system or one or more of its circuits. Pennies under fuses are put there to bypass the fuse. These are illegal and must be removed. Overfusing is done for the same reason. The latter can be prevented by the installation of modern fuse stats, which prevent use of any fuse of a higher amperage than can be handled by the circuit it serves.

b **Cords run through walls or doorways and hanging cords or wires** - This is a makeshift-type installation and most often is installed by an unqualified handyman or do-it-yourself occupant. The inspector should check with his local electrical section to determine the policy regarding this type of insulation and govern his action in accordance with the electrical section's policies.

c **Temporary wiring** - This type of installation should not be allowed, with the exception of extension cords that go directly from portable lights and electric fixtures to convenience outlets.

d **Excessively long extension cords** - This requirement does not apply to specially designed extension cords for operating portable tools and trouble lights. Cities operating under modern code standards limit the length of loose cords or extension lines to a maximum of 8 feet. This is necessary because those that are too long will overheat if overloaded or if a short circuit develops and thus create a fire hazard. Even shorter lengths are feasible in housing with new or updated wiring systems that include one convenience outlet every 12 feet around the perimeter of the room.

e **Dead or dummy outlets** - These are sometimes installed to deceive the inspection agency. This is why all outlets must be tested or the occupants questioned to see if these are alive and functioning properly. A dead outlet cannot be counted to determine compliance with the code.

XII. Steps Involved in Actual Inspection

A **Testing Tools**
The basic tools required by an inspector of housing for making an electrical inspection are a fuse and circuit tester and a flashlight.

B **Danger of Techniques**

The first thing is to remember you are in a strange house and the layout is unfamiliar to you. The second thing to remember is that you are dealing with electricity *take no chances*. Go to the water meter and check the ground. It should connect to the water line on the street side of the water meter or else be equipped with a jumper wire. Do not touch any box or wire until you are sure of the ground. Go to the main fuse box and check all fuses in all boxes. Note the condition of the wiring and of the box itself and check whether it is overfused or not. Examine all wiring in the cellar. Make sure you are standing in a dry spot before touching any electrical device. Do not disassemble the fuse box or other devices. Decisions must be made on what you see. If in doubt, consult your supervisor.

Make note whether any fuse boxes or junction boxes are uncovered. Examine all wiring for frayed or bare spots, improper splicing, or rotted, worn, or inadequate insulation. Avoid all careless touching. When in doubt DON'T! If you see bare wire, have the owner call an electrician. Look for wires or cords in use in the cellar. Many work benches are lighted by an old lamp that was once in the parlor and now has a spliced or badly frayed cord or both. Be certain all switch boxes and outlets are in a tight, sound condition.

Make sure that the emergency switch for the oil burner is at the top of the cellar stairs, not on top of the unit.

If you find an electric clothes washer-clothes dryer combination in a dwelling, it should have a 240-volt circuit 30-ampere service connected to a separate fuse or circuit breaker. Washer-dryer combinations and other portable appliances in the entire house should be served by sufficiently heavy service. If either of these special lines is not available under the above-stated conditions, consult your supervisor.

An electric range needs a 50-ampere circuit, 240 volts. A dishwasher needs a 20-ampere, 120-volt circuit. A separate three-wire circuit must be installed for an electric water heater. Continue your inspection this way through the house. In the bathroom look for the usual items, but also check for dangerous items such as radios or plug-in portable electric heaters. Have them removed immediately. Such items have killed thousands of people either has a spliced or badly frayed cord or both. Be certain all switch boxes and outlets are in a tight, sound condition. Make sure that the emergency switch for the oil burner is at the top of the cellar stairs, not on top of the unit.

If you find an electric clothes washer-clothes dryer combination in a dwelling, it should have a 240-volt circuit 30-ampere service connected to a separate fuse or circuit breaker. Washer-dryer combinations and other portable appliances in the entire house should be served by sufficiently heavy service. If either of these special lines is not available under the above-stated conditions, consult your supervisor.

An electric range needs a 50-ampere circuit, 240 volts. A dishwasher needs a 20-ampere, 120-volt circuit. A separate three-wire circuit must be installed for an electric water heater. Continue your inspection this way through the because they touched them after getting out of the bathtub or shower while still wet or because the appliance fell into the water. Look for brass pull chains in bathroom lighting fixtures. If one exists, have owner attach a string to the end of it as a temporary precaution, then order it replaced with a wall switch as required by the electrical code.

To sum up, in broad terms, the housing inspector's investigation of specified electrical elements in a house is made to detect any obvious evidence of an insufficient power supply, to ensure the availability of adequate and safe lighting and electrical facilities, and to discover and correct any obvious hazard. Because electricity is a technical, complicated field, the housing inspector, when in doubt, should consult his supervisor. He cannot, however, close the case until appropriate corrective action has been taken on all such referrals.

XIII. Wattage Consumption of Electrical Appliances

(100 watts = approximately 1 ampere)

Appliance	Watts	Appliance	Watts
Air conditioner (central)	5,000	Radio	100
Air conditioner (window)	see name plate	Range	8,000 to 16,000
Blanket	150	Refrigerator	250
Blender	250	Roaster (large)	1,380
Chaffing Dish	600	Rotisserie	1,400
Clock	3	Sewing machine	75
Coffee Maker	600	Soldering iron	200
Deep fryer	1,320	Stereo hi-fi	300
Dishwasher	1,800	Sump pump	300
Egg boiler	250	Television	300
Electric shaver	10	Toaster	1,100
Fan	75	Vacuum cleaner	400
Food mixer	200	Waffle iron	660
Furnace (fuel fixed)	800	Washing machine	5,200
Frying pan	600	Water heater	2,500-4,500
Garbage disposer	900	Water pump	300
Griddle	1,300		
Grill	600		
Heater (radiant)	1,600		
Heating pad	50		
Hot-plate (2 burners)	1,650		
Humidifier	500		
Immersion heater	300		
Iron	1,000		
Ironer	1,650		
Lighting			
Bed lamp	40		
Ceiling light	100		
Decorative lights	80		
Dining light	150		
Dresser lamps	60		
Drop light	60		
Floor lamp	400		
Fluorescent	80		
Sun lamp	275		
Table lamp	100		

XIV. Motor Currents

Horsepower	Full load amperes			
	115 v	230 1-phase	230 2-phase	230 3-phase
1/4	5.8	2.9		
1/2	9.8	4.9	2.0	2.0
3/4	13.8	6.9	2.4	2.8
1	16.0	8.0	3.2	3.6

PLUMBING ELEMENTS OF A HOUSING INSPECTION

CONTENTS

	PAGE
I. Background Factors	1
II. Definitions	1
III. Main Features of an Indoor Plumbing System	3
IV. Elements of a Plumbing System	3

PLUMBING ELEMENTS OF A HOUSING INSPECTION

Plumbing may be defined as practice, materials, and fixtures used in the installation, maintenance, and alteration of all piping, fixtures, appliances, and appurtenances in connection with sanitary or storm drainage facilities, the venting system, and the public or private water supply systems. Plumbing does not include the trade of drilling water wells, installing water softening equipment, or the business of manufacturing or selling plumbing fixtures, appliances, equipment, or hardware. A plumbing system consists of three separate parts: an adequate potable water supply system; a safe, adequate drainage system; and ample fixtures and equipment.

I. Background Factors

The generalized inspector of housing is concerned with a safe water supply system, an adequate drainage system, and ample and proper fixtures and equipment. This chapter covers the major features of a residential plumbing system and the basic plumbing terms the inspector must know and understand to identify properly housing code violations involving plumbing and the more complicated defects that he will refer to the appropriate agencies.

II. Definitions

1. **Air Chambers** — Air Chambers are pressure absorbing devices that eliminate water hammer. They should be installed as close as possible to the valves or faucet and at the end of long runs of pipe.

2. **Air Gap (Drainage System)** — The unobstructed vertical distance through the free atmosphere between the outlet of a water pipe and the flood level rim of the receptacle into which it is discharging.

3. **Air Gap (Water Distribution System)** — The unobstructed vertical distance through the free atmosphere between the lowest opening from any pipe or faucet supplying water to a tank, plumbing fixture, or other device and the flood level rim of the receptacle.

4. **Air Lock** — An air lock is a bubble of air which restricts the flow of water in a pipe.

5. **Backflow** — Backflow is the flow of water or other liquids, mixtures, or substances into the distributing pipes of a potable water supply from any source or sources other than the intended source. Back siphonage is one type of backflow.

6. **Back Siphonage** — Back siphonage is the flowing back of used, contaminated, or polluted water from a plumbing fixture or vessel into a potable water supply due to a negative pressure in the pipe.

7. **Branch** — A branch is any part of the piping system other than the main, riser, or stack.

8. **Branch Vent** — A vent connecting one or more individual vents with a vent stack.

9. **Building Drain** — The building (house) drain is the part of the lowest piping of a drainage system that receives the discharge from soil, waste, or other drainage pipes inside the walls of the building (house) and conveys it to the building sewer beginning 3 feet outside the building wall.

10. **Cross Connection** — Any physical connection or arrangement between two otherwise separate piping systems, one of which contains potable water and the other either water of unknown or questionable safety or steam, gas, or chemical whereby there may be a flow from one system to the other, the direction of flow depending on the pressure differential between the two systems. (See Backflow and Back siphonage.)

11. **Disposal Field** — An area containing a series of one or more trenches lined with coarse aggregate and conveying the effluent from the septic tank through vitrified clay pipe or

perforated, non-metallic pipe, laid in such a manner that the flow will be distributed with reasonable uniformity into natural soil.

12 **Drain** — A drain is any pipe that carries waste water or water-borne waste in a building (house) drainage system.

13 **Flood Level Rim** — The top edge of a receptacle from which water overflows.

14 **Flushometer Valve** — A device that discharges a predetermined quantity of water to fixtures for flushing purposes and is closed by direct water pressures.

15 **Flush Valve** — A device located at the bottom of the tank for flushing water closets and similar fixtures.

16 **Grease Trap** — See Interceptor

17 **Hot Water** — Hot water means potable water that is heated to at least 120°F and used for cooking, cleaning, washing dishes, and bathing.

18 **Insanitary** — Contrary to sanitary principles — injurious to health.

19 **Interceptor** — A device designed and installed so as to separate and retain deleterious, hazardous, or undesirable matter from normal wastes and permit normal sewage or liquid wastes to discharge into the drainage system by gravity.

20 **Leader** — An exterior drainage pipe for conveying storm water from roof or gutter drains to the building storm drain, combined building sewer, or other means of disposal.

21 **Main Vent** — The principal artery of the venting system, to which vent branches may be connected.

22 **Main Sewer** — See Public Sewer.

23 **Pneumatic** — The word pertains to devices making use of compressed air as in pressure tanks boosted by pumps.

24 **Potable Water** — Water having no impurities present in amounts sufficient to cause disease or harmful physiological effects and conforming in its bacteriological and chemical quality to the requirements of the Public Health Service drinking water standards or meeting the regulations of the public health authority having jurisdiction.

25 **P & T (Pressure and Temperature) Relief Valve** — A safety valve installed on a hot water storage tank to limit temperature and pressure of the water.

26 **P Trap** — A trap with a vertical inlet and a horizontal outlet.

27 **Public Sewer** — A common sewer directly controlled by public authority.

28 **Relief Vent** — An auxiliary vent that permits additional circulation of air in or between drainage and vent systems.

29 **Septic Tank** — A watertight receptacle that receives the discharge of a building's sanitary drain system or part thereof and is designed and constructed so as to separate solid from the liquid, digest organic matter through a period of detention, and allow the liquids to discharge into the soil outside of the tank through a system of open-joint or perforated piping, or through a seepage pit.

30 **Sewerage System** — A sewerage system comprises all piping, appurtenances, and treatment facilities used for the collection and disposal of sewage, except plumbing inside and in connection with buildings served, and the building drain.

31 **Soil Pipe** — The pipe that directs the sewage of a house to the receiving sewer, building drain, or building sewer.

32 **Soil Stack** — The vertical piping that terminates in a roof vent and carries off the vapors of a plumbing system.

33 **Stack Vent** — An extension of a solid or waste stack above the highest horizontal drain connected to the stack. Sometimes called a waste vent or a soil vent.

34 **Storm Sewer** — A sewer used for conveying rain water, surface water, condensate, cooling water, or similar liquid waste.

35 **Trap** – A trap is a fitting or device that provides a liquid seal to prevent the emission of sewer gases without materially affecting the flow of sewage or waste water through it.

36 **Vacuum Breaker** – A device to prevent backflow (back siphonage) by means of an opening through which air may be drawn to relieve negative pressure (vacuum).

37 **Vent Stack** – The vertical vent pipe installed to provide air circulation to and from the drainage system and that extends through one or more stories.

38 **Water Hammer** – The loud thump of water in a pipe when a valve or faucet is suddenly closed.

39 **Water Service Pipe** – The pipe from the water main or other sources of potable water supply to the water-distributing system of the building served.

40 **Water Supply System** – The water supply system consists of the water service pipe, the water-distributing pipes, the necessary connecting pipes, fittings, control valves, and all appurtenances in or adjacent to the building or premises.

41 **Wet Vent** – A vent that receives the discharge of waste other than from water closets.

42 **Yoke Vent** – A pipe connecting upward from a soil or waste stack to a vent stack for the purpose of preventing pressure changes in the stacks.

III. Main Features of an Indoor Plumbing System

The primary functions of the plumbing system within the house are as follows:

1 To bring an adequate and potable supply of hot and cold water to the users of the dwelling.

2 To drain all waste water and sewage discharged from these fixtures into the public sewer, or private disposal system.

It is, therefore, very important that the housing inspector familiarize himself fully with all elements of these systems so that he may recognize inadequacies of the structure's plumbing as well as other code violations. In order to aid the inspector in understanding the plumbing system, a series of drawings and diagrams has been included at the end of this chapter.

IV. Elements of a Plumbing System

A Supply System

1 Water Service: The piping of a house service line should be as short as possible. Elbows and bends should be kept to a minimum since these reduce the pressure and therefore the supply of water to fixtures in the house.

The house service line should also be protected from freezing. The burying of the line under 4 feet of soil is a commonly accepted depth to prevent freezing. This depth varies, however, across the country from north to south. The local or state plumbing code should be consulted for the recommended depth in your area of the country.

A typical house service installation is pictured in Figure 1.

The materials used for a house service may be copper, cast iron, steel or wrought iron. The connections used should be compatible with the type of pipe used.

a **Corporation stop** – The corporation stop is connected to the water main. This connection is usually made of brass and can be connected to the main by use of a special tool without shutting off the municipal supply. The valve incorporated in the corporation stop permits the pressure to be maintained in the main while the service to the building is completed.

b **Curb stop** – The curb stop is a similar valve used to isolate the building from the main for repairs, nonpayment of water bills, or flooded basements.

Since the corporation stop is usually under the street and would necessitate breaking the pavement to reach the valve, the curb stop is used as the isolation valve.

c **Curb stop box** – The curb stop box is an access box to the curb stop for opening and closing the valve. A long-handled wrench is used to reach the valve.

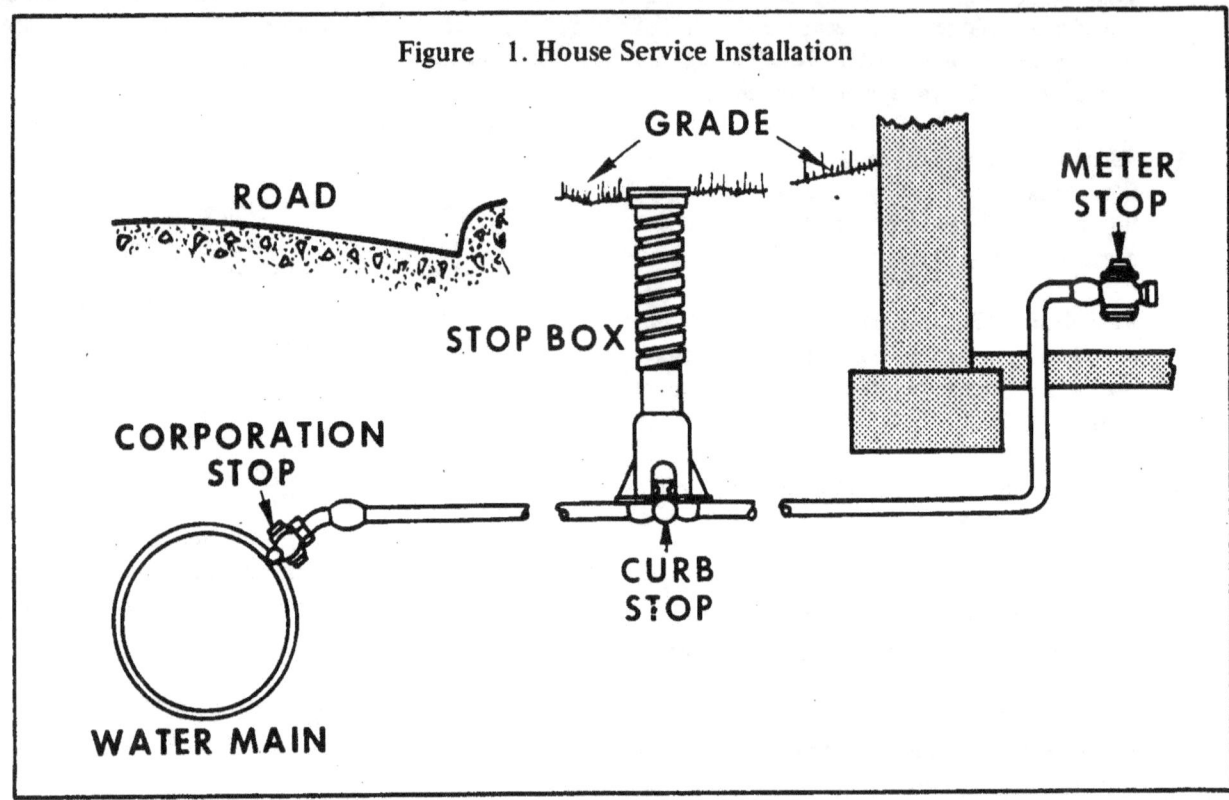

Figure 1. House Service Installation

d **Meter stop** — The meter stop is a valve placed on the street side of the water meter to isolate the meter for installation or maintenance. Many codes require a gate valve on the house side of the meter to shut off water for house plumbing repairs. The curb and meter stops are not to be used frequently and can be ruined in a short time if used very frequently.

e **Water meter** — The water meter is a device used to measure the amount of water used in the house. It is usually the property of the city and is a very delicate instrument that should not be abused.

Since the electric system is usually grounded to the water line, a grounding loop-device should be installed around the meter. Many meters come with a yoke that maintains electrical continuity even though the meter is removed.

2 **Hot and Cold Water Main Lines:** The hot and cold water main lines are usually hung from the basement ceiling and are attached to the water meter and hot-water tank on one side and the fixture supply risers on the other.

These pipes should be installed in a neat manner and should be supported by pipe hangers or straps of sufficient strength and number to prevent sagging.

Hot and cold water lines should be approximately 6 inches apart unless the hot water line is insulated. This is to insure that the cold water line does not pick up heat from the hot water line.

The supply mains should have a drain valve or stop and waste valve in order to remove water from the system for repairs. These valves should be on the low end of the line or on the end of each fixture riser.

a **The fixture risers** start at the basement main and rise vertically to the fixtures on the upper floors. In a one-family dwelling, riser branches will usually proceed from the main riser to each fixture grouping. In any event the fixture risers should not depend on the branch risers for support but should be supported with a pipe bracket.

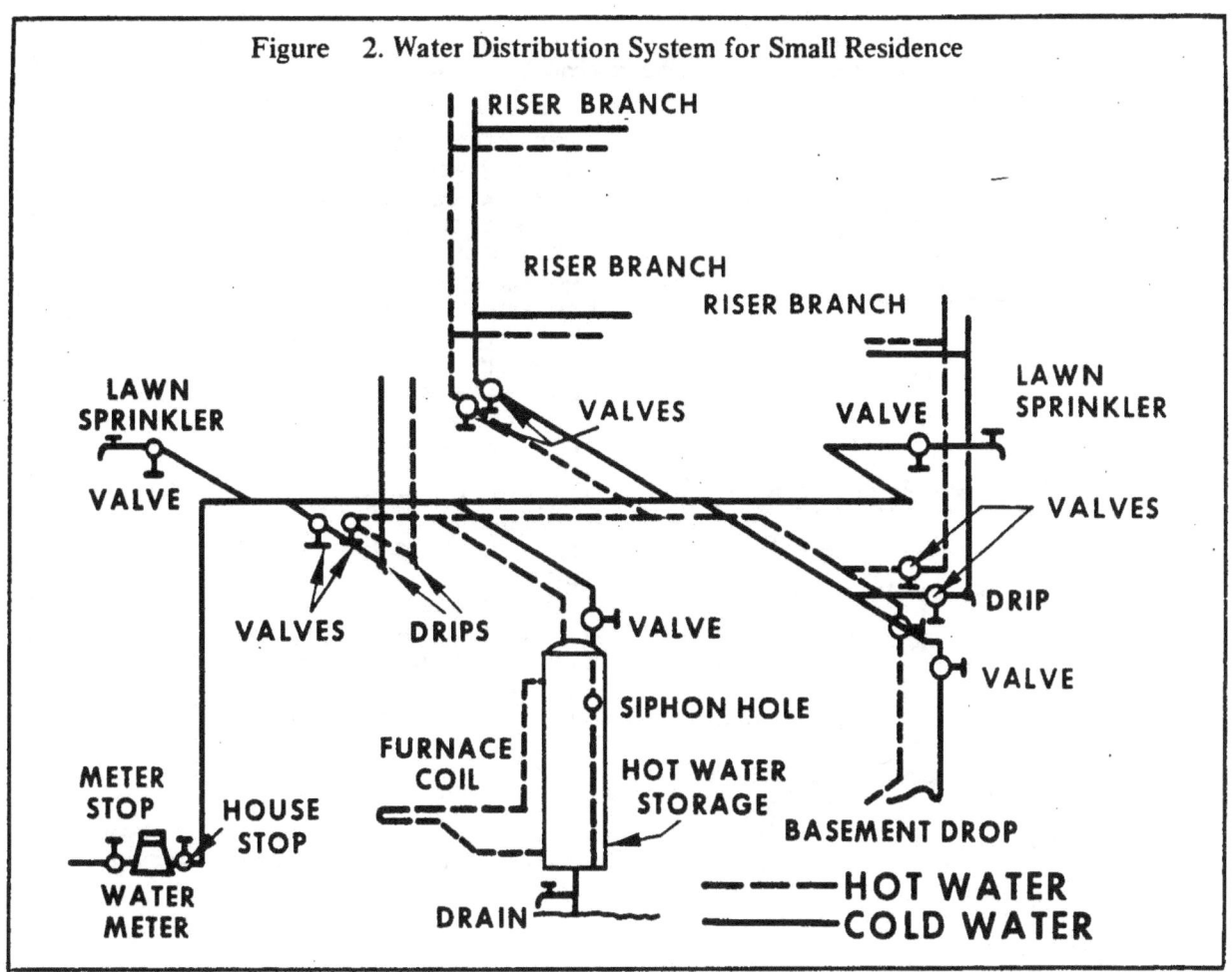

Figure 2. Water Distribution System for Small Residence

b   Each fixture is then connected to the branch riser by a separate line. The last fixture on a line is usually connected directly to the branch riser. Figure 2 is a diagram of a typical single-family-residence water supply system.

3   **Hot Water Heaters:** Hot water heaters are usually powered by electricity, fuel oil, gas, or in rare cases, coal or wood. They consist of a space for heating the water and a storage tank for providing hot water over a limited period of time.

All hot water heaters should be fitted with a temperature-pressure relief valve no matter what fuel is used.

This valve will operate when either the temperature or the pressure becomes too high due to an interruption of the water supply or a faulty thermostat.

Figure 3 shows the correct installation of a hot water heater.

4   **Pipe Sizes:** The size of basement mains and risers depends on the number of fixtures supplied. However, a ¾ inch pipe is usually the minimum size used. This allows for deposits on the pipe due to hardness in the water and will usually give satisfactory volume and pressure.

B   **Drainage System**

The water supply brought into the house and used is discharged through the drainage system. This system is either a sanitary drainage system carrying just interior waste water or a combined system carrying interior waste and roof runoff. The sanitary system will be discussed first.

1   **Sanitary Drainage System:** The proper sizing of the sanitary drain or house drain depends on the number of fixtures it serves. The usual

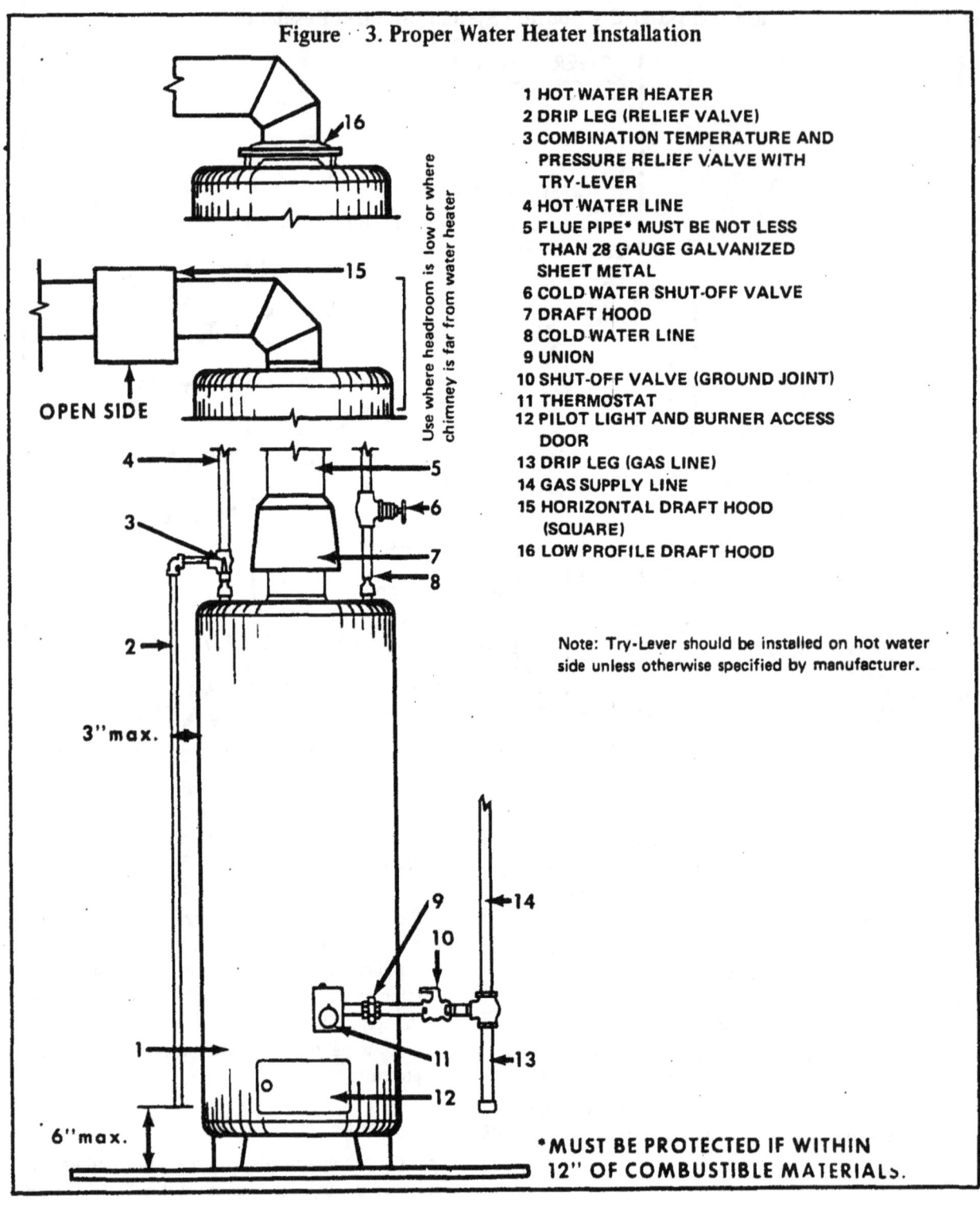

Figure 3. Proper Water Heater Installation

minimum size is 6 inches in diameter. The materials used are usually cast iron, vitrified clay, plastic, and in rare cases, lead. For proper flow in the drain the pipe should be sized so that it flows approximately one-half full. This ensures proper scouring action so that the solids contained in the waste will not be deposited in the pipe.

a **Sizing of house drain** — The Uniform Plumbing Code Committee has developed a method of sizing of house drains in terms of "fixture units." One "fixture unit" equals approximately 7½ gallons of water per minute. This is the surge flow-rate of water discharged from a wash basin in 1 minute. All other fixtures have been related to this unit.

A table fixture unit values is shown in Table 1.

The maximum number of fixture units attached to a sanitary drain is shown in Table 2.

b **Grade of house drain** — A house drain or building sewer should be sloped toward the sewer to ensure scouring of the drain. Figure 4 shows the results of proper and improper pitch of a house drain.

The usual pitch of a house or building sewer is ¼ inch fall in 1 foot of length.

Table 1. FIXTURE UNIT VALUES

Fixture	Units
Lavatory/wash basin	1
Kitchen sink	2
Bathtub	2
Laundry tub	2
Combination fixture	3
Urinal	5
Shower bath	2
Floor drain	1
Slop sinks	3
Water closet	6
One bathroom group (water closet, lavatory, bathtub, and shower; or water closet, lavatory, and shower)	8
180 square feet of roof drained	1

c **House drain installation** — A typical house drain installation is shown in Figure 5. Typical branch connections to the main are shown in Figure 6.

d **Fixture and branch drains** — A branch drain is a waste pipe that collects the waste from two or more fixtures and conveys it to the building or house sewer. It is sized in the same way as the house sewer, taking into account that all water closets must have a minimum 3-inch diameter drain, and

Table 2. SANITARY DRAIN SIZES

Maximum number of fixture units

Diameter of pipe, in.	Slope 1/8"/Ft.	Slope 1/4"/Ft.	Slope 1/2"/Ft.
1¼	1	1	1
1½	2	2	3
2	5	6	8
3	15	18	21
4	84	96	114
6	300	450	600
8	990	1,392	2,220
12	3,084	4,320	6,912

*A water closet must enter a 3 inch diameter drain and no more than 2 water closets may enter a 3 inch horizontal branch.

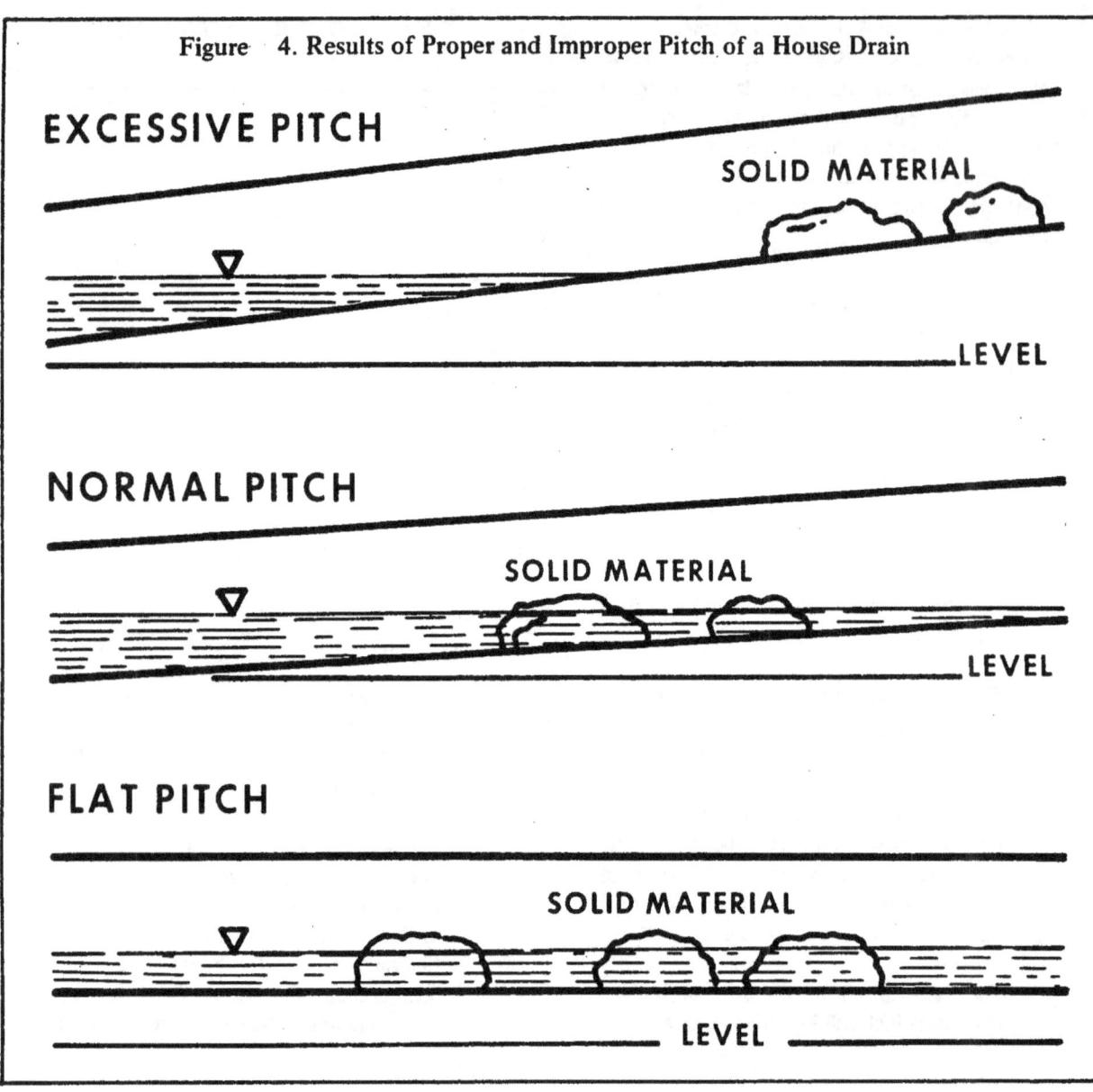

Figure 4. Results of Proper and Improper Pitch of a House Drain

only two water closets may connect into one 3-inch drain.

All branch drains must join the house drain with a "Y"-type fitting as shown in Figure 6. The same is true for fixture drains joining branch drains.

The "Y" fitting is used to eliminate, as much as possible, the deposit of solids in or near the connection. A build-up of these solids will cause a blockage in the drain.

The recommended minimum size of fixture drain is shown in Table 3.

e Traps — A plumbing trap is a device used in a waste system to prevent the passage of sewer gas into the structure and yet not hinder the fixture's discharge to any great extent. All fixtures connected to a household plumbing system should have a trap installed in the line.

Table 3. MINIMUM FIXTURE SERVICE

Fixture	Supply line, in.	Vent line, in.	Drain line, in.
Bathtub	½	1½	1½-2
Kitchen sink	½	1½	1½
Lavatory	3/8	1¼	1¼
Laundry sink	½	1½	1½
Shower	½	2	2
Water closet (tank)	3/8	3	3

Figure 5. Typical House Drain Installation

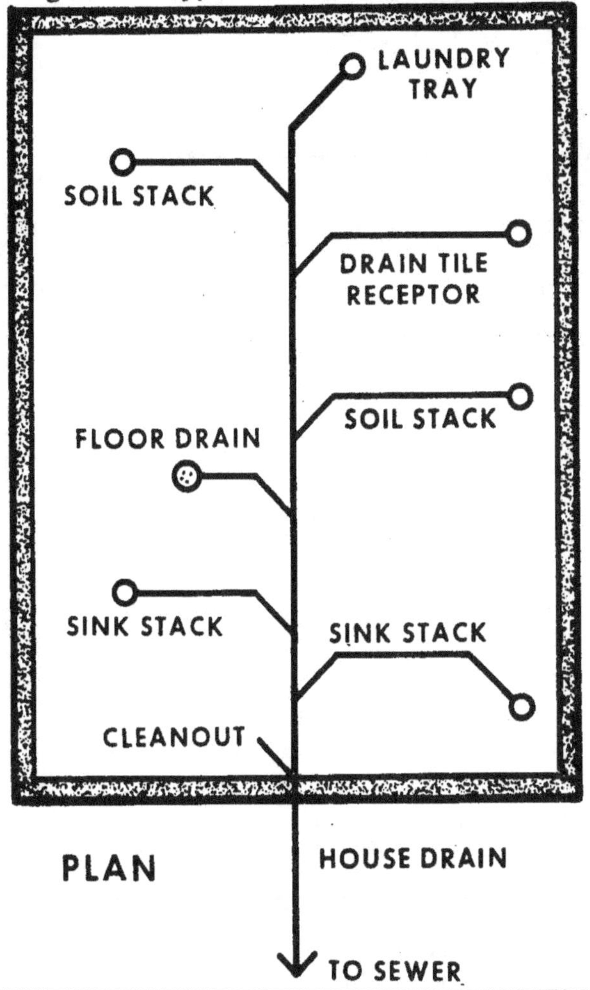

LAUNDRY TRAY
SOIL STACK
DRAIN TILE RECEPTOR
SOIL STACK
FLOOR DRAIN
SINK STACK
SINK STACK
CLEANOUT
PLAN
HOUSE DRAIN
TO SEWER

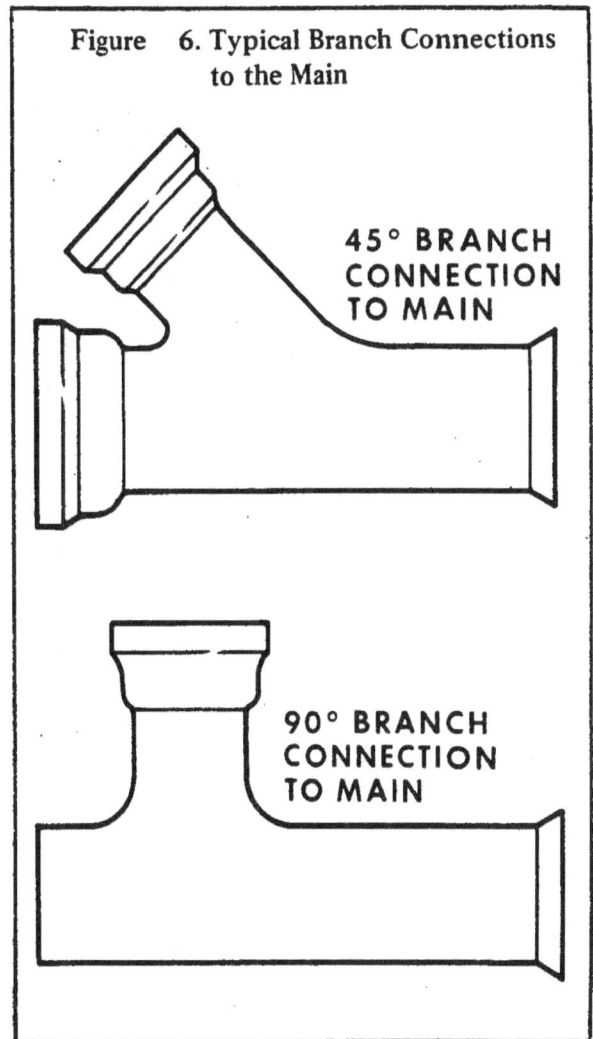

Figure 6. Typical Branch Connections to the Main

45° BRANCH CONNECTION TO MAIN
90° BRANCH CONNECTION TO MAIN

The effect of sewer gases on the human body are known; many are extremely harmful. Additionally, certain sewer gases are explosive. A trap will prevent these gases from passing into the structure.

1) "P" trap – The most common trap found today is the "P" trap. Figure 6-7 is a drawing of a "P" trap.

   The depth of the seal in a trap is usually 2 inches. A deep seal trap has a 4-inch seal.

   As was mentioned earlier, the purpose of a trap is to seal out sewer gases from the structure. Since a plumbing system is subject to wide variations in flow, and this flow originates in many different sections of the system, there is a wide variation in pressures in the waste lines. These pressure differences tend to destroy the water seal in the trap.

To counteract this problem mechanical traps were introduced. It has been found, however, that the corrosive liquids flowing in the system corrode or jam these mechanical traps. It is for this reason that most plumbing codes prohibit mechanical traps.

There are many manufacturers of traps, and all have varied the design somewhat. Figures 8 and 9 show various types of "P" traps. The "P" trap is usually found in lavatories, sinks, urinals, drinking fountains, showers, and other installations that do not discharge a great deal of water.

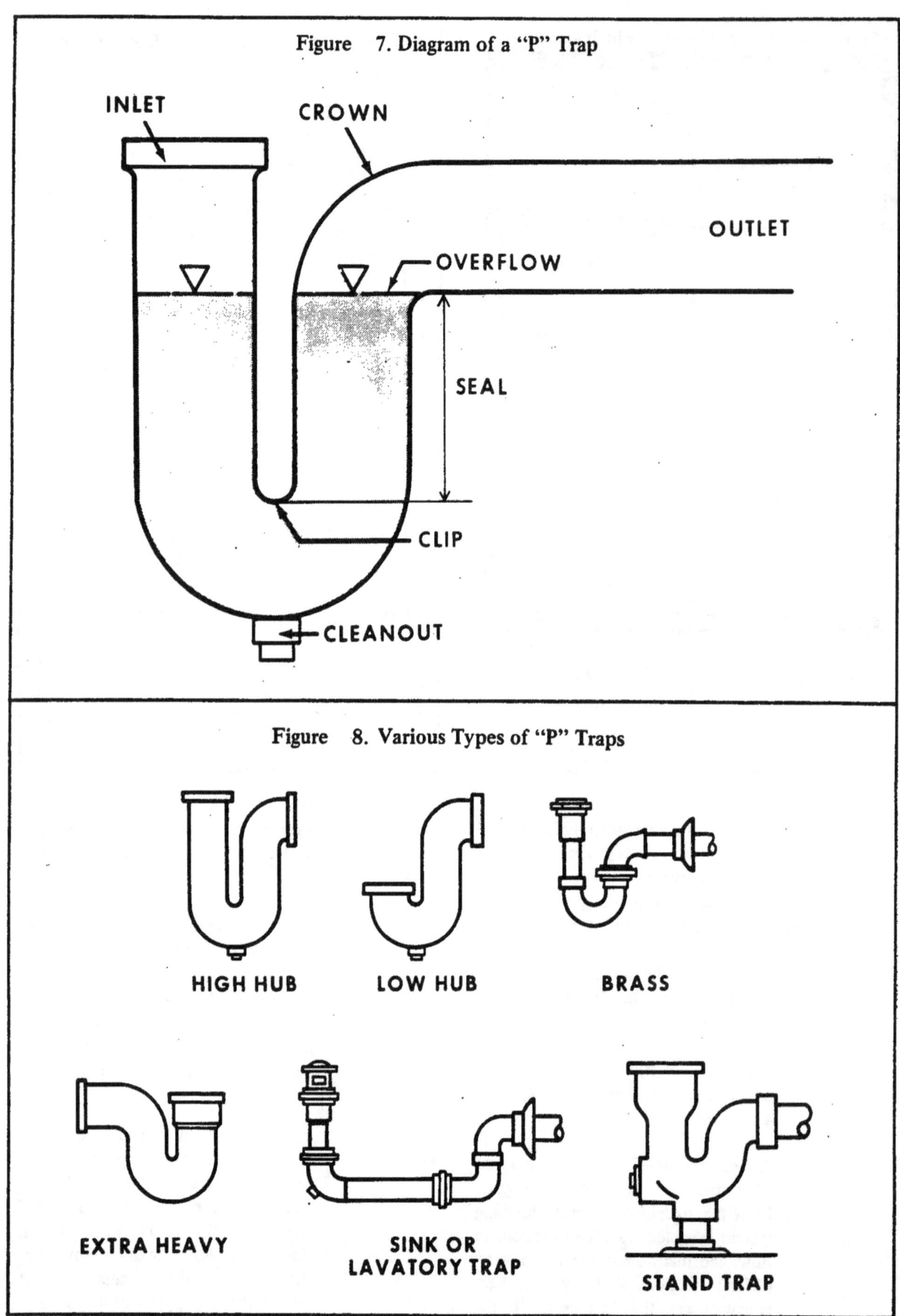

Figure 7. Diagram of a "P" Trap

Figure 8. Various Types of "P" Traps

2) Drum trap — The drum trap is another water seal-type trap. They are usually used in the 4- x 5-inch or 4- x 8-inch sizes. These traps have a greater sealing capacity than the "P" trap and pass large amounts of water quickly. Figure 10 shows a drum trap.

Drum traps are commonly connected to bathtubs, foot baths, sitz baths, and modified shower baths. Figure 11 shows a drum trap connected to a bathtub and shower.

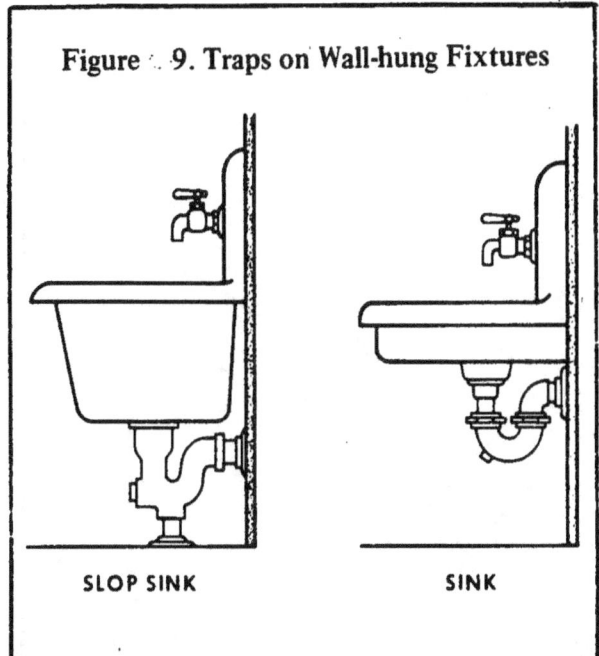

Figure 9. Traps on Wall-hung Fixtures

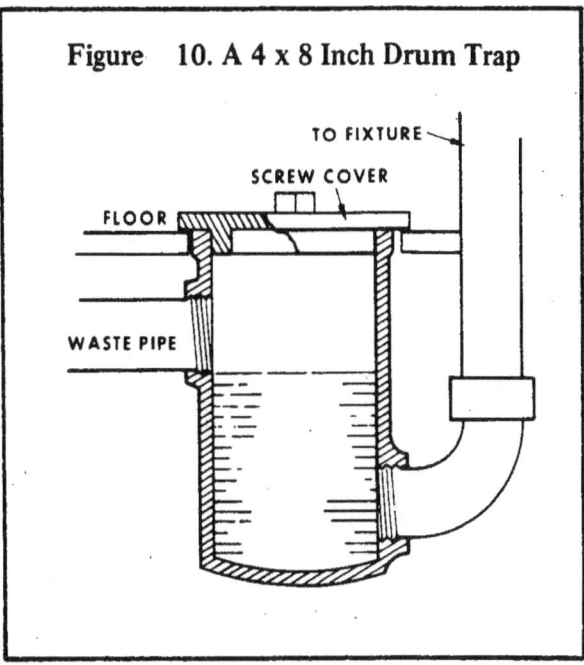

Figure 10. A 4 x 8 Inch Drum Trap

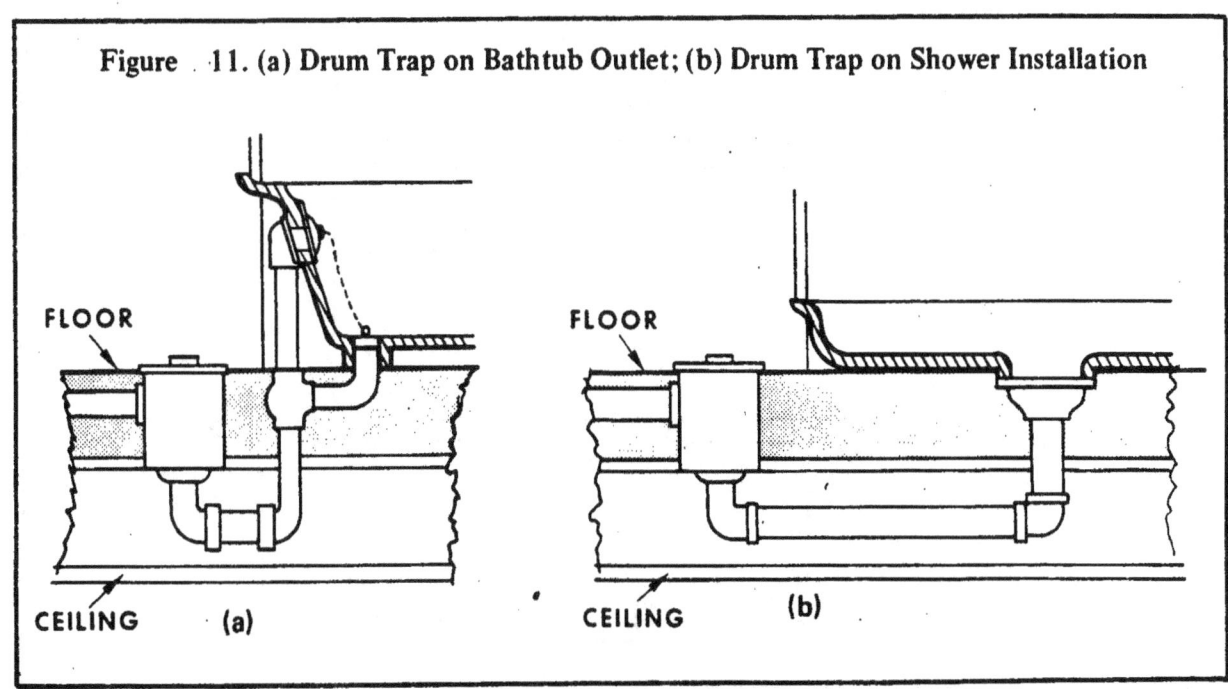

Figure 11. (a) Drum Trap on Bathtub Outlet; (b) Drum Trap on Shower Installation

3) Objectionable traps — The "S" trap and the ¾ "S" trap should not be used in plumbing installations. They are almost impossible to ventilate properly, and the ¾ "S" trap forms a perfect siphon.

The bag trap, an extreme form of "S" trap, is seldom found. Figure 12 shows these types of "S" traps.

Figure 13 shows one type of mechanically sealed trap. Any trap that depends on a moving part for its effectiveness is usually inadequate and has been prohibited by the local plumbing codes.

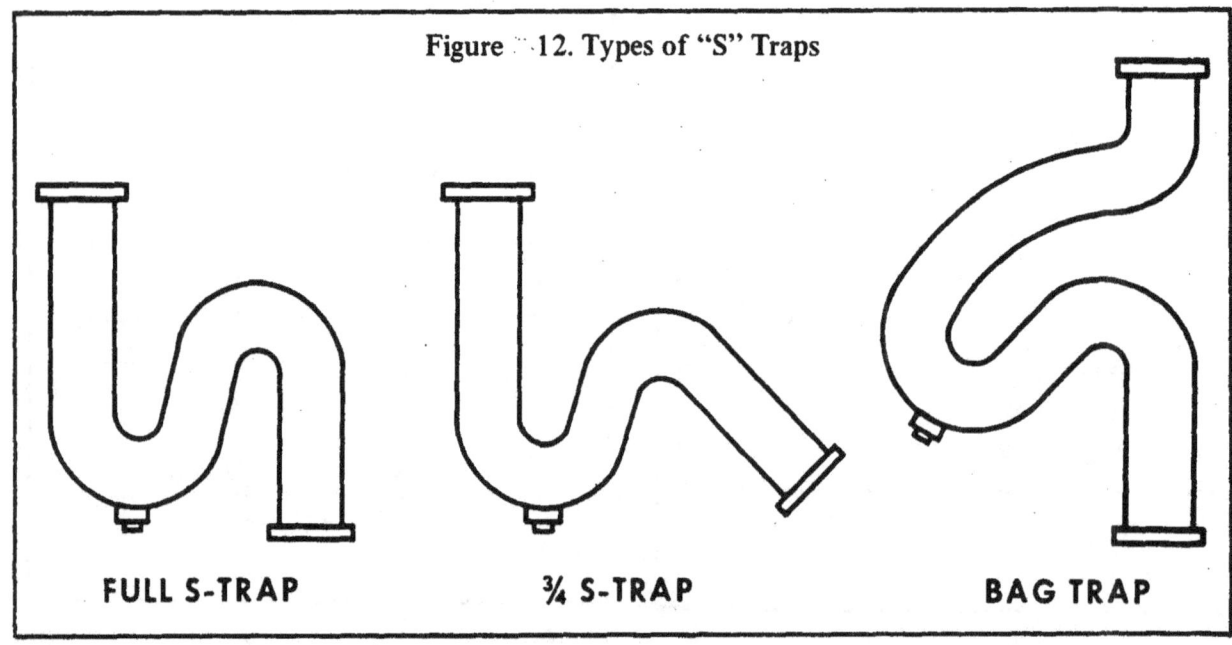

Figure 12. Types of "S" Traps

FULL S-TRAP   ¾ S-TRAP   BAG TRAP

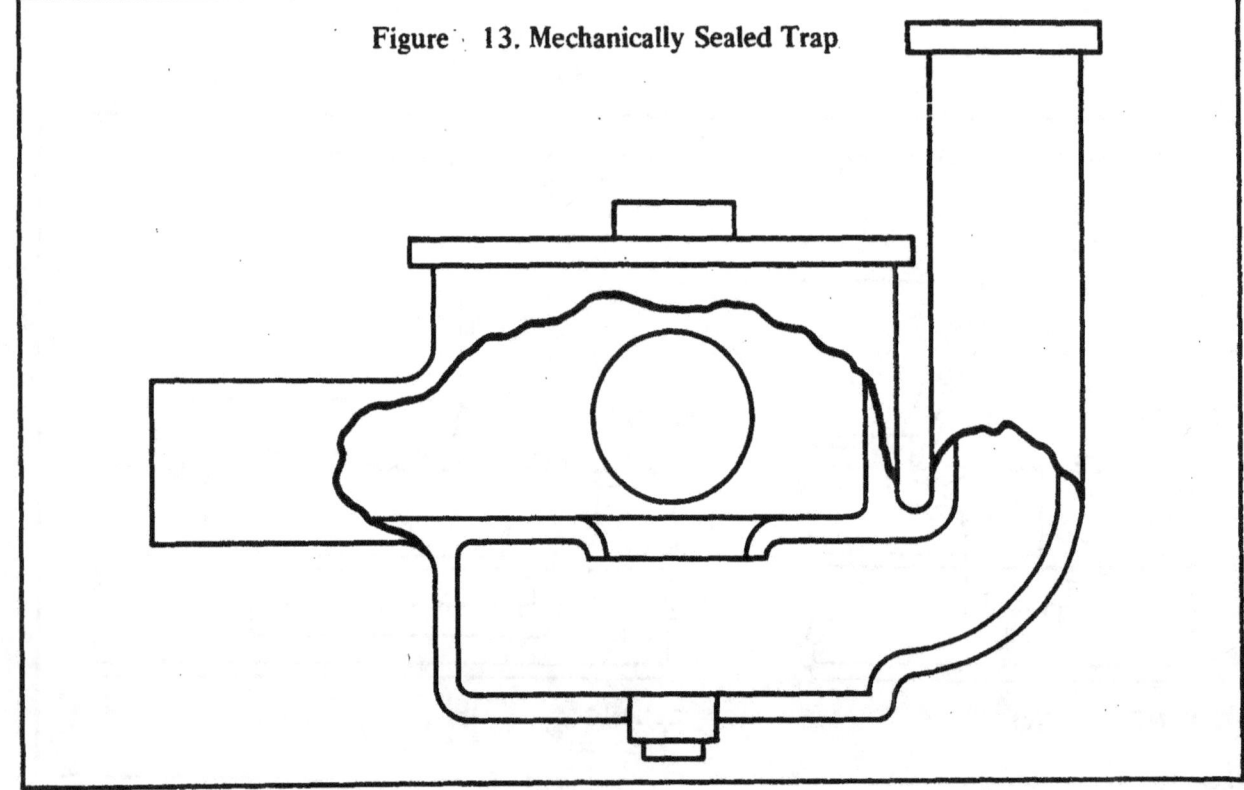

Figure 13. Mechanically Sealed Trap

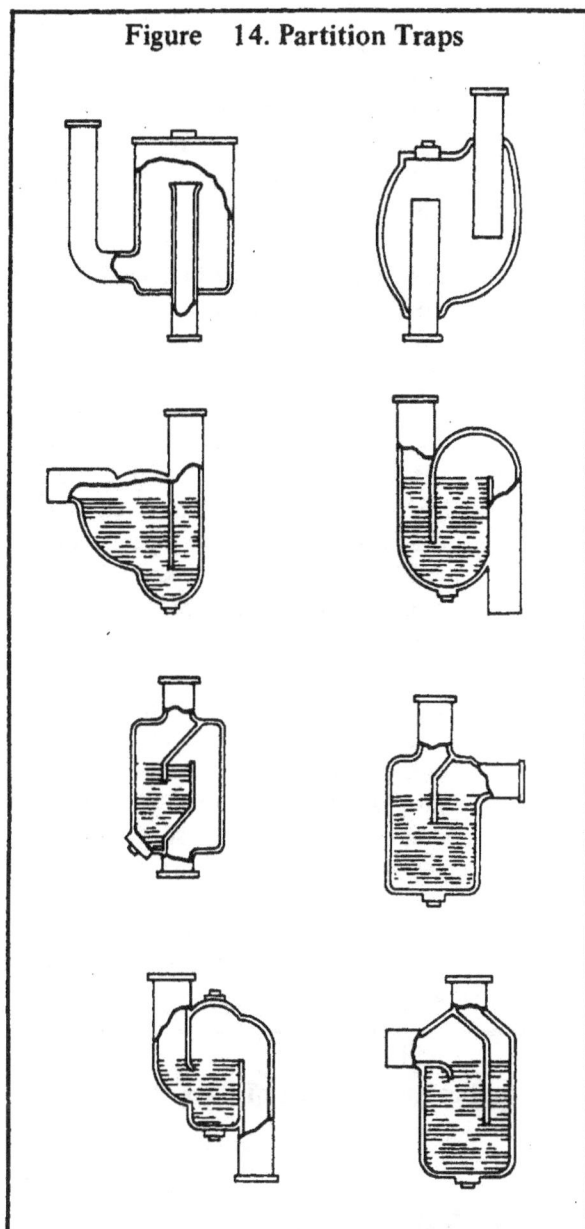

Figure 14. Partition Traps

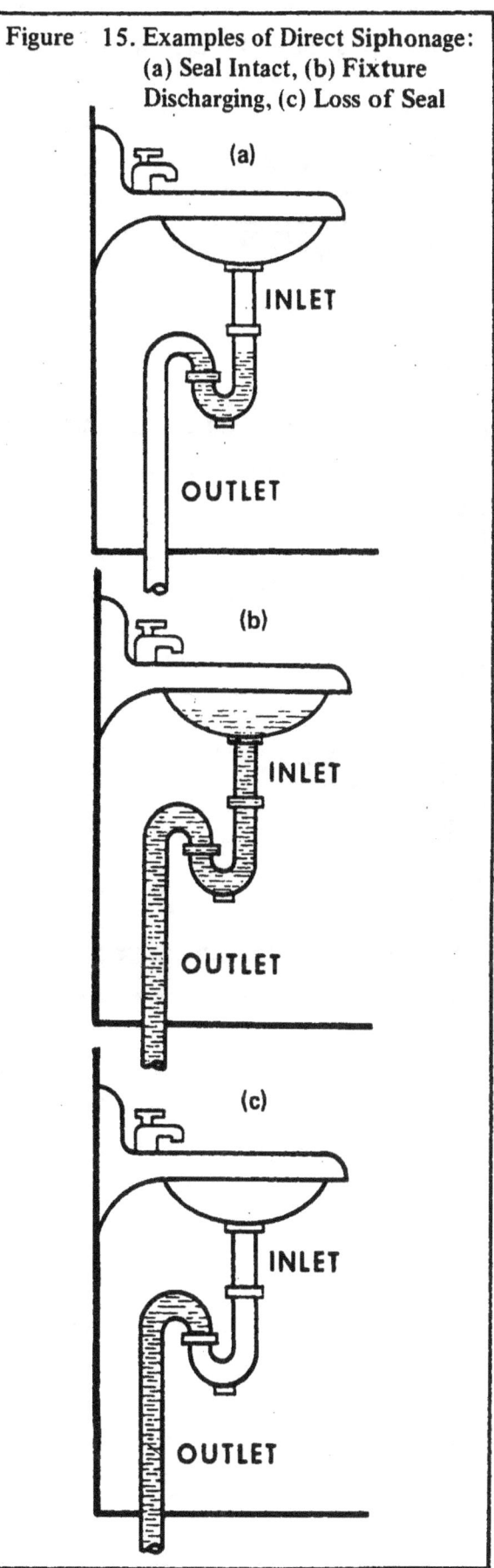

Figure 15. Examples of Direct Siphonage: (a) Seal Intact, (b) Fixture Discharging, (c) Loss of Seal

Figure 14 shows various types of internal partition traps. These traps work, but their design usually results in their being higher priced than the "P" or drum traps.

It should be remembered that traps are used only to prevent the escape of sewer gas into the structure. They do not compensate for pressure variations. Only proper venting will eliminate pressure problems.

f **Ventilation** — A plumbing system is ventilated to prevent trap seal loss, material deterioration, and flow retardation.

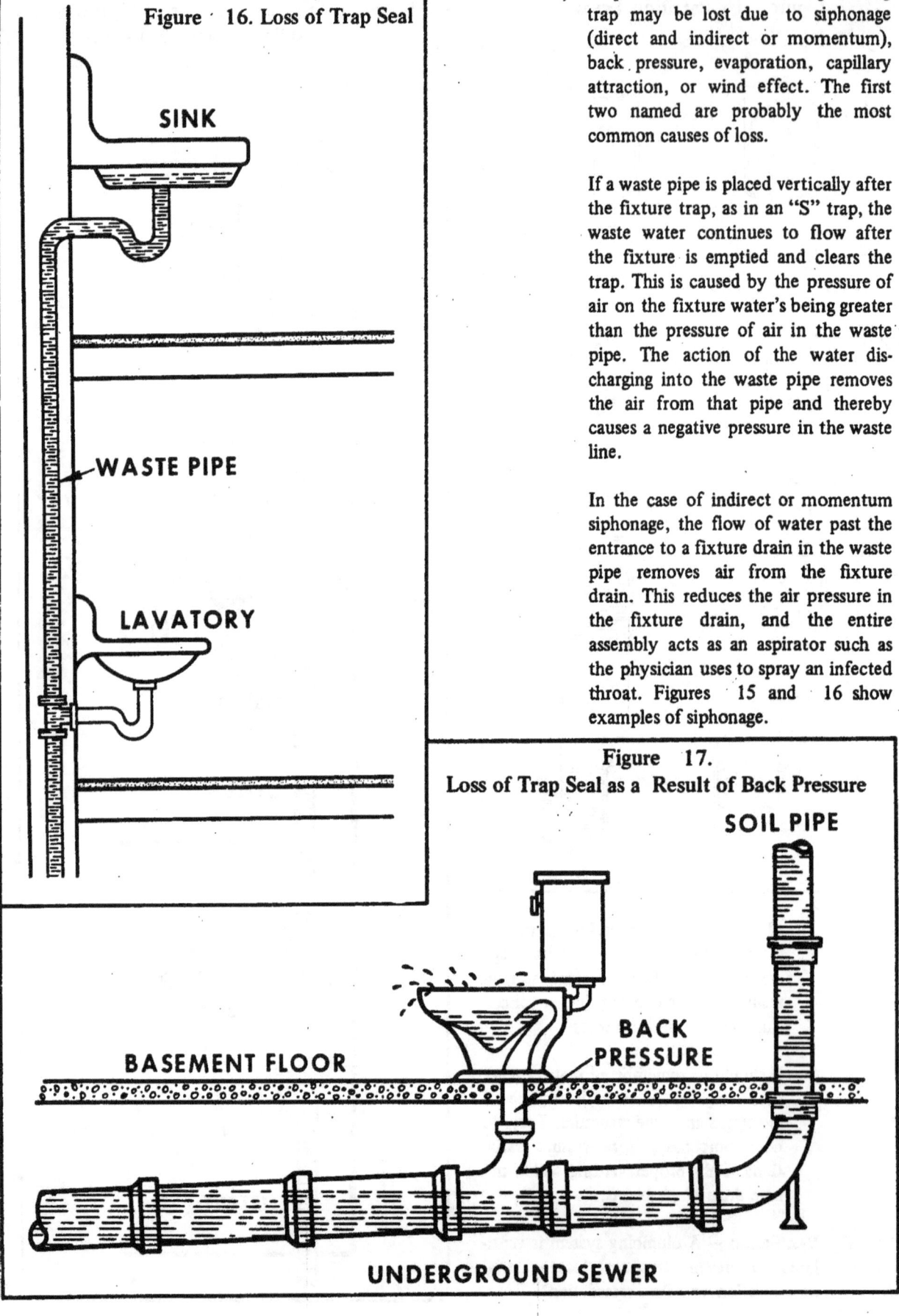

Figure 16. Loss of Trap Seal

Figure 17. Loss of Trap Seal as a Result of Back Pressure

1) Trap seal loss — The seal in a plumbing trap may be lost due to siphonage (direct and indirect or momentum), back pressure, evaporation, capillary attraction, or wind effect. The first two named are probably the most common causes of loss.

If a waste pipe is placed vertically after the fixture trap, as in an "S" trap, the waste water continues to flow after the fixture is emptied and clears the trap. This is caused by the pressure of air on the fixture water's being greater than the pressure of air in the waste pipe. The action of the water discharging into the waste pipe removes the air from that pipe and thereby causes a negative pressure in the waste line.

In the case of indirect or momentum siphonage, the flow of water past the entrance to a fixture drain in the waste pipe removes air from the fixture drain. This reduces the air pressure in the fixture drain, and the entire assembly acts as an aspirator such as the physician uses to spray an infected throat. Figures 15 and 16 show examples of siphonage.

2) Back pressure — The flow of water in a soil pipe varies according to the fixtures being used. A lavatory gives a small flow and a water closet a large flow. Small flows tend to cling to the sides of the pipe, but large ones form a slug of waste as they drop. As this slug of water falls down the pipe the air in front of it becomes pressurized. As the pressure builds it seeks an escape point. This point is either a vent or a fixture outlet. If the vent is plugged or there is no vent, the only escape for this air is the fixture outlet. The air pressure forces the trap seal up the pipe into the fixture. If the pressure is great enough the seal is blown out of the fixture entirely. Figures 17 and 18 illustrate this type of problem.

3) Vent sizing — Vent pipe installation is similar to that of soil and waste pipe. The same fixture unit criteria are used. Table 3 shows minimum vent pipe sizes.

Vent pipes of less than 1¼ inches in diameter should not be used. Vents smaller than this diameter tend to clog and do not perform their function.

4) Individual fixture ventilation — Figure 19 shows a typical installation of a wall-hung plumbing unit. This type of ventilation is generally used for sinks, lavatories, drinking fountains, and so forth.

Figure 20 shows a typical installation of a bathtub or shower ventilation system.

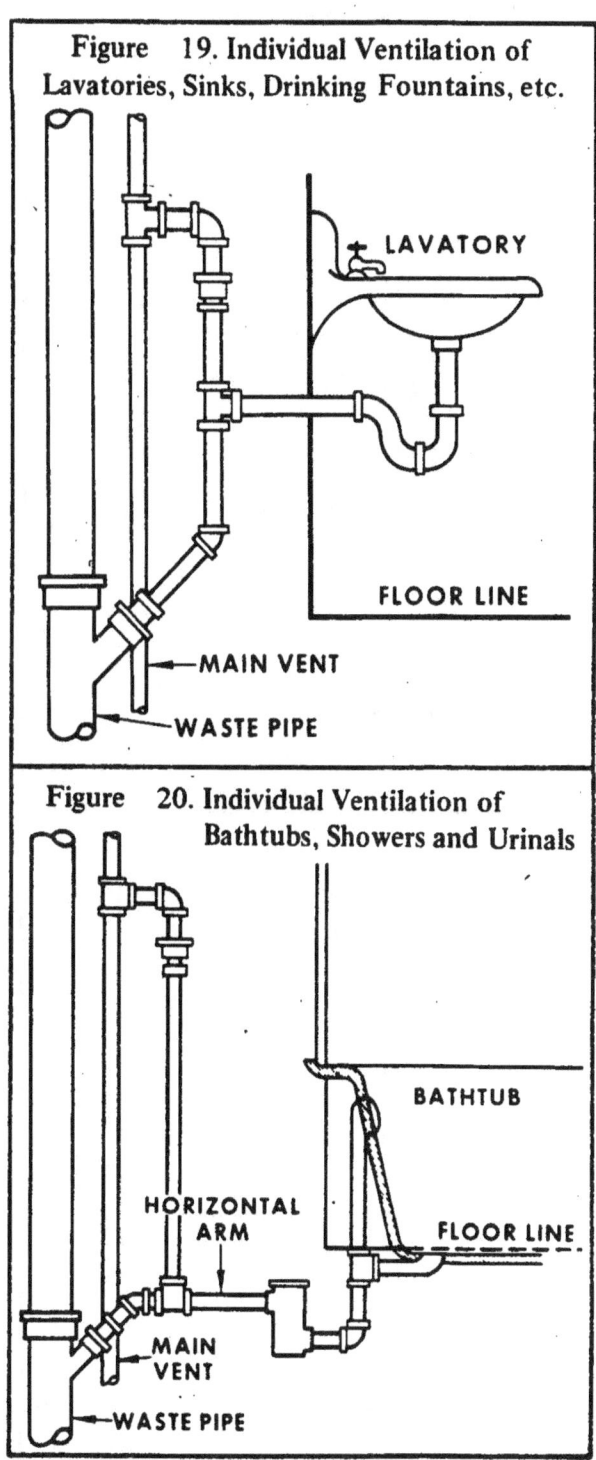

Figure 19. Individual Ventilation of Lavatories, Sinks, Drinking Fountains, etc.

Figure 20. Individual Ventilation of Bathtubs, Showers and Urinals

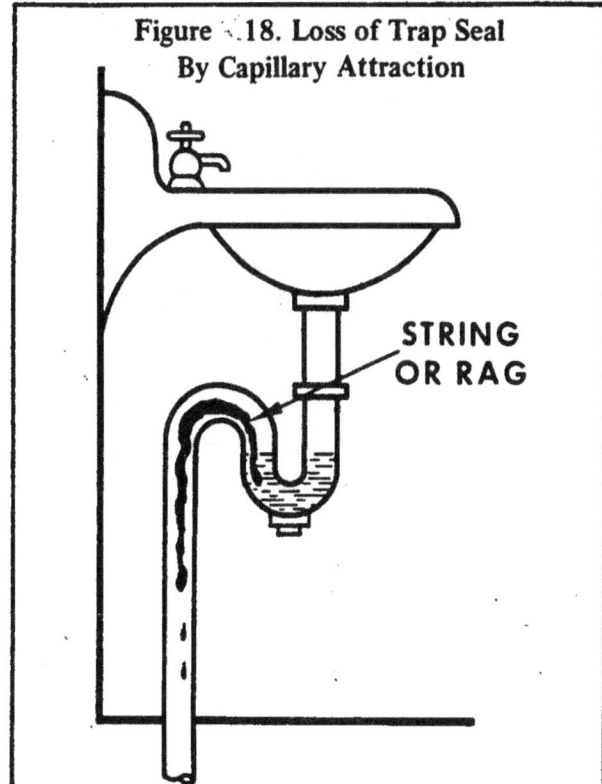

Figure 18. Loss of Trap Seal By Capillary Attraction

Figure 21 shows the proper vent connection for a water closet or slop sink. The water closet can be either a tank type or a flushometer valve type.

5) Unit venting — Figures 22 to 24 picture a back-to-back ventilation system for various common plumbing fixtures. The unit venting system is commonly used in apartment buildings. This type of system saves a great deal of money and space when fixtures are placed back to back in separate apartments.

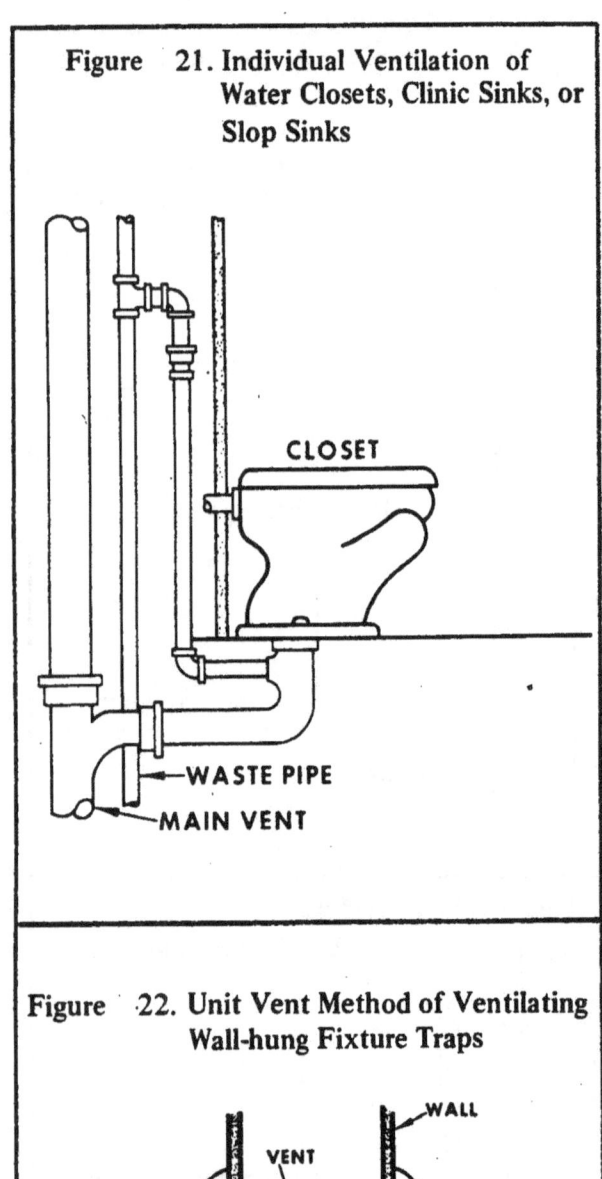

Figure 21. Individual Ventilation of Water Closets, Clinic Sinks, or Slop Sinks

Figure 22. Unit Vent Method of Ventilating Wall-hung Fixture Traps

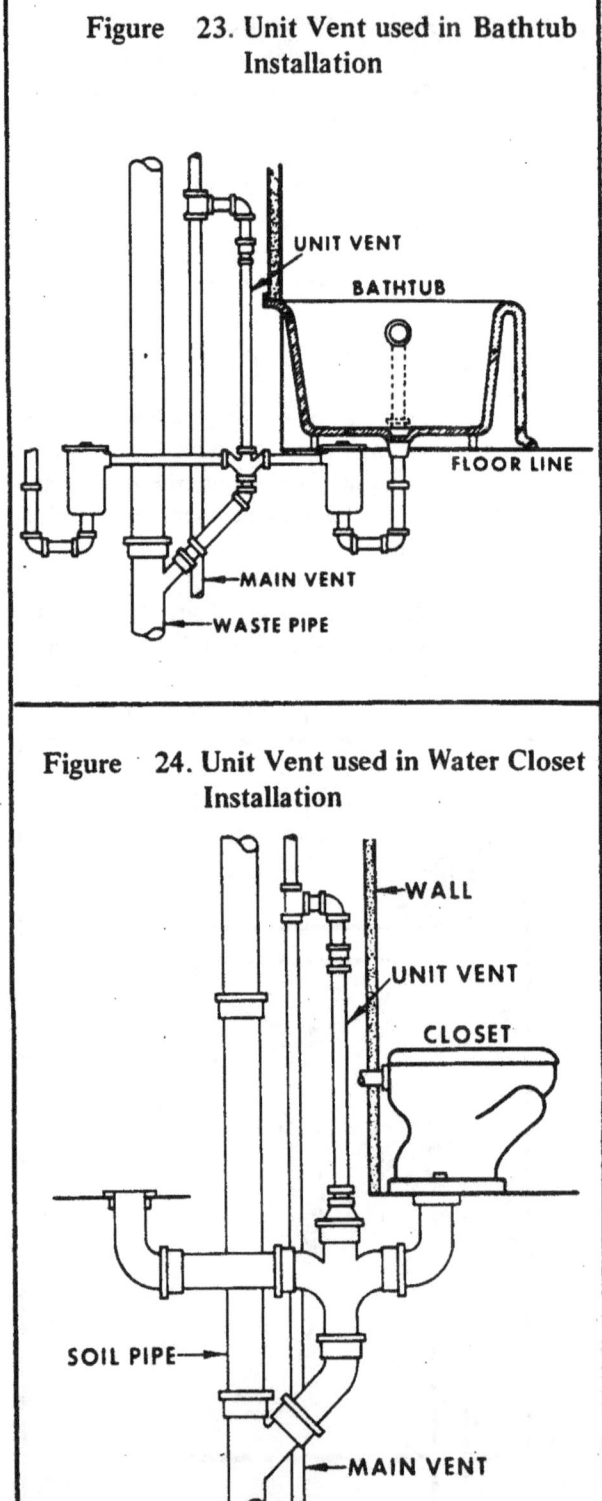

Figure 23. Unit Vent used in Bathtub Installation

Figure 24. Unit Vent used in Water Closet Installation

Figure 25 shows a double combination "Y" used for joining the fixtures to the common soil pipe. The deflectors are to prevent waste from one fixture flowing back up into the waste in the attached fixture on the other side of the wall.

6) Wet venting — Wet venting of a plumbing system is common in household bathroom fixture grouping. It is exactly what the name implies: the vent pipe is used as a waste line. Figure 26 shows a typical wet-vent installation in a home.

7) Total drainage system — Up to now we have talked about the drain, soil waste, and vent systems of a plumbing system separately. For a working system, however, they must all be connected. Figures 27 through 32 show some typical drainage systems that are found in homes and small apartment buildings.

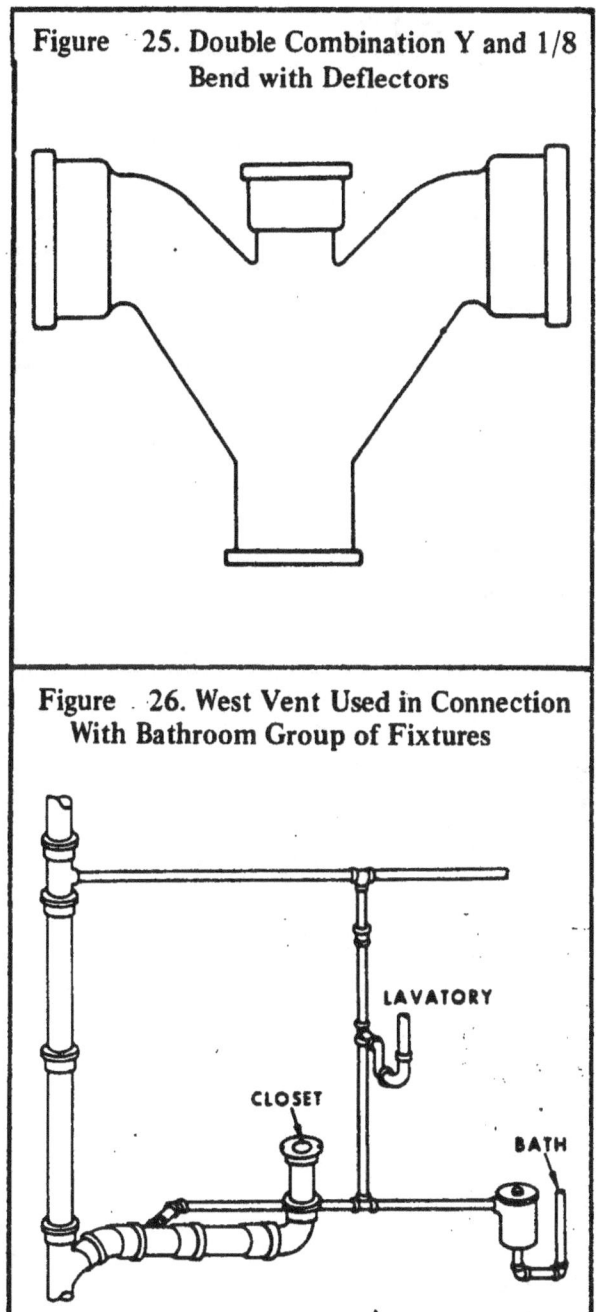

Figure 25. Double Combination Y and 1/8 Bend with Deflectors

Figure 26. West Vent Used in Connection With Bathroom Group of Fixtures

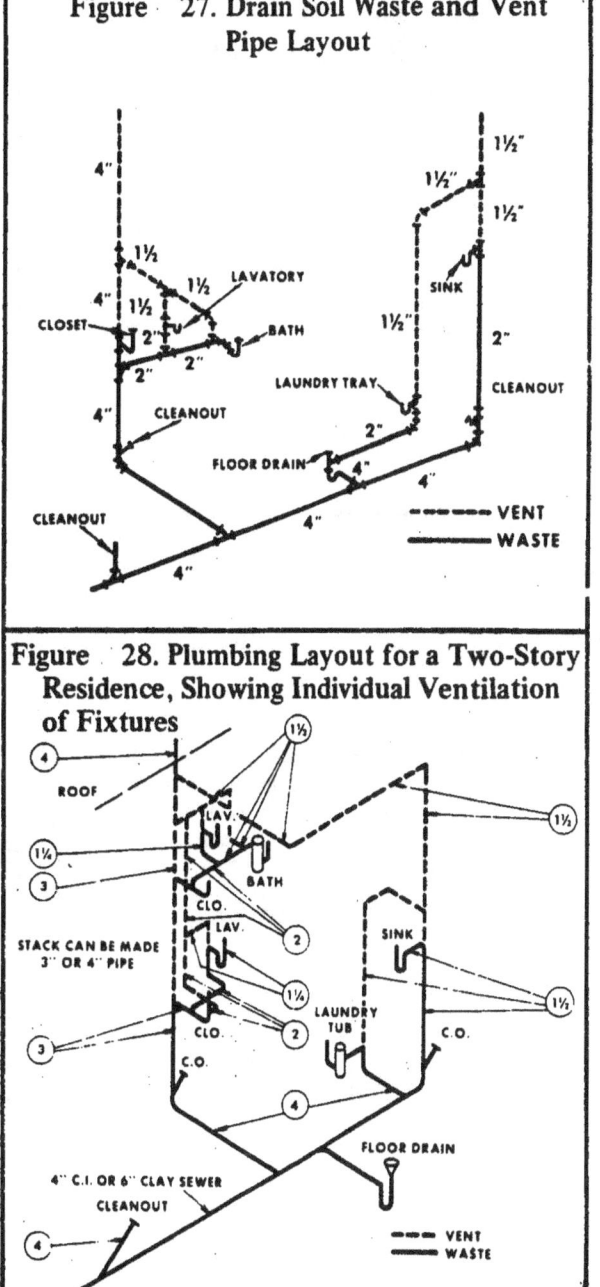

Figure 27. Drain Soil Waste and Vent Pipe Layout

Figure 28. Plumbing Layout for a Two-Story Residence, Showing Individual Ventilation of Fixtures

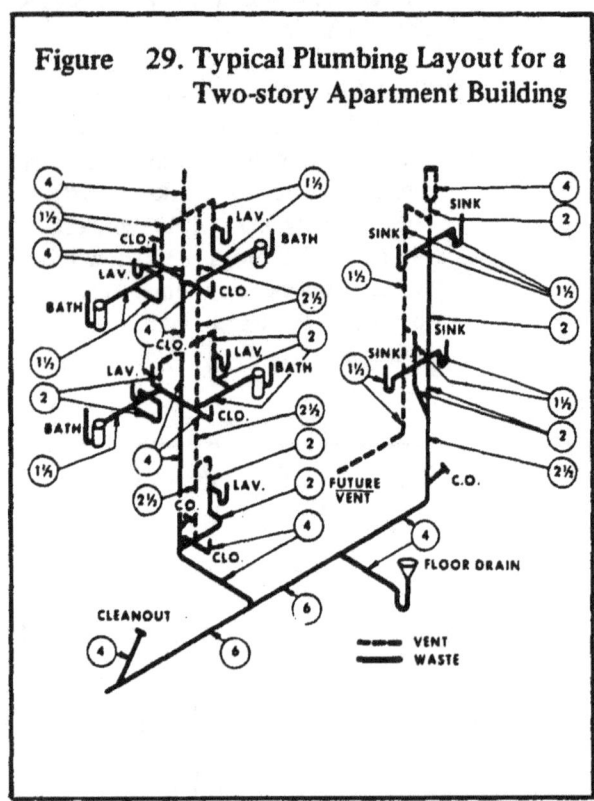

Figure 29. Typical Plumbing Layout for a Two-story Apartment Building

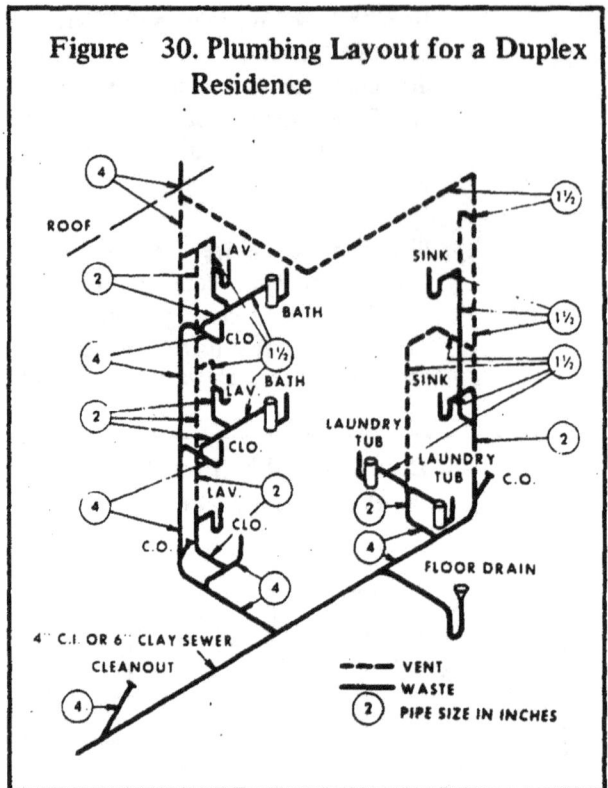

Figure 30. Plumbing Layout for a Duplex Residence

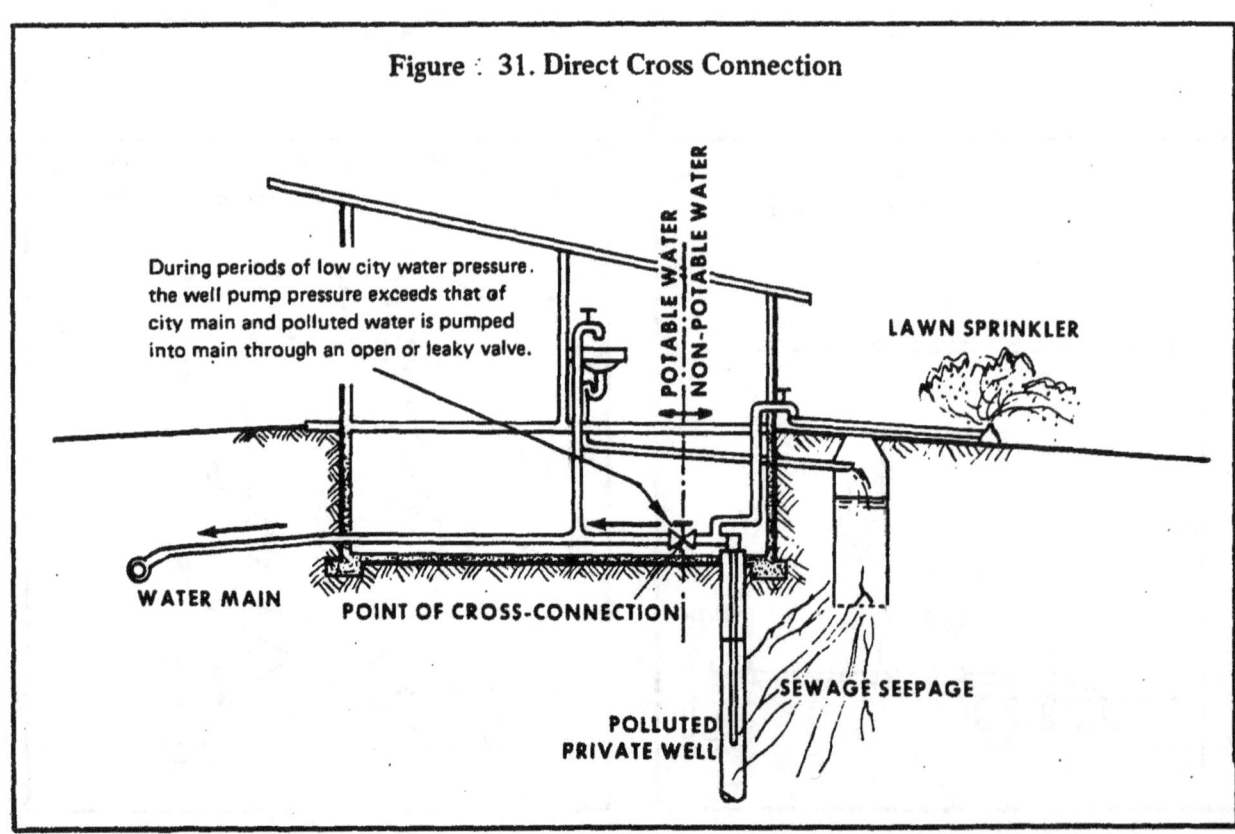

Figure 31. Direct Cross Connection

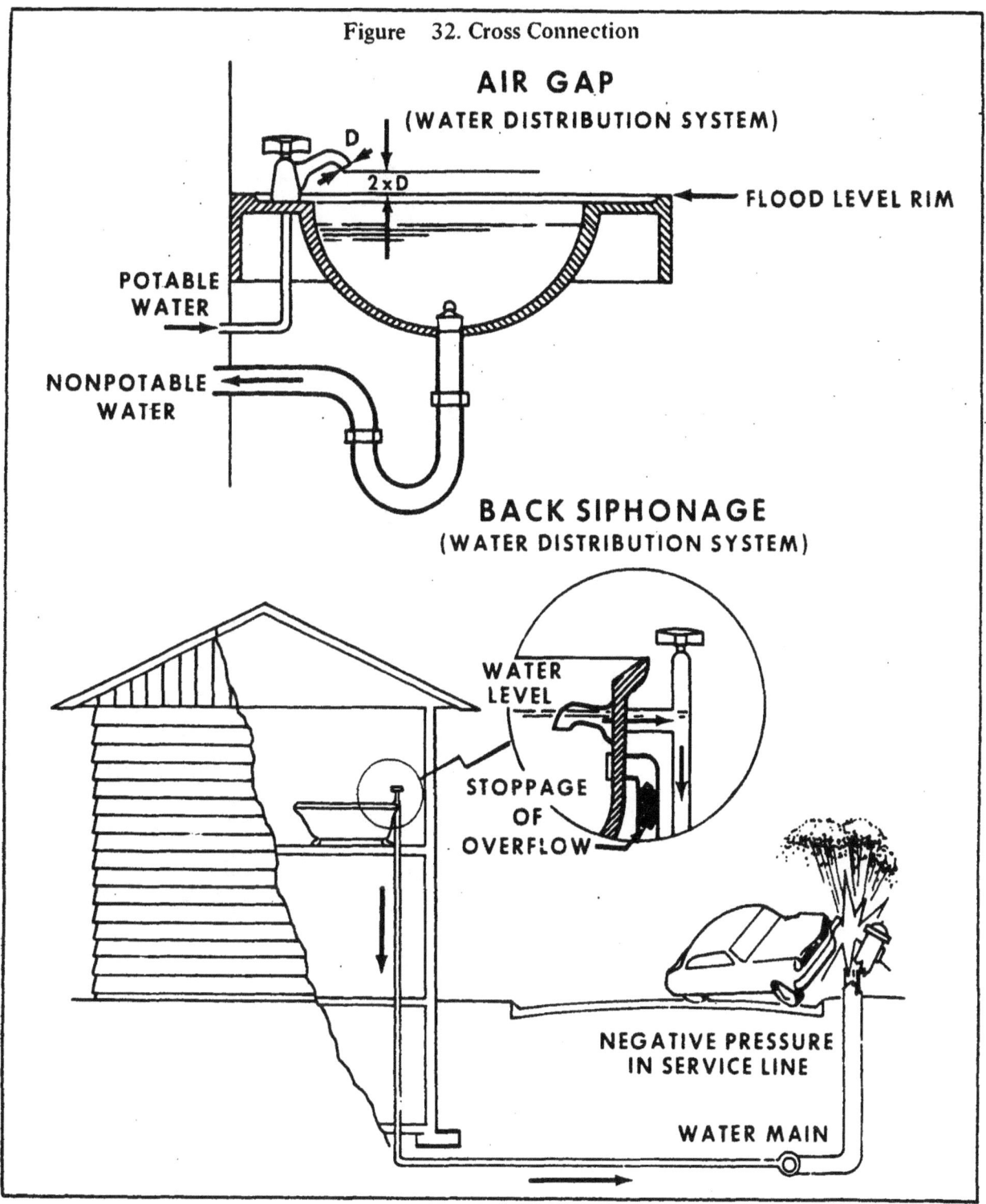

Figure 32. Cross Connection

BASIC FUNDAMENTALS OF
DRAWINGS AND SPECIFICATIONS

A building project may be broadly divided into two major phases: (1) the DESIGN phase, and (2) the CONSTRUCTION phase. In accordance with a number of considerations, of which the function and desired appearance of the building are perhaps the most important, the architect first conceives the building in his mind's eye, as it were, and then sets his concept down on paper in the form of PRESENTATION drawings. Presentation drawings are usually done in PERSPECTIVE, by employing the PICTORIAL drawing techniques.

Next the architect and the engineer, working together, decide upon the materials to be used in the structure and the construction methods which are to be followed. The engineer determines the loads which supporting members will carry and the strength qualities the members must have to bear the loads. He also designs the mechanical systems of the structure, such as the lighting, heating, and plumbing systems. The end-result of all this is the preparation of architectural and engineering DESIGN SKETCHES. The purpose of these sketches is to guide draftsmen in the preparation of CONSTRUCTION DRAWINGS.

The construction drawings, plus the SPECIFICATIONS to be described later, are the chief sources of information for the supervisors and craftsman responsible for the actual work of construction. Construction drawings consist mostly of ORTHOGRAPHIC views, prepared by draftsmen who employ the standard technical drawing techniques, and who use the symbols and other designations

You should make a thorough study of symbols before proceeding further with this chapter. Figure 1 illustrates the conventional symbols for the more common types of material used on structures. Figure 2 shows the more common symbols used for doors and windows.

Before you can interpret construction drawings correctly, you must also have some knowledge of the structure and of the terminology for common structural members.

I. STRUCTURES

The main parts of a structure are the LOAD-BEARING STRUCTURAL MEMBERS, which support and transfer the loads on the structure while remaining in equilibrium with each other. The places where members are connected to other members are called JOINTS. The sum total of the load supported by the structural members at a particular instant is equal to the total DEAD LOAD plus the total LIVE LOAD.

The total dead load is the total weight of the structure, which gradually increases, of course, as the structure rises, and remains constant once it is completed. The total live load is the total weight of movable objects (such as people, furniture, bridge traffic or the like) which the structure happens to be supporting at a particular instant.

The live loads in a structure are transmitted through the various load-bearing structural members to the ultimate support of the earth as follows. Immediate or direct support for the live loads is provided by HORIZTONAL members; these are in turn supported by VERTICAL members; which in turn are supported by FOUNDATIONS and/or FOOTINGS; and these are, finally, supported by the earth.

The ability of the earth to support a load is called the SOIL BEARING CAPACITY; it is determined by test and measured in pounds per square foot. Soil bearing capacity varies considerably with different types of soil, and a soil of given bearing capacity will bear a heavier load on a wide foundation or footing than it will on a narrow one.

VERTICAL STRUCTURAL MEMBERS

Vertical structural members are high-strength columns; they are sometimes called PILLARS in buildings. Outside wall columns and inside bottom-floor columns, usually rest directly on footings. Outside-wall columns usually extend from the footing or foundation to the roof line. Inside bottom-floor columns extend upward from footings or foundations to horizontal members which in turn support the

DRAWINGS AND SPECIFICATIONS

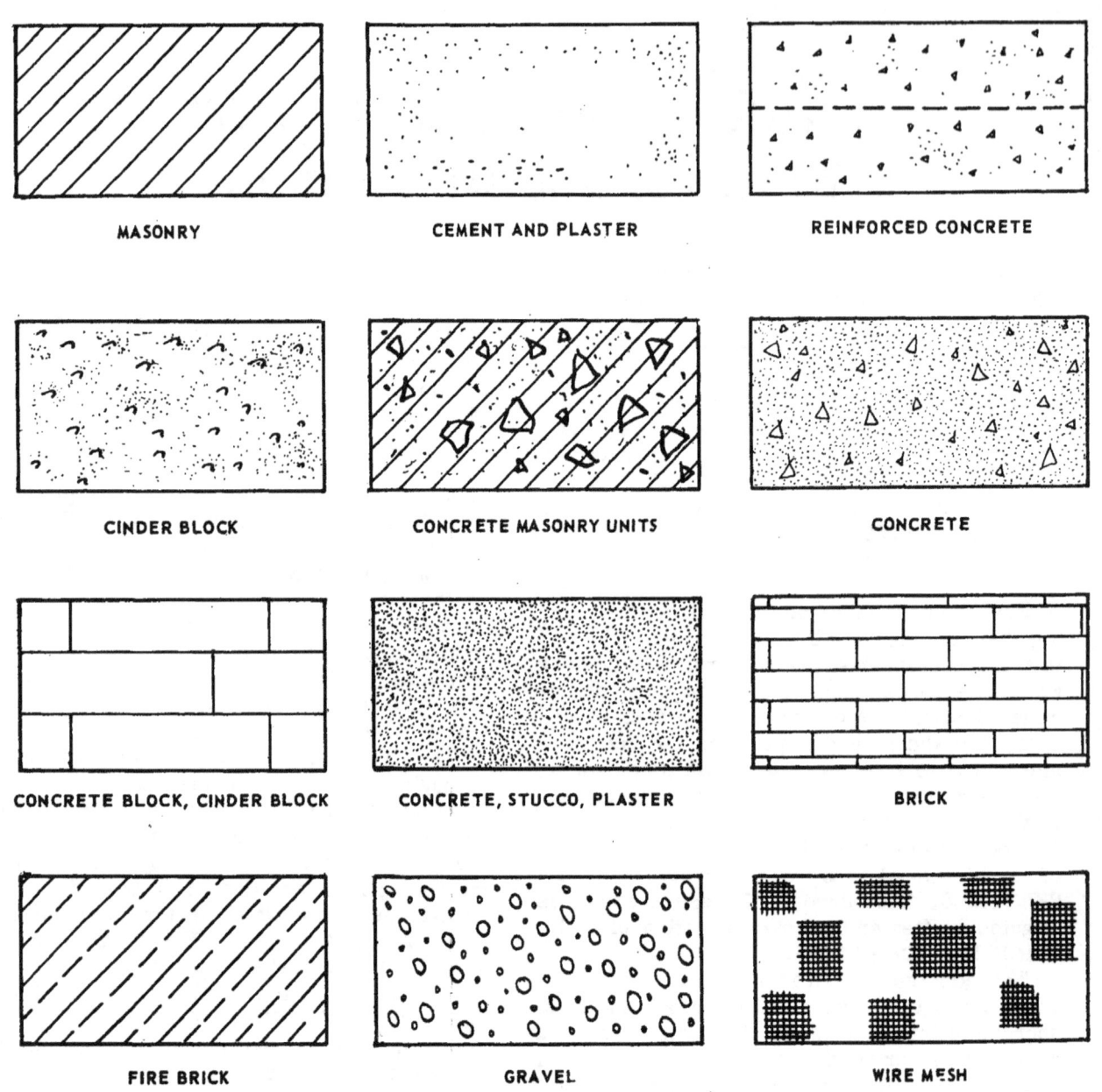

Figure 1.—Material symbols.

first floor. Upper floor columns usually are located directly over lower floor columns.

A PIER in building construction might be called a short column. It may rest directly on a footing, or it may be simply set or driven in the ground. Building piers usually support the lowermost horizontal structural members.

In bridge construction a pier is a vertical member which provides intermediate support for the bridge superstructure.

The chief vertical structural members in light frame construction are called STUDS. They are supported on horizontal members called SILLS or SOLE PLATES, and are topped by horizontal members called TOP PLATES or RAFTER PLATES. CORNER POSTS are enlarged studs, as it were, located at the building corners. In early FULL-FRAME construction a corner post was usually a solid piece of larger timber. In most modern construction BUILT-UP

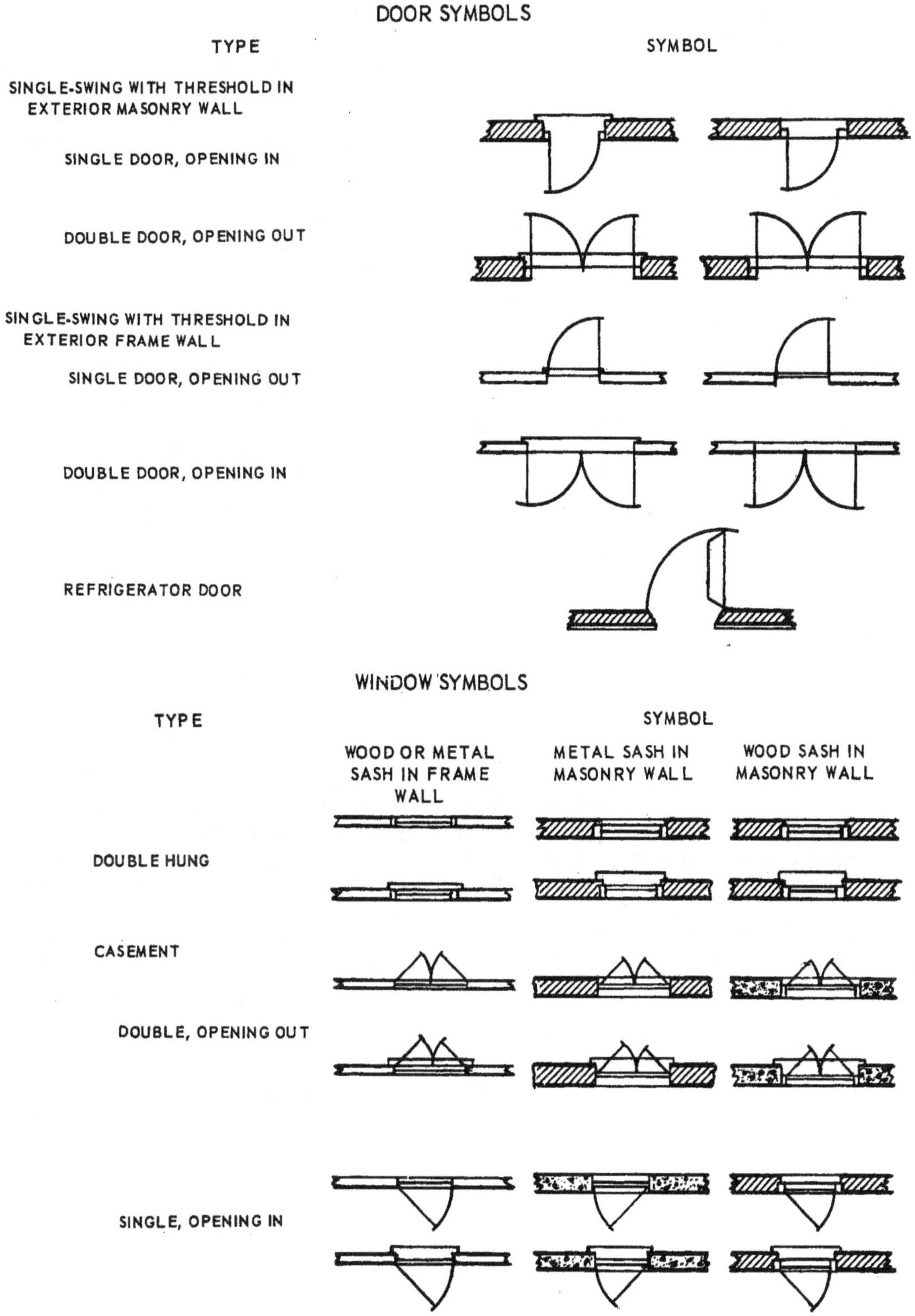

DOOR SYMBOLS

TYPE	SYMBOL
SINGLE-SWING WITH THRESHOLD IN EXTERIOR MASONRY WALL	
SINGLE DOOR, OPENING IN	
DOUBLE DOOR, OPENING OUT	
SINGLE-SWING WITH THRESHOLD IN EXTERIOR FRAME WALL	
SINGLE DOOR, OPENING OUT	
DOUBLE DOOR, OPENING IN	
REFRIGERATOR DOOR	

WINDOW SYMBOLS

TYPE	WOOD OR METAL SASH IN FRAME WALL	METAL SASH IN MASONRY WALL	WOOD SASH IN MASONRY WALL
DOUBLE HUNG			
CASEMENT DOUBLE, OPENING OUT			
SINGLE, OPENING IN			

Figure 2 —Architectural symbols (door and windows).

corner posts are used, consisting of various numbers of ordinary studs, nailed together in various ways.

HORIZONTAL STRUCTURAL MEMBERS

In technical terminology, a horizontal load-bearing structural member which spans a space, and which is supported at both ends, is called a BEAM. A member which is FIXED at one end only is called a CANTILEVER. Steel members which consist of solid pieces of the regular structural steel shapes are called beams, but a type of steel member which is actually a light truss is called an OPEN-WEB STEEL JOIST or a BAR STEEL JOIST.

Horizontal structural members which support the ends of floor beams or joists in wood frame construction are called SILLS, GIRTS, or GIRDERS, depending on the type of framing being done and the location of the member in the structure. Horizontal members which support studs are called SILL or SOLE PLATES. Horizontal members which support the wall-ends of rafters are called RAFTER PLATES. Horizontal members which assume the weight of concrete or masonry walls above door and window openings are called LINTELS.

TRUSSES

A beam of given strength, without intermediate supports below, can support a given load over only a certain maximum span. If the span is wider than this maximum, intermediate supports, such as a column must be provided for the beam. Sometimes it is not feasible or possible to install intermediate supports. When such is the case, a TRUSS may be used instead of a beam.

A beam consists of a single horizontal member. A truss, however, is a framework, consisting of two horizontal (or nearly horizontal) members, joined together by a number of vertical and/or inclined members. The horizontal members are called the UPPER and LOWER CHORDS; the vertical and/or inclined members are called the WEB MEMBERS.

ROOF MEMBERS

The horizontal or inclined members which provide support to a roof are called RAFTERS. The lengthwise (right angle to the rafters) member which support the peak ends of the rafters in a roof is called the RIDGE. (The ridge may be called the Ridge board, the Ridge PIECE, or the Ridge pole.) Lengthwise members other than ridges are called PURLINS. In wood frame construction the wall ends of rafters are supported on horizontal members called RAFTER PLATES, which are in turn supported by the outside wall studs. In concrete or masonry wall construction, the wall ends of rafters may be anchored directly on the walls, or on plates bolted to the walls.

II. CONSTRUCTION DRAWINGS

Construction drawings are drawings in which as much construction information as possible is presented GRAPHICALLY, or by means of pictures. Most construction drawings consist of ORTHOGRAPHIC views. GENERAL drawings consist of PLANS AND ELEVATIONS, drawn on a relatively small scale. DETAIL drawings consist of SECTIONS and DETAILS, drawn on a relatively large scale.

PLANS

A PLAN view is, as you know, a view of an object or area as it would appear if projected onto a horizontal plane passed through or held above the object or area. The most common construction plans are PLOT PLANS (also called SITE PLANS), FOUNDATION PLANS, FLOOR PLANS, and FRAMING PLANS.

A PLOT PLAN shows the contours, boundaries, roads, utilities, trees, structures, and any other significant physical features pertaining to or located on the site. The locations of proposed structures are indicated by appropriate outlines or floor plans. By locating the corners of a proposed structure at given distances from a REFERENCE or BASE line (which is shown on the plan and which can be located on the site), the plot plan provides essential data for those who will lay out the building lines. By indicating the elevations of existing and proposed earth surfaces (by means of CONTOUR lines), the plot plan provides essential data for the graders and excavators.

A FOUNDATION PLAN (fig. 3) is a plan view of a structure projected on a horizontal plane passed through (in imagination, of course) at the level of the tops of the foundations. The plan shown in figure 3 tells you that the main foundation of this structure will consist of a rectangular 12-in. concrete block wall, 22 ft

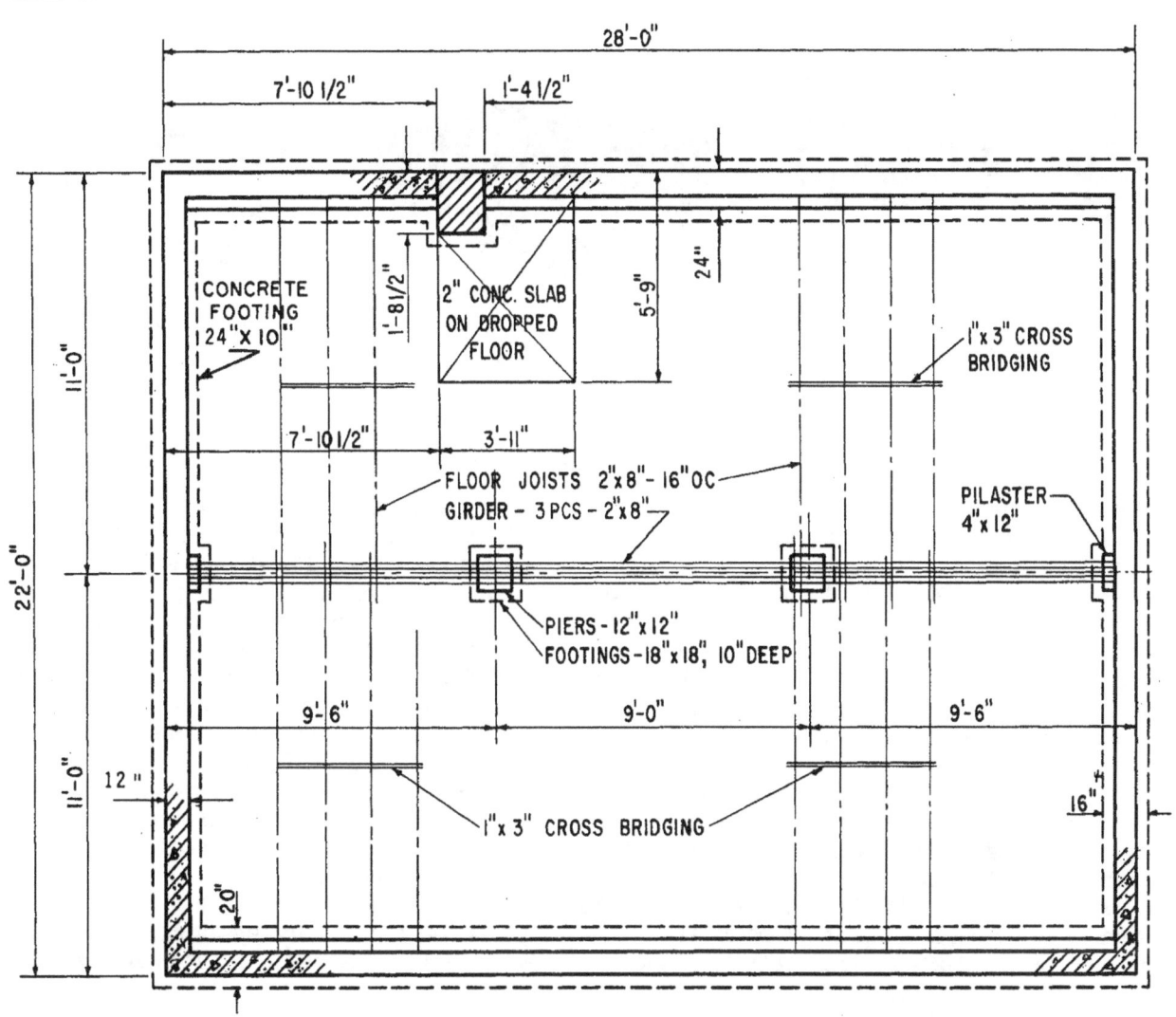

Figure 3.—Foundation plan.

wide by 28 ft long, centered on a concrete footing 24 in. wide. Besides the outside wall and footing, there will be two 12-in. square piers, centered on 18-in. square footings, and located on center 9 ft 6 in. from the end wall building lines. These piers will support a ground floor center-line girder.

A FLOOR PLAN (also called a BUILDING PLAN) is developed as shown in figure 4. Information on a floor plan includes the lengths, thicknesses, and character of the building walls at that particular floor, the widths and locations of door and window openings, the lengths and character of partitions, the number and arrangement of rooms, and the types and locations of utility installations. A typical floor plan is shown in figure 5.

FRAMING PLANS show the dimensions, numbers, and arrangement of structural members in wood frame construction. A simple FLOOR FRAMING PLAN is superimposed on the foundation plan shown in figure 3. From this foundation plan you learn that the ground-floor joists in this structure will consist of 2 x 8's, lapped at the girder, and spaced 16 in. O. C. The plan also shows that each row of joists is to be braced by a row of 1 x 3 cross bridging. For a more complicated floor framing problem, a framing plan like the one shown in figure 2-6 would be required. This plan

201

  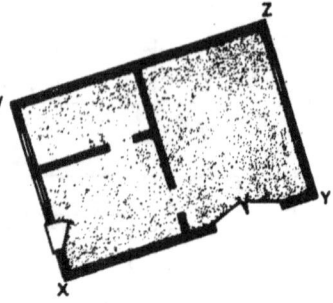

Figure 4.—Floor plan development.

shows, among other things, the arrangement of joists and other members around stair wells and other floor openings.

A WALL FRAMING PLAN gives similar information with regard to the studs, corner posts, bracing, sills, plates, and other structural members in the walls. Since it is a view on a vertical plane, a wall framing plan is not a plan in the strict technical sense. However, the practice of calling it a plan has become a general custom. A ROOF FRAMING PLAN gives similar information with regard to the rafters, ridge, purlins, and other structural members in the roof.

A UTILITY PLAN is a floor plan which shows the layout of a heating, electrical, plumbing, or other utility system. Utility plans are used primarily by the ratings responsible for the utilities, but they are important to the Builder as well. Most utility installations require the leaving of openings in walls, floors, and roofs for the admission or installation of utility features. The Builder who is placing a concrete foundation wall must study the utility plans to determine the number, sizes, and locations of the openings he must leave for utilities.

Figure 7 shows a heating plan. Figure 8 shows an electrical plan.

ELEVATIONS

ELEVATIONS show the front, rear, and sides of a structure projected on vertical planes parallel to the planes of the sides. Front, rear, right side, and left side elevations of a small building are shown in figure 9.

As you can see, the elevations give you a number of important vertical dimensions, such as the perpendicular distance from the finish floor to the top of the rafter plate and from the finish floor to the tops of door and window finished openings. They also show the locations and characters of doors and windows. Dimensions of window sash and dimensions and character of lintels, however, are usually set forth in a WINDOW SCHEDULE.

A SECTION view is a view of a cross-section, developed as indicated in figure 10. By general custom, the term is confined to views of cross-sections cut by vertical planes. A floor plan or foundation plan, cut by a horizontal plane, is, technically speaking, a section view as well as a plan view, but it is seldom called a section.

The most important sections are the WALL sections. Figure 11 shows three wall sections for three alternate types of construction for the building shown in figures 3, 5, 7 and 8. The angled arrows marked "A" in figure 5 indicate the location of the cutting plane for the sections.

The wall sections are of primary importance to the supervisors of construction and to the craftsmen who will do the actual building. Take the first wall section, marked "masonry construction," for example. Starting at the bottom, you learn that the footing will be concrete, 2 ft wide and 10 in. high. The vertical distance of the bottom of the footing below FINISHED GRADE (level of the finished earth surface around the house) "varies"—meaning that it will depend on the soil-bearing capacity at the particular site. The foundation wall will consist of

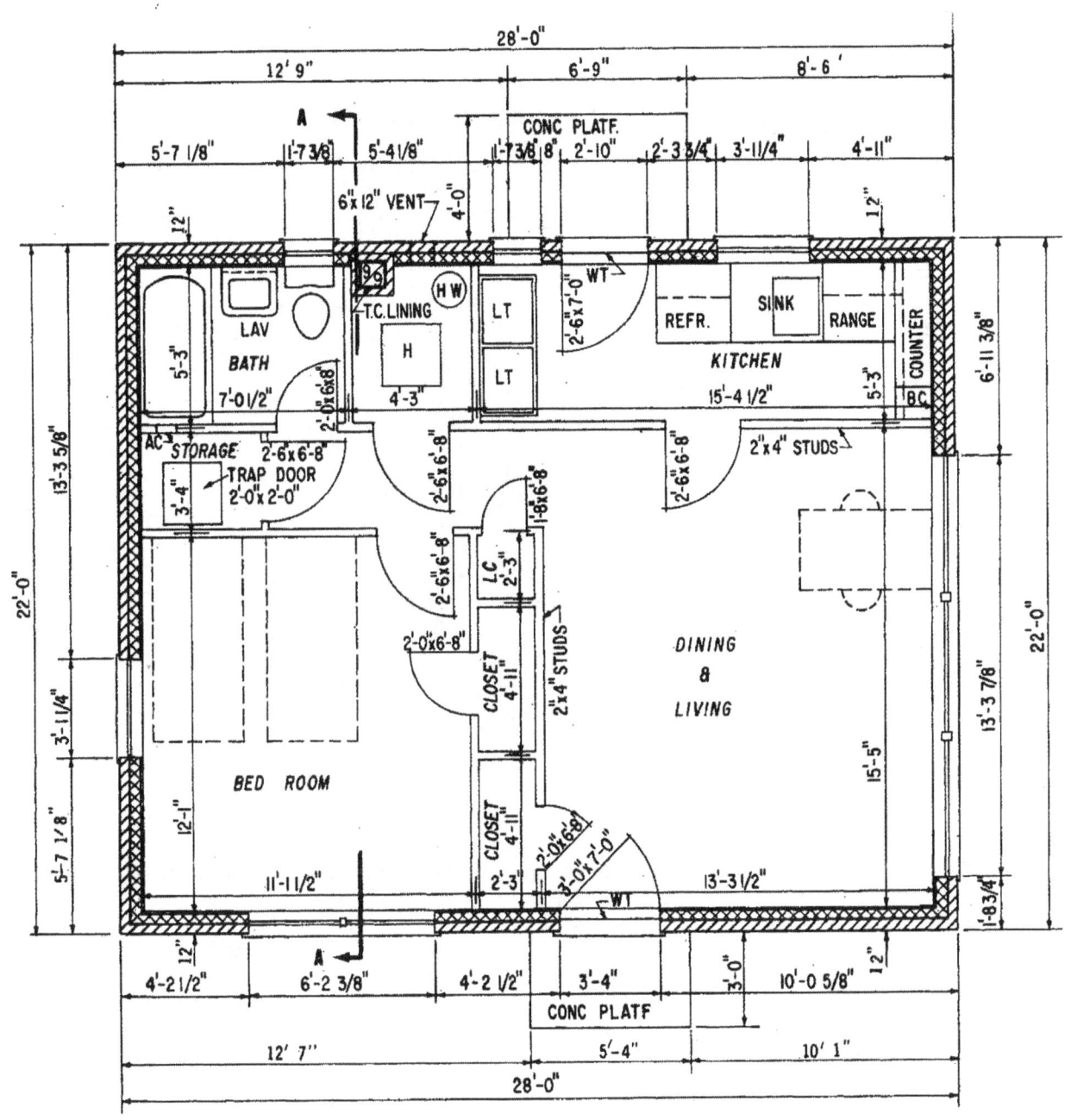

Figure 5.—Floor plan.

12-in. CMU, centered on the footing. Twelve-inch blocks will extend up to an unspecified distance below grade, where a 4-in. brick FACING (dimension indicated in the middle wall section) begins. Above the line of the bottom of the facing, it is obvious that 8-in. instead of 12-in. blocks will be used in the foundation wall.

The building wall above grade will consist of a 4-in. brick FACING TIER, backed by a BACKING TIER of 4-in. cinder blocks. The floor joists, consisting of 2 x 8's placed 16 in. O.C., will be anchored on 2 x 4 sills bolted to the top of the foundation wall. Every third joist will be additionally secured by a 2 x 1/4 STRAP ANCHOR embedded in the cinder block backing tier of the building wall.

The window (window B in the plan front elevation, fig. 9) will have a finished opening

203

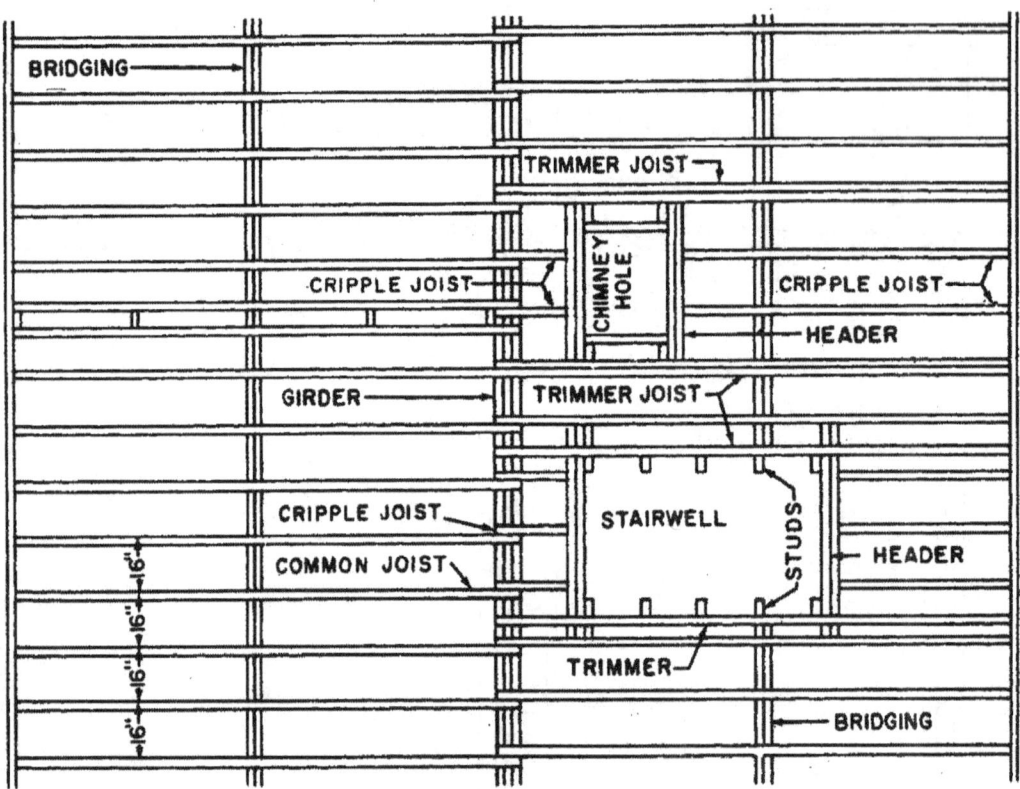

Figure 6.—Floor framing plan.

4 ft 2-5/8 in. high. The bottom of the opening will come 2 ft 11-3/4 in. above the line of the finished floor. As indicated in the wall section, (fig. 11) 13 masonry COURSES (layers of masonry units) above the finished floor line will amount to a vertical distance of 2 ft 11-3/4 in. As also indicated, another 19 courses will amount to the prescribed vertical dimension of the finished window opening.

Window framing details, including the placement and cross-sectional character of the lintel, are shown. The building wall will be carried 10-1/4 in., less the thickness of a 2 x 8 RAFTER PLATE, above the top of the window finished opening. The total vertical distance from the top of the finished floor to the top of the rafter plate will be 8 ft 2-1/4 in. Ceiling joists and rafters will consist of 2 x 6's, and the roof covering will consist of composition shingles laid on wood sheathing.

Flooring will consist of a wood finisher floor laid on a wood subfloor. Inside walls will be finished with plaster on lath (except on masonry wall which would be with or without lath as directed). A minimum of 2 vertical feet of crawl space will extend below the bottoms of the floor joists.

The middle wall section in figure 2-11 gives you similar information for a similar building constructed with wood frame walls and a DOUBLE-HUNG window. The third wall section shown in the figure gives you similar information for a similar building constructed with a steel frame, a casement window, and a concrete floor finished with asphalt tile.

DETAILS

DETAIL drawings are drawings which are done on a larger scale than that of the general drawings, and which show features not appearing at all, or appearing on too small a scale, on the general drawings. The wall sections just described are details as well as sections, since

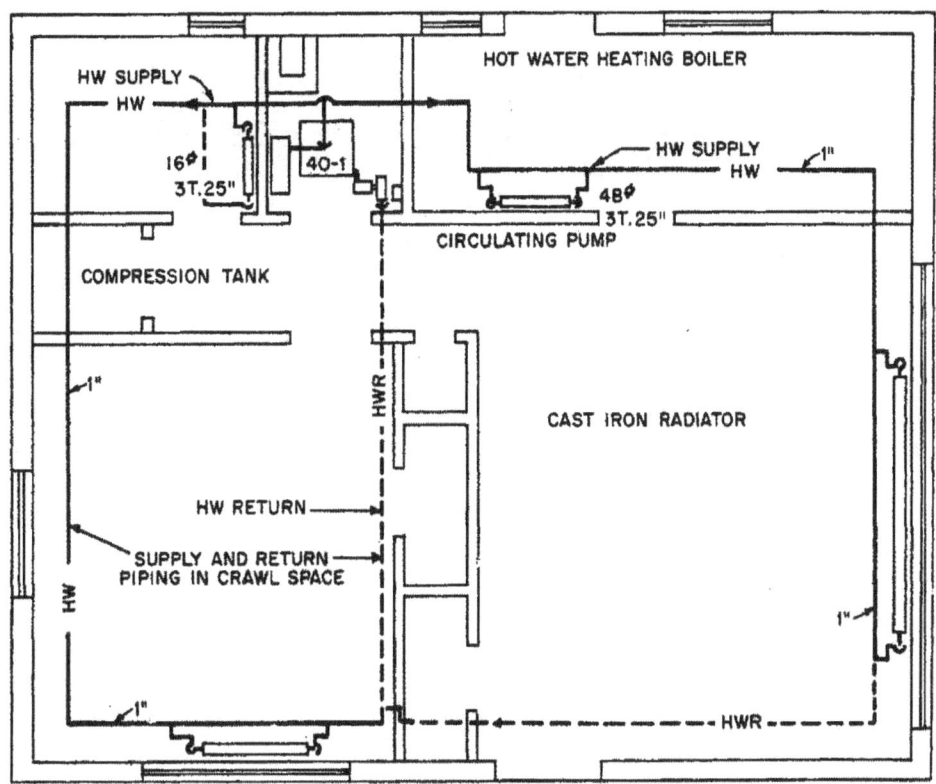

Figure 7.—Heating plan.

they are drawn on a considerable larger scale than the plans and elevations. Framing details at doors, windows, and cornices, which are the most common types of details, are practically always sections.

Details are included whenever the information given in the plans, elevations, and wall sections is not sufficiently "detailed" to guide the craftsmen on the job. Figure 12 shows some typical door and window wood framing details, and an eave detail for a very simple type of CORNICE. You should study these details closely to learn the terminology of framing members.

III. SPECIFICATIONS

The construction drawings contain much of the information about a structure which can be presented GRAPHICALLY (that is, in drawings). A very considerable amount of information can be presented this way, but there is more information which the construction supervisors and artisans must have and which is not adaptable to the graphic form of presentation. Information of this kind includes quality criteria for materials (maximum amounts of aggregate per sack of cement, for example), specified standards of workmanship, prescribed construction methods, and the like.

Information of this kind is presented in a list of written SPECIFICATIONS, familiarly known as the "SPECS." A list of specifications usually begins with a section on GENERAL CONDITIONS. This section starts with a GENERAL DESCRIPTION of the building, including the type of foundation, type or types of windows, character of framing, utilities to be installed, and the like. Next comes a list of DEFINITIONS of terms used in the specs, and next certain routine declarations of responsibility and certain conditions to be maintained on the job.

SPECIFIC CONDITIONS are grouped in sections under headings which describe each of the major construction phases of the job. Separate specifications are written for each phase, and the phases are then combined to more or less follow the usual order of construction sequences on the job. A typical list of sections under "Specific Conditions" follows:

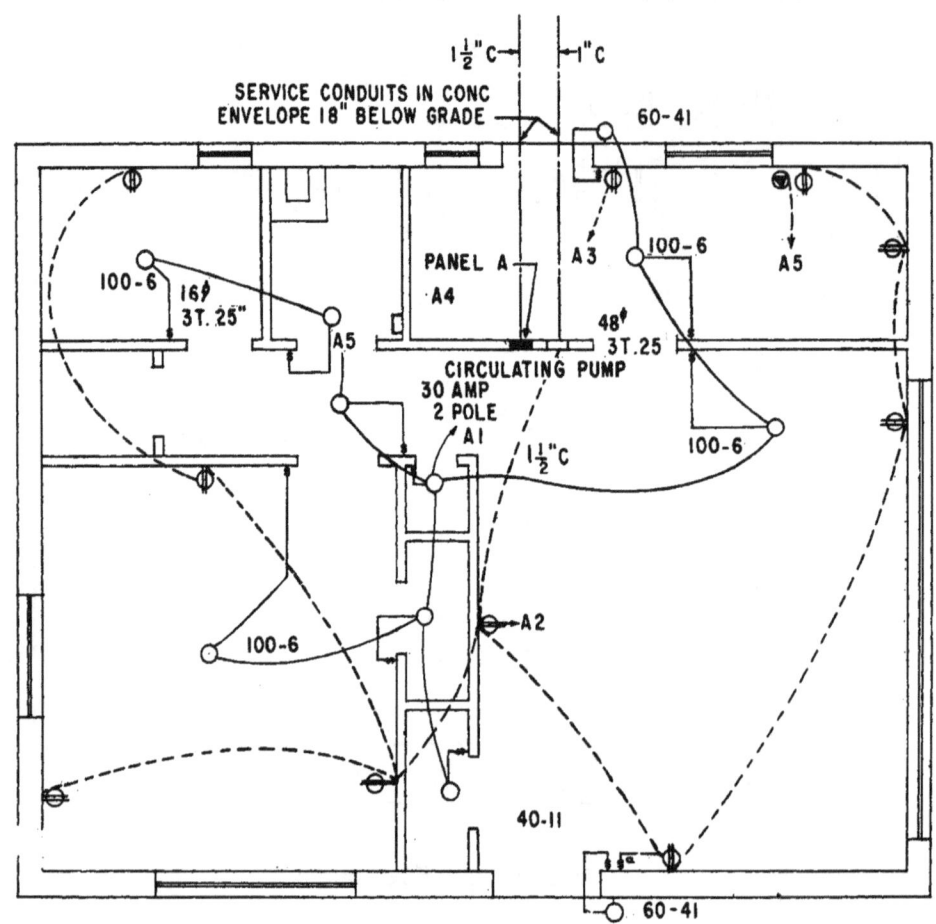

Figure 8.—Electrical plan.

2.—EARTHWORK 3.—CONCRETE 4.—MASONRY 5.—MISCELLANEOUS STEEL AND IRON 6.—CARPENTRY AND JOINERY 7.—LATHING AND PLASTERING 8.—TILE WORK 9.—FINISH FLOORING 10.—GLAZING 11.—FINISHING HARDWARE 12.—PLUMBING 13.—HEATING 14.—ELECTRICAL WORK 15.—FIELD PAINTING.

A section under "Specific Conditions" usually begins with a subsection of GENERAL REQUIREMENTS which apply to the phase of construction being considered. Under Section 6, CARPENTRY AND JOINERY, for example, the first section might go as follows:

6-01. GENERAL REQUIREMENTS. All framing, rough carpentry, and finishing woodwork required for the proper completion of the building shall be provided. All woodwork shall be protected from the weather, and the building shall be thoroughly dry before the finish is placed. All finish shall be dressed, smoothed, and sandpapered at the mill, and in addition shall be hand smoothed and sandpapered at the building where necessary to produce proper finish. Nailing shall be done, as far as practicable, in concealed places, and all nails in finishing work shall be set. All lumber shall be S4S (meaning, "surfaced on 4 sides"); all materials for millwork and finish shall be kiln-dried; all rough and framing lumber shall be air- or kiln-dried. Any cutting, fitting, framing, and blocking necessary for the accommodation of other work shall be provided. All nails, spikes, screws, bolts, plates, clips, and other fastenings and rough hardware necessary for the proper completion of the building shall be provided.

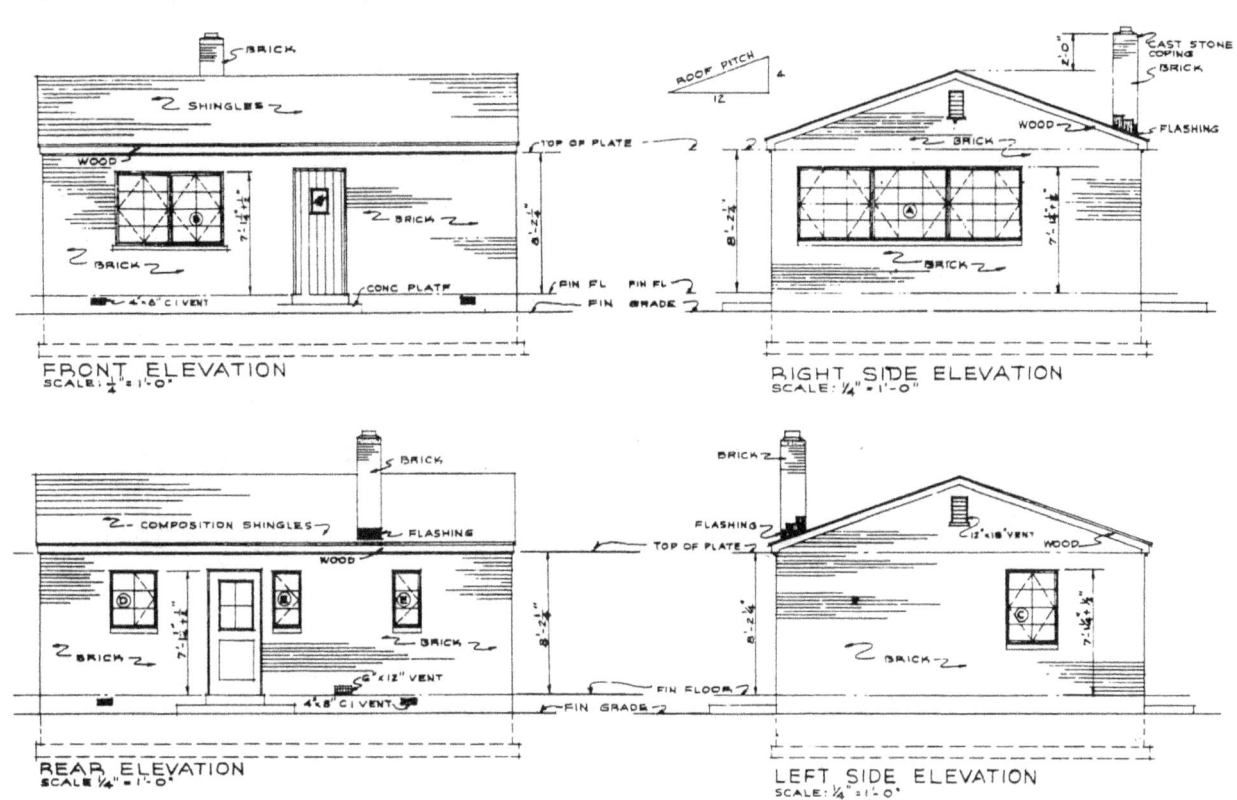

Figure 2-9.—Elevations.

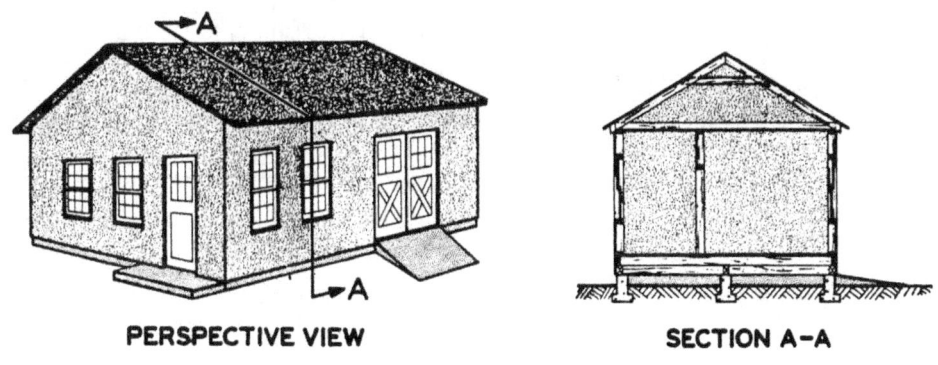

Figure 10.—Development of a section view.

All finishing hardware shall be installed in accordance with the manufacturers' directions. Calking and flashing shall be provided where indicated, or where necessary to provide weathertight construction.

Next after the General Requirements for Carpentry and Joinery, there is generally a subsection on "Grading," in which the kinds and grades of the various woods to be used in the structure are specified. Subsequent subsections

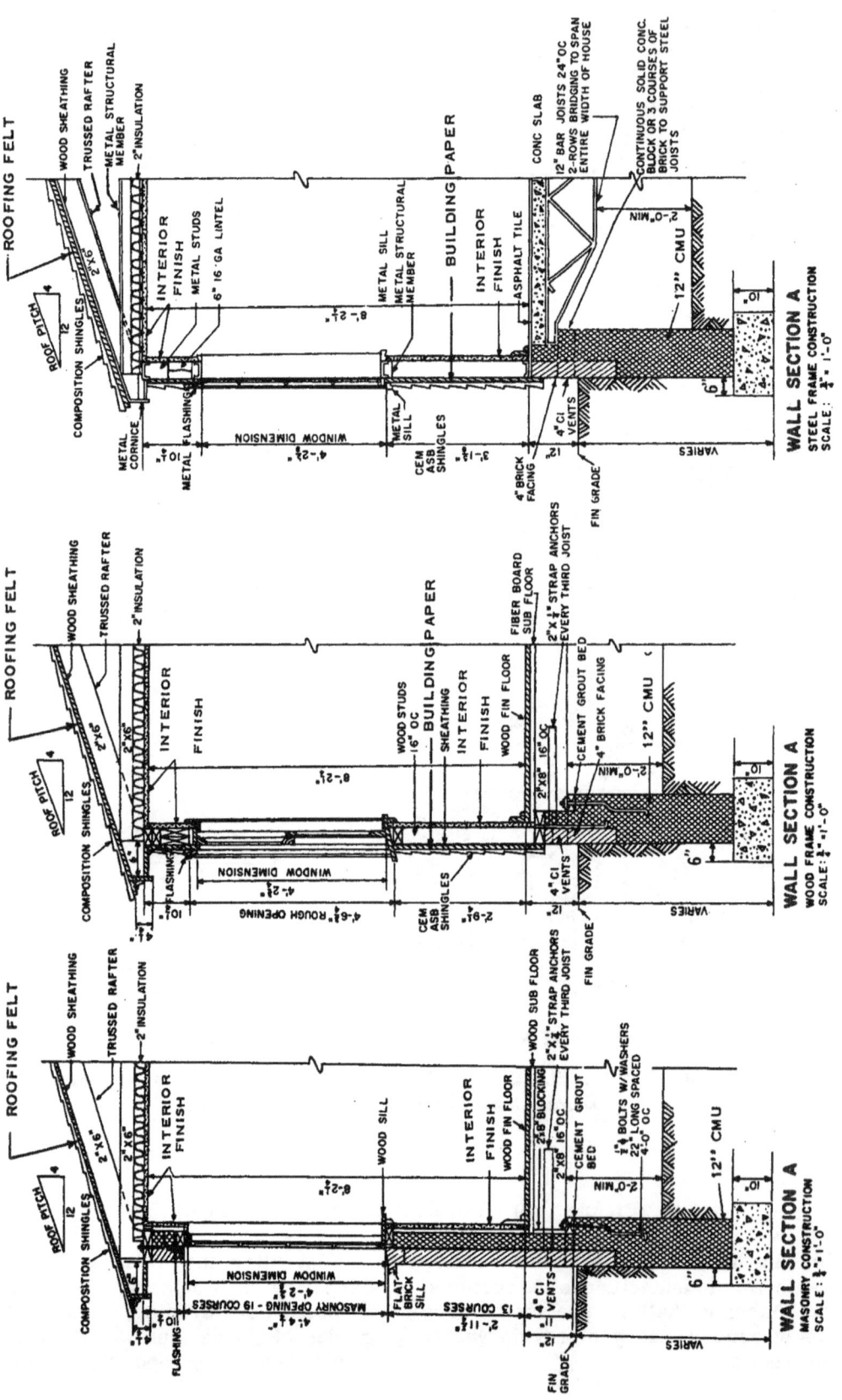

Figure 11.—Wall sections

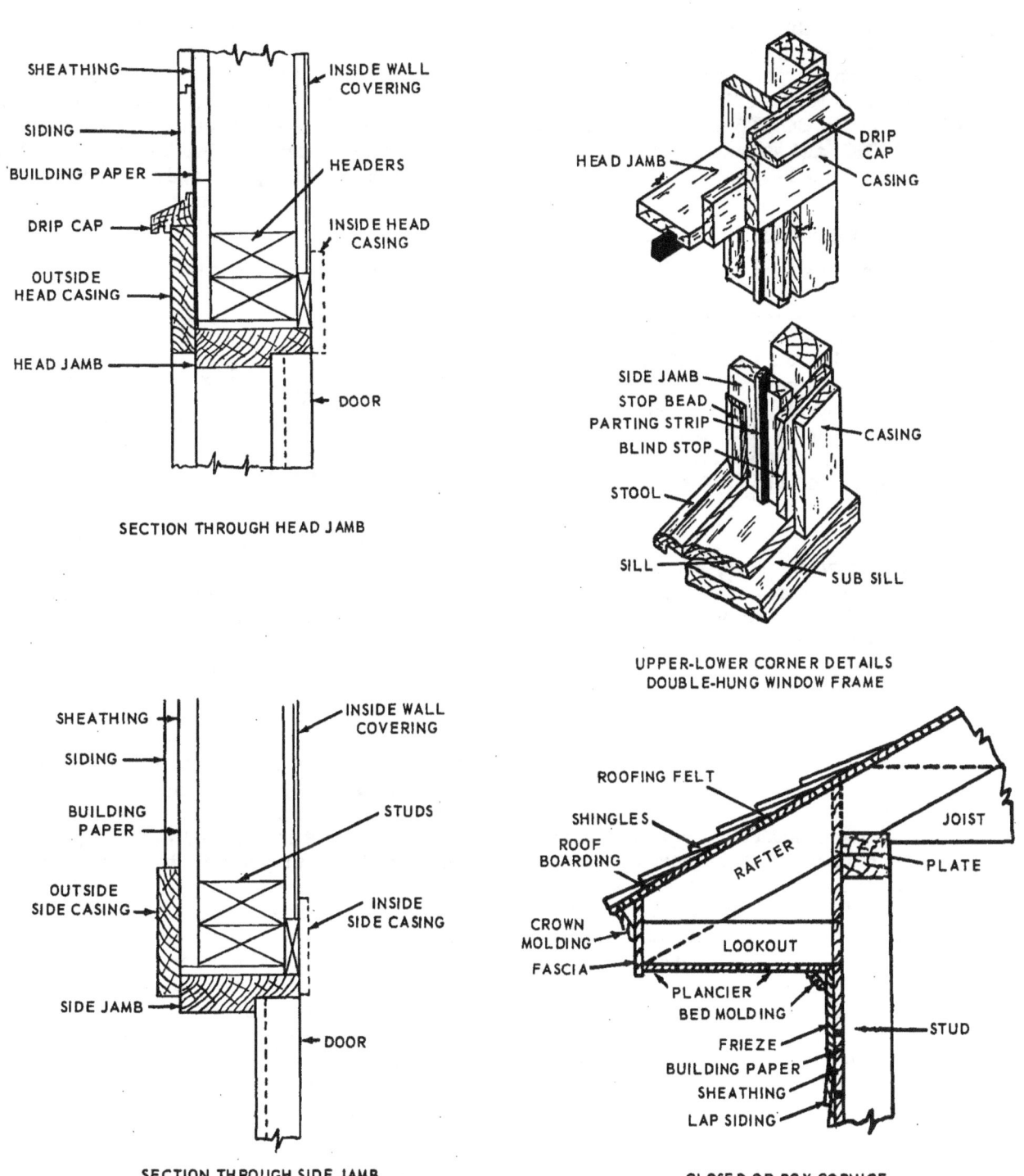

Figure 12.—Door, window and eave details.

specify various quality criteria and standards of workmanship for the various aspects of the rough and finish carpentry work, under such headings as FRAMING; SILLS, PLATES, AND GIRDERS; FLOOR JOISTS AND ROOF RAFTERS; STUDDING; and so on. An example of one of these subsections follows:

STUDDING for walls and partitions shall have doubled plates and doubled stud caps. Studs shall be set plumb and not to exceed 16-in. centers and in true alignment; they shall be bridged with one row of 2 x 4 pieces, set flatwise, fitted tightly, and nailed securely to each stud. Studding shall be doubled around openings and the heads of openings shall rest on the inner studs. Openings in partitions having widths of 4 ft and over shall be trussed. In wood frame construction, studs shall be trebled at corners to form posts.

From the above samples, you can see that a knowledge of the relevant specifications is as essential to the construction supervisor and the construction artisan as a knowledge of the construction drawings.

It is very important that the proper spec be used to cover the material requested. In cases in which the material is not covered by a Government spec, the ASTM (American Society for Testing Materials) spec or some other approved commercial spec may be used. It is EXTREMELY IMPORTANT in using specifications to cite all amendments, including the latest changes.

As a rule, the specs are provided for each project by the A/E (ARCHITECT-ENGINEERS). These are the OFFICIAL guidelines approved by the chief engineer or his representative for use during construction. These requirements should NOT be deviated from without prior approval from proper authority. This approval is usually obtained by means of a change order. When there is disagreement between the specifications and drawings, the specifications should normally be followed; however, check with higher authority in each case.

IV. BUILDER'S MATHEMATICS

The Builder has many occasions for the employment of the processes of ordinary arithmetic, and he must be thoroughly familiar with the methods of determining the areas and volumes of the various plane and solid geometrical figures. Only a few practical applications and a few practical suggestions, will be given here.

RATIO AND PROPORTION

There are a great many practical applications of ratio and proportion in the construction field. A few examples are as follows:

Some dimensions on construction drawings (such as, for example, distances from base lines and elevations of surfaces) are given in ENGINEER'S instead of CARPENTER's measure. Engineer's measure is measure in feet and decimal parts of a foot, or in inches and decimal parts of an inch, such as 100.15 ft or 11.14 in. Carpenter's measure is measure in yards, feet, inches, and even-denominator fractions of an inch, such as 1/2 in., 1/4 in., 1/16 in., 1/32 in., and 1/64 in.

You must know how to convert an engineer's measure given on a construction drawing to a carpenter's measure. Besides this, it will often happen that calculations you make yourself may produce a result in feet and decimal parts of a foot, which result you will have to convert to carpenter's measure. To convert engineer's to carpenter's measure you can use ratio and proportion as follows:

Let's say that you want to convert 100.14 ft to feet and inches to the nearest 1/16 in. The 100 you don't need to convert, since it is already in feet. What you need to do, first, is to find out how many twelfths of a foot (that is, how many inches) there are in 14/100 ft. Set this up as a proportional equation as follows: $x:12::14:100$.

You know that in a proportional equation the product of the means equals the product of the extremes. Consequently, $100x = (12 \times 14)$, or 168. Then $x = 168/100$, or 1.68 in. Next question is, how many 16ths of an in. are there in 68/100 in.? Set this up, too, as a proportional equation, thus: $x:16::68:100$. Then $100x = 1088$, and $x = 10\ 88/100$ sixteenths. Since 88/100 of a sixteenth is more than one-half of a sixteenth, you ROUND OFF by calling it 11/16. In 100.14 ft, then, there are 100 ft 1 11/16 in. For example:

A. $\underbrace{x:12::14:100}_{\text{Extremes}}$ means

Product of extremes = product of means:

$$100\ x = 168$$
$$x = 1.68 \text{ IN.}$$

B. $x:16::68:100$

$$100\ x = 1088$$
$$x = 10.88$$
$$x = 10\frac{88}{100} \text{ sixteenths}$$

Rounded off to 11/16

Another way to convert engineer's measurements to carpenter's measurements is to multiply the decimal portion of a foot by 12 to get inches; multiply the decimal by 16 to get the fraction of an inch.

There are many other practical applications of ratio and proportion in the construction field. Suppose, for example, that a table tells you that, for the size and type of brick wall you happen to be laying, 12,321 bricks and 195 cu ft of mortar are required per every 1000 sq ft of wall. How many bricks and how much mortar will be needed for 750 sq ft of the same wall? You simply set up equations as follows; for example:

Brick: $x:750::12,321:1000$
Mortar: $x:750::195:1000$

Brick: $\dfrac{X}{750} = \dfrac{12,321}{1000}$ Cross multiply

$$1000\ X = 9,240,750 \quad \text{Divide}$$
$$X = 9,240.75 = 9241 \text{ Brick.}$$

Mortar: $\dfrac{X}{750} = \dfrac{195}{1000}$ Cross multiply

$$1000\ X = 146,250 \quad \text{Divide}$$
$$X = 146.25 = 146\ 1/4 \text{ cu ft}$$

Suppose, for another example, that the ingredient proportions by volume for the type of concrete you are making are 1 cu ft cement to 1.7 cu ft sand to 2.8 cu ft coarse aggregate. Suppose you know as well, by reference to a table, that ingredients combined in the amounts indicated will produce 4.07 cu ft of concrete. How much of each ingredient will be required to make a cu yd of concrete?

Remember here, first, that there are not 9, but 27 (3 ft x 3 ft x 3 ft) cu ft in a cu yd. Your proportional equations will be as follows:

Cement: $x:27::1:4.07$

Sand: $x:27::1.7:4.07$

Coarse aggregate: $x:27::2.8:4.07$

Cement: $x:27::1:4.07$

$$\frac{x}{27} = \frac{1}{4.07}$$

$$4.07\ x = 27$$

$$x = 6.63 \text{ cu ft Cement}$$

Sand: $x:27::1.7:4.07$

$$\frac{x}{27} = \frac{1.7}{4.07}$$

$$4.07\ x = 45.9$$

$$x = 11.28 \text{ cu ft Sand}$$

Coarse aggregate: $x:27::2.8:407$

$$\frac{x}{27} = \frac{2.8}{4.07}$$

$$4.07\ x = 75.6$$

$$x = 18.57 \text{ cu ft Coarse aggregate}$$

ARITHMETICAL OPERATIONS

The formulas for finding the area and volume of geometric figures are expressed in algebraic equations which are called formulas. A few of the more important formulas and their mathematical solutions will be discussed in this section.

To get an area, you multiply 2 linear measures together, and to get a volume you multiply 3 linear measures together. The linear measures you multiply together must all be expressed in the SAME UNITS; you cannot, for example, multiply a length in feet by a width in inches to get a result in square feet or in square inches.

Dimensions of a feature on a construction drawing are not always given in the same units. For a concrete wall, for example, the length and height are usually given in feet and the thickness in inches. Furthermore, you may want to get a result in units which are different from any shown on the drawing. Concrete volume, for example, is usually expressed in cubic yards, while the dimensions of concrete work are given on the drawings in feet and inches.

You can save yourself a good many steps in calculating by using fractions to convert the original dimension units into the desired end-result units. Take 1 in., for example. To express 1 in. in feet, you simply put it over 12, thus: 1/12 ft. To express 1 in. in yards, you simply put it over 36, thus: 1/36 yd. In the same manner, to express 1 ft in yards you simply put it over 3, thus 1/3 yd.

Suppose now that you want to calculate the number of cu yd of concrete in a wall 32 ft long by 14 ft high by 8 in. thick. You can express all these in yards and set up your problem thus:

$$\frac{32}{3} \times \frac{14}{3} \times \frac{8}{36}$$

Next you can cancel out, thus:

$$\frac{32}{3} \times \frac{14}{3} \times \frac{8}{36} = \frac{896}{81}$$

Dividing 896 by 81, you get 11.06 cu yds of concrete in the wall.

The right triangle is a triangle which contains one right (90°) angle. The following letters will denote the parts of the triangle indicated in figure 2-13—a = altitude, b = base, c = hypotenuse.

In solving a right triangle, the length of any side may be found if the lengths of the other two sides are given. The combinations of 3-4-5 (lengths of sides) or any multiple of these combinations will come out to a whole number. The following examples show the formula for finding

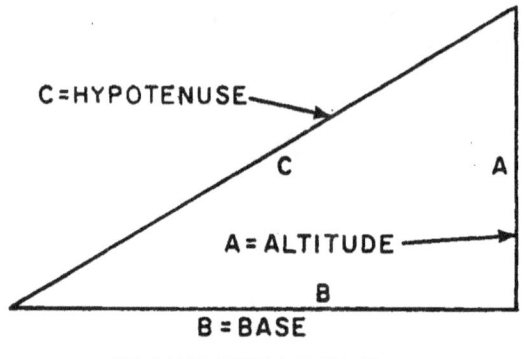

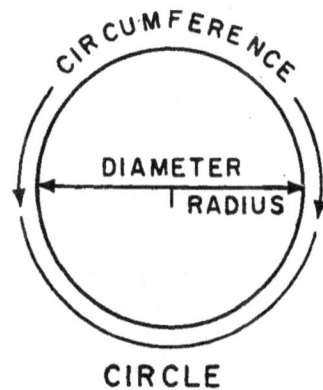

Figure 13.—Right triangle and circle.

each side. Each of these formulas is derived from the master formula $c^2 = a^2 + b^2$.

(1) Find c when a = 3, and b = 4.

$$c = \sqrt{a^2 + b^2} = \sqrt{3^2 + 4^2} = \sqrt{9 + 16} = \sqrt{25} = 5$$

(2) Find a when b = 8, and c = 10.

$$a = \sqrt{c^2 - b^2} = \sqrt{10^2 - 8^2} = \sqrt{100 - 64} = \sqrt{36} = 6$$

(3) Find b when a = 9, and c = 15.

$$b = \sqrt{c^2 - a^2} = \sqrt{15^2 - 9^2} = \sqrt{225 - 81} = \sqrt{144} = 12.$$

There are tables from which the square roots of numbers may be found; otherwise, they may be found arithmetically as explained later in this chapter.

Areas And Volumes Of
Geometric Figures

This section on areas and volumes of geometric figures will be limited to the most commonly used geometric figures. Reference books, such as Mathematics, Vol. 1, are available for additional information if needed. Areas are expressed in square units and volumes in cubic units.

1. A circle is a plane figure bounded by a curved line every point of which is the same distance from the center.
   a. The curved line is called the circumference.
   b. A straight line drawn from the center to any point on the circumference is called a radius. (r = 1/2 the diameter.)
   c. A straight line drawn from one point of the circumference through the center and terminating on the opposite point of the circumference is called a diameter. (d = 2 times the radius.) See figure 2-13.
   d. The area of a circle is found by the following formulas: $A = \pi r^2$ or $A = .7854 d^2$. (π is pronounced pie = 3.1416 or 3 1/7, .7854 is 1/4 of π.) Example: Find the area of a circle whose radius is 7". $A = \pi r^2 = 3\ 1/7 \times 7^2 = 22/7 \times 49 = 154$ sq in. If you use the second formula you obtain the same results.
   e. The circumference of a circle is found by multiplying π times the diameter or 2 times π times the radius. Example: Find the circumference of a circle whose diameter is 56 inches. $C = \pi d = 3.1415 \times 56 = 175.9296$ inches.

2. The area of a right triangle is equal to one-half the product of the base by the altitude. (Area = 1/2 base x altitude.) Example: Find the area of a triangle whose base is 16" and altitude 6". Solution:

$A = 1/2\ bh = 1/2 \times 16 \times 6 = 48$ sq in.

3. The volume of a cylinder is found by multiplying the area of the base times the height. ($V = 3.1416 \times r^2 \times h$). Example: Find the volume of a cylinder which has a radius of 8 in. and a height of 4 ft. Solution:

8 in $= \frac{2}{3}$ ft and $\left(\frac{2}{3}\right)^2 = \frac{4}{9}$ sq ft.

$V = 3.1416 \times \frac{4}{9} \times 4 = \frac{50.2656}{9} = 5.59$ cu ft.

4. The volume of a rectangular solid equals the length x width x height. (V = lwh.) Example: Find the volume of a rectangular solid which has a length of 6 ft, a width of 3 ft, and a height of 2 ft. Solution:

$V = lwh = 6 \times 3 \times 2 = 36$ cu ft.

5. The volume of a cone may be found by multiplying one-third times the area of the base times the height.

$$\left(V = \frac{1}{3} \pi r^2 h\right)$$

Example: Find the volume of a cone when the radius of its base is 2 ft and its height is 9 ft. Solution:

$$\pi = 3.1416, r = 2, 2^2 = 4$$

$$V = \frac{1}{3} r^2 h = \frac{1}{3} \times 3.1416 \times 4 \times 9 = 37.70 \text{ cu ft.}$$

Powers And Roots

1. Powers—When we multiply several numbers together, as 2 x 3 x 4 = 24, the numbers 2, 3, and 4 are factors and 24 the product. The operation of raising a number to a power is a special case of multiplication in which the factors are all equal. The power of a number is the number of times the number itself is to be taken as a factor. Example: 2^4 is 16. The second power is called the square of the number, as 3^2. The third power of a number is called the cube of the number, as 5^3. The exponent of a number is a number placed to the right and above a base to show how many times the base is used as a factor. Example:

4^3 ← exponent =
← base

$4 \times 4 \times 4 = 64.$

2. Roots—To indicate a root, use the sign $\sqrt{}$, which is called the radical sign. A small figure, called the index of the root, is placed in the opening of the sign to show which root is to be taken. The square root of a number is one of the two equal factors into which a number is

divided. Example: $\sqrt{81} = \sqrt{9 \times 9} = 9$. The cube root is one of the three equal factors into which a number is divided. Example: $\sqrt[3]{125} = \sqrt[3]{5 \times 5 \times 5} = 5$.

Square Root

1. The square root of any number is that number which, when multiplied by itself, will produce the first number. For example; the square root of 121 is 11 because 11 times 11 equals 121.

2. How to extract the square root arithmetically:

```
                        95.
    √9025     √90'25.
              : -81
      180 :    925
       +5 :   -925
      185 :    000
```

a. Begin at the decimal point and divide the given number into groups of 2 digits each (as far as possible), going from right to left and/or left to right.
b. Find the greatest number (9) whose square is contained in the first or left hand group (90). Square this number (9) and place it under the first pair of digits (90), then subtract.
c. Bring down the next pair of digits (25) and add it to the remainder (9).
d. Multiply the first digit in the root by 20 and use it as a trial divisor (180). This trial divisor (180) will go into the new dividend (925) five times. This number, 5 (second digit in the root), is added back to the trial divisor, obtaining the true divisor (185).
e. The true divisor (185) is multiplied by the second digit (5) and placed under the remainder (925). Subtract and the problem is solved.
f. If there is still a remainder and you want to carry the problem further, add zeros (in pairs) and continue the above process.

Coverage Calculations

You will frequently have occasion to estimate the number of linear feet of boards of a given size, or the number of tiles, asbestos shingles, and the like, required to cover a given area. Let's take the matter of linear feet of boards first.

What you do here is calculate, first, the number of linear feet of board required to cover 1 sq ft. For boards laid edge-to-edge, you base your calculations on the total width of a board. For boards which will lap each other, you base your calculations on the width laid TO THE WEATHER, meaning the total width minus the width of the lap.

Since there are 144 sq in. in a sq ft, linear footage to cover a given area can be calculated as follows. Suppose your boards are to be laid 8 in. to the weather. If you divide 8 in. into 144 sq in., the result (which is 18 in., or 1.5 ft) will be the linear footage required to cover a sq ft. If you have, say, 100 sq ft to cover, the linear footage required will be 100 x 1.5, or 150 ft.

To estimate the number of tiles, asbestos shingles, and the like required to cover a given area, you first calculate the number of units required to cover a sq ft. Suppose, for example, you are dealing with 9 in. x 9 in. asphalt tiles. The area of one of these is 9 in. x 9 in. or 81 sq in. In a sq ft there are 144 sq in. If it takes 1 to cover 81 sq in., how many will it take to cover 144 sq in.? Just set up a proportional equation, as follows.

$$1:81::x:144$$

When you work this out, you will find that it takes 1.77 tiles to cover a sq ft. To find the number of tiles required to cover 100 sq ft, simply multiply by 100. How do you multiply anything by 100? Just move the decimal point 2 places to the right. Consequently, it takes 177 9 x 9 asphalt tiles to cover 100 sq ft of area.

Board Measure

BOARD MEASURE is a method of measuring lumber in which the basic unit is an abstract volume 1 ft long by 1 ft wide by 1 in. thick. This abstract volume or unit is called a BOARD FOOT.

There are several formulas for calculating the number of board feet in a piece of given dimensions. Since lumber dimensions are most frequently indicated by width and thickness in inches and length in feet, the following formula is probably the most practical.

$$\frac{\text{Thickness in in.} \times \text{width in in.} \times \text{length in ft}}{12}$$

= board feet

Suppose you are calculating the number of board feet in a 14-ft length of 2 x 4. Applying the formula, you get:

$$\frac{\overset{1}{\cancel{2}} \times \overset{2}{\cancel{4}} \times 14}{\underset{3}{\cancel{\underset{6}{\cancel{12}}}}} = \frac{28}{3} = 9\ 1/3\ \text{bd ft}$$

The chief practical use of board measure is in cost calculations, since lumber is bought and sold by the board foot. Any lumber less than 1 in. thick is presumed to be 1 in. thick for board measure purposes. Board measure is calculated on the basis of the NOMINAL, not the ACTUAL, dimensions of lumber.

The actual size of a piece of dimension lumber (such as a 2 x 4, for example) is usually less than the nominal size.

www.ingramcontent.com/pod-product-compliance
Lightning Source LLC
Chambersburg PA
CBHW081807300426
44116CB00014B/2274